FASHION TECHNOLOGY
AND
MANAGEMENT

FASHION TECHNOLOGY AND MANAGEMENT

PARUL GUPTA

MD Publications Pvt Ltd
New Delhi

Published by
MD Publications Pvt Ltd
"MD House", 11, Darya Ganj
New Delhi-110002
Tel. : +91-11-41563325, 41562846
E-mail : contact@mdppl.com
Website : www.mdppl.com

ISBN: 978-81-7533-122-8

PRICE: Rs. 995.00

Published and Printed by **MD Publications Pvt Ltd** at Times Press,
910, Jatwara Street, Darya Ganj, New Delhi.

CONTENTS

Preface

The term 'fashion' usually applies to a prevailing mode of expression, but quite often applies to a personal mode of expression that may or may not apply to all. Inherent in the term is the idea that the mode will change more quickly than the culture as a whole. The terms "fashionable" and "unfashionable" are employed to describe whether someone or something fits in with the current popular mode of expression. The term "fashion" is frequently used in a positive sense, as a synonym for glamour and style. In this sense, fashions are a sort of communal art, through which a culture examines its notions of beauty and goodness. The term "fashion" is also sometimes used in a negative sense, as a synonym for fads, trends and materialism.

The fashions of the West are unparalleled either in antiquity or in the other great civilizations of the world.

Fashion in clothes has allowed wearers to express emotion or solidarity with other people for millennia. Modern Westerners have a wide choice available in the selection of their clothes. What a person chooses to wear can reflect that person's personality or likes. When people who have cultural status start to wear new or different clothes a fashion trend may start. People who like or respect them may start to wear clothes of a similar style.

Fashions may vary significantly within a society according to age, social class, generation, occupation and geography as well as over time. If, for example, an older person dresses according to the fashion of young people, he or she may look ridiculous in the eyes of both young and older people. The terms "fashionista" or "fashion victim" refer to someone who slavishly follows the current fashions.

By the late nineteenth century a division had occurred between the provision of male and female clothing. Tailors continued to produce men's tailored garments, but female dressmakers undertook the making of women's clothing, with the exception of riding habits and corsets. A limited democratization of fashion occurred in the eighteenth century as some ready made and partly made clothing allowed the less wealthy to keep in step with the growing pace of changes in fashion. The principle of exclusivity was reasserted by the continued use of the finest tailors and dressmakers by those able to afford their services and the expensive fabrics they recommended. By the twenty first century the rise of the couturier whose name and clientele implied the height of fashion reinforced such distinctions. The idea of men being equally as interested in fashion as women declined sharply in the nineteenth century. The beaus, macaronis, and dandies of the eighteenth and early nineteenth centuries, who were caricatured and ridiculed for their dedication to the more details of personal appearance, were replaced by dour, dark-suited men of business.

The origins of the late twentieth century's multi-billion pound fashion industry can be traced back to Worth and his two sons. He created new designs to show to his clients rather than deferring to their ideas, a notable change from previous practice. These garments were displayed on human models for his clientele of royalties, aristocrats, and the rich bourgeoisie. His clothes were bought by foreign buyers, and became available in the capitals of Europe, India and the US, and he was treated like an artist rather than as a tradesman by his clients, although he always thought of himself as the latter. He also reinvented the idea that a man can understand and design for women as well, if not better, than another woman.

I am thankful to my colleagues and friends who inspired me directly and indirectly to formulate thoughts concerning this work. I am also thankful to various sources whose work I have consulted and used to compile this book in this form. Last, but not the least, I wish to thank my family members for their loving support during various stages of this work. I would also like to thanks Mr. Pranav Gupta of **MD Publications Pvt. Ltd.**, New Delhi for the elegant and timely production of this book.

Parul Gupta

1

Fashion Technology and Management: An Overview

Introduction

We are not all identically dressed in a unisex uniform of tee-shirts and chinos. Nor are we likely to be. Many people still care passionately about the way they look. Yet fashion, as we have known it, is definitely disappearing. Certainly, over the past fifty years, fashion has been completely transformed.

The empire of fashion has fragmented into hundreds of competing looks what Ted Polhemus calls "style tribes". Polhemus has spent years studying the effect of youth culture on street styles, and he uses the term "style tribes" to describe the looks associated with groups such as goths, punks, and rappers. I would argue, though, that adults also fall into different style tribes, epitomized by different fashion labels. The Modernists, for example, (represented by, say, Jil Sander) are an entirely different breed than the Sex Machines (Tom Ford for Gucci). The Rebels (Alexander McQueen) can easily be distinguished from the Romantics (John Galliano). This is not a question of socio-economic status or age. Members of the Status Symbol tribe (Marc Jacobs for Louis Vuitton) have neither more nor less money than members of the Artistic Avant-Garde (Rei Kawakubo for Commes des Garçons), but they do have very different values and lifestyles.

As a result of this stylistic proliferation, we can safely predict that there will be no New Look next year, at least not in the sense that Christian Dior launched his "New Look" in 1947. At that time it was still possible for a fashion designer radically to transform the way women dressed. Dior's first couture collection featured dresses with small shoulders, a voluptuously curved torso with a nipped-in waist and padded bust and hips, and long, full skirts. It was a dramatic change from the broad shoulders, boxy torsos, and short skirts of the war years. Some women tried to salvage their old clothes by lowering hemlines and removing shoulder pads; others focused on acquiring an entirely new wardrobe. There were protests in Great Britain from Labour Party politicians and some members of the public, who argued that the New Look was profligate and retrograde.

But the style was wildly popular with many women, who felt starved for glamour and femininity after the war years. "We are saved," wrote Susan Mary Alsop, "becoming clothes are back, gone the stern padded shoulders, in are soft rounded shoulders without padding, nipped-in waists, wide, wide skirts about four inches below the knee. And such well-made armor inside the dress that one doesn't need underclothes; a tight bodice keeps bust and waist small as small, then a crinoline-like underskirt of tulle, stiffened, keeps the skirt to the ballet skirt tutu effect that Mr. Dior wants to set off the tiny waist."

The cost of a couture dress was "very high", she admitted. However, the New Look was soon "knocked off" at all price points. Already the structure of the fashion system was changing, as the haute couture was transformed from a system based on the atelier to one dominated by the global corporate conglomerate. Paris was the capital of fashion, but its mode of influence owed much to American-style licensing and mass-manufacturing. To a far greater extent than hitherto, this was a mass society when "fashion for all" became a reality. This trend has only accelerated in subsequent decades.

The profile of fashion designers was already very different in the 1950s than it had been in the 1920s. "Women are bad fashion designers. The only role a woman should have in fashion is wearing clothes," declared Jacques Fath in 1954. Behind Fath's provocative rhetoric lurked an undeniable fact. In the 1920s and 1930s, women had dominated the French couture. After the war, however, the new stars of the couture were men like Christian Dior, Christobal Balenciaga, and Jacques Fath. As fashion was reconceived as big business and high art, rather than a small-scale luxury craft that required a minimal investment, women designers lost ground. At the turn of the century Jeanne Lanvin had opened her own business with a loan of 300 francs. Marcel Boussac invested $500,000 in establishing the House of Dior.

Only a few women were able to marshal this type of financial backing, notably Coco Chanel whose perfume business was lucrative. Chanel herself was not above exploiting the prejudices of her day. Fath claimed that "Fashion is an Art and men are the Artists." But Chanel insisted that "Men were not meant to design for women." The sight of women in Dior's New Look fashions acted on her as "a red flag to a bull", recalled Franco Zeffirelli. In his autobiography he described how Chanel voiced ugly homophobic sentiments: "Look at them. Fools, dressed by queens living out their fantasies. They dream of being women, so they make real women look like transvestites."

It took a very long time before women designers began to approach gender equality, and when they did it was the result both of social changes (such as women's liberation) and further structural changes in the fashion industry (especially the growth of ready to wear). Although there are many gay fashion designers, homosexuals continue to face widespread social prejudice, which has been exacerbated in the age of AIDS.

If we look back at the post-war period, it is clear that, almost immediately after World War II ended, the Cold War began, ushering in an atmosphere of conformity and paranoia. As one American advertisement for men's clothing put it: "You're being watched! Dress right you can't afford not to!" If men were pushed towards stereotyped masculinity and sartorial uniformity, women were pressured into the world of the Feminine Mystique.

Fashion writer Eve Merriam noted how the women's fashion press emphasized conformity: "The language is hortatory, a summons. You have been Called. Would you keep the Lord waiting?...Therefore accept the dicta from on high and do not question. Today, thick textures, nubby, palpable. Tomorrow, diaphanous draperies, fluid, evanescent. Mauve Is. Don it, or go back to supermarket suburbia where perhaps you really belong."

"Think pink!" ordered the fashion editor in the 1950s movie Funny Face, and immediately women obeyed. (Only the fashion editor herself remained above the diktat.) Today, of course, this type of direct order is no longer seen in fashion magazines, because it would arouse anger and ridicule, rather than obedience. To understand why this shift occurred, it is necessary to examine the course of fashion in the 1960s and 1970s, in particular the rise of Youthquake fashions and the spread of anti-fashion sentiment.

Self-trained British designer Mary Quant reacted against the conformity of mainstream women's fashions. As early as 1955, she opened her first boutique on the King's Road, a fashion promenade for London's Mods and Rockers, youth groups obsessed with music and style. In her autobiography, she wrote: "I had always wanted young people to have a fashion of their own. To me adult appearance was very unattractive, alarming and terrifying, stilted, confined, and ugly. It was something I knew I didn't want to grow into." The clothes she made were simple and inexpensive variations on the Chelsea Girl or Art Student look, unmistakably young in feeling, and with rising hemlines.

"People were very shocked by the clothes, which seem so demure and simple now," Quant's husband and partner, Alexander Plunket Greene, told *Rolling Stone* in 1987. "At the time they seemed outrageous. I think there was a slightly sort of paedophile thing about it, wasn't there?" The fashionable woman of the Fifties, "all high heels and rock-hard tits", was replaced in London by a girl with a "childish... shape" and "a great deal of long leg".

In 1961, the year the Beatles were discovered, Quant began to mass-produce miniskirts. It was several years before the hemlines of adult women started to rise above the knee, but the styles of "Swinging London" gradually made an impact around the world, even in Paris. In 1961 French designer André Courrèges showed his first miniskirts. Courrèges later claimed, "I was the man who invented the mini. Mary Quant only commercialized the idea." But Quant dismissed his claim: "It wasn't me or Courrèges who invented the miniskirt anyway it was the girls in the street who did it." Although Quant's success did not herald the rise of a new generation of women designers, it did mark the official beginning of a revolution in fashion based on youth.

Styles began on the street, among a core group of working-class youths who were obsessively concerned with issues of personal style. They were known as "mods" - an abbreviation of "modern". In the 1950s, menswear tended to be staid and sober. But as England's youth culture blossomed, clothing for young men became increasingly colourful, modish, and body conscious, advertising the wearer's sex appeal. This transformation was called the "Peacock Revolution".

Youth culture was based on music and fashion, sex and drugs. According to boutique owner John Stephen, when the Beatles and the Rolling Stones adopted a style, "fans noticed what they wore and wanted to buy the same clothes." Just as the miniskirt was probably indirectly influenced by the greater availability of contraception, especially the birth-control pill, so also did changing sexual attitudes influence men's fashions. Sir Mark Palmer recalled that "There was a time when men wouldn't wear coloured clothes for fear of being thought queer." However, after homosexuality was decriminalized in Britain in 1967, gay men felt less need to disguise their sexual orientation to avoid persecution.

"Sexual intercourse began in 1963," declared the poet Philip Larkin with pardonable exaggeration. Certainly, the sexual revolution influenced the course of fashion history. As we move into the twenty-first century and fashion becomes ever more erotic and taboo-breaking, it is clear that the youthquake of the 1960s played a pivotal role in the development in modern fashion.

Soon the "mod" style became an international phenomenon. "Even the peers are going "mod"" declared *Life* International in a piece on the "Spread of the Swinging Revolution", published in July 1966.

It all began with the teenage 'mods' who spent most of their pocket money on flamboyant clothes. Now the frills and flowers are being adopted in other strata of Britain's society, and the male-fashions born in London have joined the theatre among the British exports that aren't lagging. The way-out styles already have appeared in such disparate metropolises as Paris and Chicago and may eventually change the whole *raison d'etre* of male dress.

Meanwhile, some designers in Paris also began to explore new directions in fashion. Yves Saint Laurent designed his controversial "Beat Look" for the House of Dior in 1960. Inspired by the beatniks, Saint Laurent drew on other rebellious youth styles, such as the biker's black leather jacket. A few years later, Saint Laurent also developed a ready-to-wear line, Rive Gauche. "Ready to wear, for me, is not a last resource, a sub-couture; it is the future," said Saint Laurent. "One dresses women who are younger, more receptive. With them, one can finally be more audacious."

Fashion futurism also served as a metaphor for youth. This was especially important in France, which had no real youth culture or music scene comparable to that in Britain or America. André Courrèges designed his "Space Age" or "Moon Girl" collection in 1964, which included white pantsuits and minidresses worn with vinyl go-go boots and other space-age accessories. "The Courrèges message is loud and clear: bold stark simple clothes, exquisitely balanced with scientific precision to achieve a dazzling new mathematical beauty," declared a British magazine. "It's a look that couldn't have been dreamed of in pre-Sputnik days." High tech from plastic and stretch fabric to industrial zippers was associated with progress and a happy future. "Zip up, pop on and just go zing!" advised American Vogue in 1965. "No hooks, no ties everything clings, swings, ready to orbit."

The rise of the hippies, first in America and then around the world, heralded a new shift in youth culture. Fashion historian Bruno de Roselle has analysed the significance of "anti-fashion sentiment" among young people associated with the hippy culture. Fashion, the hippies believed, was a "system that Society imposes on all of us, restricting our freedom". Fashion change turns us into "consumers" who have to buy new clothes "even if the old ones are not worn out". In part an economic criticism of capitalism, the hippies' argument also implied, philosophically, that "fashion is a perpetual lie".

Fashion is damaging, because "this uniformity and this change keep us from being ourselves. Clothing is a means of communication about the self, but we are not allowed to be honest and individual." The solution to this dilemma, according to the hippies, was "to abandon received fashion, in order to invent our own personal fashions". Theoretically, each individual would create his own unique style. He would "express himself" and "do his own thing" as the clichés of the time put it. In this way, the individual would defeat "the System", whether this was conceived of as the fashion system, advanced global capitalism, or society in general.

Rejecting contemporary fashion, the hippies looked for inspiration in the clothing of long ago and far away. The ethnic look and the romantic-pastoral look were especially significant. Hippy women gravitated toward long skirts, while men adopted evocative garments such as fringed suede shirts, like those worn by native Americans. Initially handmade or scavenged from thrift shops, these clothes were soon produced by savvy entrepreneurs.

Hippy styles rapidly entered the fashion mainstream. In 1967, American Vogue solemnly announced that "Timothy Leary's paradigm "Turn on, tune in, drop out" remains the classic statement of the hippy weltanschauung." Rock critic Richard Goldstein wrote: "Now beauty is free. Liberated from hang-ups over form and function, unencumbered by tradition or design. A freaky goddess surveying her realm. Kite-high, moon-pure. Groovy, powerful and weird! The style of the 60s is creative anarchy."

People are mistaken in thinking of the 1970s as a period of calm after the "uproar" of the 1960s. Although political radicalism faded after the end of the Vietnam War, both the drug culture and the sexual revolution became mass phenomena. From about 1970 through 1974, fashion was characterized by a continuation of many late 1960s themes, such as conspicuous outrageousness (epitomized by platform shoes and hot pants), retro fantasies, and ethnic influences. In its orientation toward youth, freedom, and other counterculture virtues like equality and anti-capitalism, the first phase of 1970s style might be described as late hippie diffusion.

From 1975 through 1979, however, fashion became simultaneously harsher and more conservative. On the level of street fashion, the peace and love ethos of the hippies was followed by the sex and violence of the punks and the macho style of gay "clones". In the world of high fashion, a deliberately decadent style of "Terrorist Chic" dominated. Yet at the same time, middleclass people increasingly gravitated toward sportswear separates and Dressfor-Success uniformity.

When the 1970s began, however, the most striking development was the sound of hemlines falling. In January 1970, the Paris collections emphasized long skirts. After almost a decade of rapidly rising hemlines, the new, longer length made news around the world. *Life* published a cover article on "The Great Hemline Hassle", bemoaning the demise of the mini-skirt, symbol of youth and sexual allure. Many women reacted against the new fashion of midi skirts, because they were tired of fashion's excesses – and sympathetic to the hippies' creed of dressing to suit oneself. (The hippies themselves, of course, had already adopted long skirts, and within a few years hemlines would, in fact, fall.) Yet the resistance to the midi was historically significant. Never again would the majority of women change their hemlines just to be in fashion.

Increasingly, women chose to wear trousers, the traditional symbol of masculine power. They even began wearing trouser suits to work, another important turning point in twentieth-century fashion. Meanwhile, for casual occasions, both men and women favoured denim jeans. Although blue jeans are popularly associated with the 1960s, in fact they became more important in the 1970s than ever before. Even as jeans became "co-opted" by the fashion system (with the appearance of various fashion jeans), their signifying value grew more powerful, as they symbolized youth, freedom, and sex appeal.

"Let us grant to the seventies its claim to antifashion, for the freedom to wear what you want, where and when you want, is finally here," declared journalist Clara Pierre in her 1976 book, *Looking Good: The Liberation of Fashion*. The hippies had destroyed every rule, except the injunction to please oneself. Now the arbiters of fashion, editors and designers alike, risked being dismissed as "fashion fascists" if they dared tell women what was "in" or "out". As a result, fashion journalists quickly adopted a new language of "freedom" and "choice". They constantly reassured readers that "fashion now is the expression of women who are free, happy, and doing what they want to be doing". As British Vogue put it: "The real star of the fashion picture is the wearer you."

Certain designers understood the mood of the time. Yves Saint Laurent is "today's Chanel", declared *Women's Wear Daily* in 1972. Like Chanel, he pioneered the masculine look in women's fashion, but he did not neglect erotic allure. According to actress Catherine Deneuve: "Saint Laurent designs for women with double lives. His day clothes help a woman confront the world of strangers. They permit her to go everywhere without drawing unwelcome attention and, with their somewhat masculine quality, they give her a certain force, prepare her for encounters that may become a conflict of wills. In the evening when a woman chooses to be with those she is fond of, he makes her seductive."

Seduction took many forms in the 1970s, however. Many young people adopted "wild styles", such as hot pants and platform shoes. Traditional rules of taste and propriety were deliberately violated. "Trashy" styles proliferated, including see-through blouses, crushed vinyl burgundy maxicoats, electric blue lycra "second-skin" bodystockings, and silver lurex halter tops. Polyester shirts were open to the waist, and dresses were slit up to the crotch. "Is bad taste a bad thing?" demanded British *Vogue* in 1971, with the clear implication that the freedom to violate social conventions was liberating. No wonder the 1970s have been called "The Decade that Taste Forgot".

At the same time, however, fashion designers such as Halston and Calvin Klein spear-headed a new kind of minimalist modernism. Simple cashmere or Ultrasuede dresses gave women a sensuous but grown-up appearance. In the evening, sex came out of the closet and music continued to be a major influence on fashion. Disco was originally a gay phenomenon, but soon it had spread to the wider society. Disco dressing emphasized materials that picked up the light, and clothes that showed off the body. Indeed, disco helped introduce underwear as outerwear. Especially popular were silken slip dresses with spaghetti straps.

By contrast, punk rock spawned a deliberately "revolting style". The punks are most notorious for their ripped tee-shirts, Doc Marten boots, and "tribal" hairstyles. As Dick Hebdige writes in *Subculture: The Meaning of Style:*

> *Safety pins were worn as gruesome ornaments through the cheek, ear or lip. 'Cheap' trashy fabrics (plastic, lurex, etc.) in vulgar designs (e.g. mock leopard skin) and 'nasty' colors, long discarded by the quality end of the fashion industry as obsolete kitsch, were salvaged by the punks and turned into garments which offered self-conscious commentaries on the notions of modernity and taste. In particular, the illicit iconography of sexual fetishism was exhumed from the boudoir, closet and the pornographic film and placed on the street.*

More important than safety-pins and mohawks was the way the punks used the visual strategy of *bricolage,* throwing together wildly unrelated elements, like army surplus and fetish underwear. The punk style was initially greeted with horror. Yet within a very short time, it was a major influence on international fashion. Vivienne Westwood was a pivotal figure in the transmission of punk style, with her notorious pornographic tee-shirts and bondage trousers. Soon Jean Paul Gaultier was producing underwear-asouterwear, and black leather became mainstream.

Fashion photographers like Guy Bourdin and Helmut Newton also drew on violent and pornographic iconography. Newton often depicted women fighting, in positions of dominance, or posed as sex workers. He was hired as a consultant for the horror film *The Eyes of Laura Mars,* which depicted Faye Dunaway as a fashion photographer whose work mixed sex and violence. In one scene, two models wearing nothing but underwear, high heels and fur coats engage in a violent hair-pulling catfight in front of a burning car. Guy Bourdin focused explicitly on the connections between sex and death. His shoe advertisements for Charles Jourdain were especially notorious: In one advertisement he depicted what appeared to be the aftermath of a fatal car crash; one of the victim's shoes lay at the side of the road. Fashion advertising of the 1990s continued this trend, especially with the vogue for "heroin chic". Aspects of aggression proved erotically alluring to many people.

Saint Laurent exploited the eroticism of sexual ambiguity, most famously in his female version of the tuxedo suit, *le smoking,* which Helmut Newton photographed for French *Vogue.* Saint Laurent's evening clothes, on the other hand, revelled in the "retro" and "ethnic" influences so beloved of the hippies. With his Russian or Ballets Russes collection of 1976–7 Saint Laurent launched a phantasmagoria of Oriental influences, creating spectacularly luxurious costumes, such as sable-trimmed gold brocade Cossack coats and long gypsy skirts in iridescent silks. "A revolution ... that will change the course of fashion around the world," proclaimed the *New York Times* in a front-page article. "The most dramatic and expensive show ever seen in Paris," declared the *International Herald Tribune.*

Some observers complained that the collection was "nostalgic" and too close to "costume" to be really wearable, but American Vogue defiantly insisted that "What Yves Saint Laurent has done is to remind us that fashion, in its radical form of haute couture, is costume. It strikingly illustrates the degree of sophistication attained by fashion's analysis of history." This issue continues to recur in fashion today, as designers like John Galliano pillage the past to create romantic fantasy fashions.

Paris remained the capital of fantasy fashion, but in the late 1970s, the rise of ready to wear in Milan began to threaten French fashion hegemony. Whereas the Roman couture was essentially an imitation of Paris, Milan offered a genuine alternative to Paris. "Weary of French fantasy clothes and rude treatment on Parisian showroom floors, buyers were happy to take their order books next store," announced *Newsweek* in 1978. The clothes coming out of Milan were, admittedly, not couture, but they were extremely stylish. "They were classically cut but not stodgy, innovative but never theatrical. They were for real people albeit rich people to wear to real places."

Backed by the Italian textile producers, designers in Milan produced highquality ready-to-wear clothes that combined the casual qualities of American sportswear with European luxury and status. "The Italians were the first to make refined sportswear," recalled John Fairchild of Women's Wear Daily. Significantly, the international clientele for Italian style included both men and women. Moreover, they increasingly wore clothing that was not only "made in Italy", but that also expressed some version of "the Italian Look".

In 1982, when Giorgio Armani was featured on the cover of *Time Magazine,* the lead article began with a quote from Pierre Berge, the business partner of Yves Saint Laurent. Asked about Italian fashion, Berge insisted that except for "pasta and opera, the Italians can't be credited with anything!" Berge demanded, "Give me one piece of clothing, one fashion statement that Armani has made that truly influenced the world." It was a rash challenge to make to an American journalist, and Jay Cocks impudently replied, "Alors, Pierre. The unstructured jacket. An easeful elegance. Tailoring of a kind thought possible only when done by hand. A new sort of freedom in clothes."

Already in the mid-1970s, Armani had begun to soften men's clothes. He rejected the stiffly tailored business suits that traditionally symbolized masculine rectitude, introducing instead "deconstructed" jackets, without padding and stiff interlinings. The shoulders dropped and broadened, the lapels and buttons crept downward. Armani used softer, more easily draped "luxury" fabrics (such as cashmere and silk-and-wool blends), which have a greater tactile appeal than the tightly woven wools more typical of men's suits. He also expanded the repertoire of colours available to men; in addition to traditionally masculine colours like navy blue and steel grey, he added softer warmer shades, like camel. Then Armani turned around and interpreted his menswear look for the female.

Much of Armani's popularity and the appeal of the Italian look in general derived from the way it "came to bridge the gap between the anti-Establishment 60's and the money-gathering 80's" (as fashion journalist Woody Hochswender astutely noted). If the tailored suit had long signified businesslike respectability, now it also projected an image combining sensuality and physical power for men and women alike. An Armani suit symbolized easy self-assurance and understated elegance. As gender stereotypes became less rigid, women appreciated the powerful image created by an Italian suit, while men were increasingly willing to present themselves as sex objects.

Gianni Versace was the other pivotal figure in the emergence of Italian fashion. The favourite designer of extroverted musicians and actors, he brought colour and Baroque vitality to rock 'n roll fashion. Not since Pucci's psychedelic prints had fashion seen such a riot of colour and design. His use of leather was also brilliant, especially in his so-called S&M collection of 1991, which introduced hundreds of socialites to a style derived from the gay leatherman look. Perhaps his most famous single dress, however, was the neo-punk safety-pin dress worn by Elizabeth Hurley. The murder of Gianni Versace brought an untimely end to a larger-than-life talent, but his sister Donatella continued to design for the company.

New talents have continued to flourish in Italy. Miuccia Prada, for example, is the designer of choice for many chic fashion editors. The heir to a leather goods company, she first received international attention in the mid-1980s with her black nylon backpack, which brilliantly undermined contemporary status symbols, like the "gilt 'n quilt" Chanel purse. Prada soon became known for her fashion-forward styles, which unerringly combined classicism and audacity. For younger and/or more playful women, she launched her secondary line Miu Miu.

Meanwhile, over the course of the 1990s, Tom Ford, the American designer at Gucci, transformed that near-moribund company into one of the world's hottest fashion labels, known for ultra-sexy clothes and must-have accessories. Yet, as Ford demonstrates, fashion today is no longer rigidly segmented by country.

An American designer can work for an Italian company, an Englishman can design for a French couture house, and an Austrian can set up shop in New York. The German Jil Sander and the Belgian Anne Demeulemeester are major international talents. Of course, there is evidence of crossculturalism in the past as well: neither Schiaparelli nor Balenciaga were French, although both flourished in Paris. Yet the internalization of fashion has become especially noticeable ever since the Japanese invasion of the 1980s, which also marked a new phase in avant-garde fashion.

Suzy Menkes has described the sensational effect of Kawakubo's Spring/ Summer 1983 collection for Commes des Garcons: "Down the catwalk, marching to a rhythmic beat like a race of warrior women, came models wearing ink-black coat dresses, cut big, square, away from the body with no line, form, or recognizable silhouette." Menkes recognized that Kawakubo was "search[ing] for clothing that owes nothing to outworn concepts of femininity". Most journalists were just shocked, and they used the language of mourning, poverty, and atomic warfare, arguing that the clothes made women look like "nuclear bag ladies".

When American *Vogue* featured Kawakubo's clothes in 1983, an outraged reader demanded to know why anyone would want to pay $230 for "a torn ... shroud". Joan Kaner, then vice-president and fashion director at Bergdorf Goodman said that "Rei's clothes are interesting to look at, difficult to wear. How much do people want to look tattered?" The new Japanese clothes also tended to be oversized and loose; to a hostile viewer, big and bulky. "They do nothing for the figure," complained Kaner, "and for all the money going into health and fitness, why look like a shopping bag lady?"

As time went on, however, avant-garde fashion began to be accepted, at least among certain artistic style tribes. The cognoscenti recognized that Kawakubo's infamous "ripped" sweater, for example, was not ripped at all. The seemingly random pattern of holes was the result of careful thought and technology. According to Kawakubo: "The machines that make fabric are more and more making uniform, flawless textures. I like it when something is *off*, not perfect. Handweaving is the best way to achieve this. Since this isn't always possible, we loosen a screw of the machines here and there so they can't do exactly what they're supposed to do." Her sweater is today in the fashion collection of the Victoria and Albert Museum, where it is recognized as an important development in late twentieth-century design.

In addition to Rei Kawakubo, the most influential Japanese designers were Yohji Yamamoto and Issey Miyake. Both are the kind of designer that other designers admire. Miyake was recognized early as a true artist of fashion, whose explorations into textile technology have revolutionized fashion.

Yamamoto has become ever more influential, as he combines the aspirations of the haute couture with the daring of the iconoclast. By the 1990s, the Japanese avant-garde had given birth to a European avant-garde, spearheaded by Martin Margiela, who, like Kawakubo, espoused an aesthetic of deconstruction and radical experimentation. Margiela's use of recycled clothing was especially influential. He unravelled French Army socks and knitted them into sweaters, and cut up old leather coats to make into evening dresses. The young Belgian designer Anne Demeulemeester revels in the inky black that Kawakubo herself has now renounced in favour of newly transgressive colors like pink.

Sex and gender continue to be central issues in the cultural construction of contemporary fashion. But whereas Yves Saint Laurent politely combined seduction and subversion, designers like Jean-Paul Gaultier have upped the ante. "A woman, like a man, can be feminine," insisted Gaultier, whose work travesties traditional gender expectations. His collection 'And God Created Man' featured the skirt for men, while 'Wardrobe for Two' focused on androgyny. As Gaultier said in 1984: "Gender-bending, huh! It's a game. Young people understand that to dress like a tart doesn't reflect one's moral stance perhaps those *jolies madames* in their little Chanel suits are the real tarts? I'm offering equality of sex appeal."

Gaultier was also notorious as the apostle of bad taste. "Me, I like everything," he said. "Everything can be beautiful or ugly. I like different kinds of beauty." He showed his strange clothes on unconventional models fat women, old people, heavily tattooed and pierced people. When French *Vogue* went to Brooklyn to photograph Jean-Paul Gaultier's collection of Hasidic fashions, many Jews complained. His use of fetishism has been especially influential, epitomized in his corsets created for Madonna. Less obvious are the ways in which he has subverted traditional ideas of class distinction.

Social class is no longer clearly defined in terms of fashion, in part because of the excess associated with the nouveaux-riches styles of the 1980s. The 1980s have been stereotyped as a "decade of greed" and "excess". Journalists have focused on themes such as the money culture, junk bonds, and status symbols. As it happened, the stock market crash of 1987 coincided with Christian Lacroix's New York opening, and there were those who drew a connection between the two events. In her essay, "Dancing on the Lip of the Volcano: Christian Lacroix's Crash Chic", society journalist Julie Baumgold argued that "Lacroix makes clothes of such extravagant, gorgeous excess as to divide the classes once and for all."

The frivolous and theatrical look of Lacroix's dresses extended over hoops or bustles, and adorned with garlands, fringe and ribbons, in a riot of red, pink and gold, stripes, polka dots and roses, and costing some $15,000 to $30,000 per dress seemed to signify a decadent society wholely abandoned to the cult of conspicuous consumption. The reality, however, was much more complex. Class distinctions were important in the 1980s, as they are today, but now the desire for status increasingly coexists with the desire to look young and "cool", however this is defined by one's style tribe.

Even venerable couture houses have required injections of youthful style. Thus, in 1982 Karl Lagerfeld was invited to design for Chanel. Journalist Javier Arroyello credits Lagerfeld with being:

> *the man who broke the spell of the Chanel mummy. He likes to picture himself as an emergency doctor who rejuvenated the famous Chanel suit, the exhausted uniform of the* grandes bourgeoises, *through repeated shock treatments (he brought leather and even denim to the kingdom of gold-trimmed tweed) and intensive corrective surgery (wider shoulders, roomier jackets, a sharper silhouette that included even pants).*

There were occasional complaints that Lagerfeld had "vulgarized" the Chanel look. But sales increased dramatically, and the average age of the Chanel customer dropped from the mid-fifties to the late thirties. "All the stuff before pre-Karl was so-o-o square," said Caroline Kellett, a young English fashion editor. Innovative and iconoclastic, Lagerfeld wore the Chanel mantle lightly. He admitted that "Chanel has to stay Chanel in a way," but he also stressed that there was room to expand beyond "those knit suits".

Drawing on influences from the street, Lagerfeld put his Chanel models in rappers' chunky gold chains, big gold earrings, and the kind of skin-tight shorts worn by New York City bicycle messengers. The influence moved both ways, however. Some rappers have mixed baggy shorts and baseball caps by Home Boyz with combat boots by Chanel. "We have the Chanel combat boots now, which are more upscale," explained one performer. "They're also really easy to dance in."

Together with popular music, sports are one of the most important influences on contemporary fashion. This trend has long been evident throughout society, and can even be observed in, for example, the Mattel toy catalogue in 1984, the year when "Great Shape Barbie" was launched. As the advertising copy put it: "Hot new trend in fashion aerobics," adding that the Barbie doll looked "trim 'n terrific" in her "trendy looking" athletic clothes. The 1980s were indeed characterized by a pronounced emphasis on physical fitness especially aerobics, jogging, and body-building which had a significant impact on the culture of fashion.

The trend towards more body-conscious clothing was as radical a development as the rise of the miniskirt in the 1960s. Whereas Dior's New Look squeezed and padded women into an approximation of the ideal shape (and men were covered with boxy grey flannel suits), by the end of the twentieth century women could simply pull on a leotard and leggings. Meanwhile, young men cruised through the urban landscape wearing lycra bicycle shorts and sleeveless undershirts. New fabric technologies provide impetus for fashion-forward styles. Along with various stretch fabrics, there are an increasing variety of "smart" materials that can do useful things, such as providing warmth with minimal bulk and weight. Today many designers in both Europe and America cater to the sculpted bodies of fashion trendsetters. It is, however, incumbent upon men and women alike to *internalize* the corrective aspects of fashion, and to mould their bodies into a fashionably muscular shape. As the culture of fashion has changed, so also has the fashion industry and the image of fashion. But fashion itself remains alive and well, always new, always changing.

❑❑❑

2

Fashion in Collective and Consumer Behaviour

Introduction

It is important to realize that it covers a much wider domain. It is to be found in manners, the arts, literature, and philosophy, and may even reach into certain areas of science. In fact, it may operate in any field of group life, apart from the technological and utilitarian area and the area of the sacred. Its operation requires a class society, for in its essential character it does not occur either in a homogenous society like a primitive group, nor in a caste society.

Fashion behaves as a movement, and on this basis it is different from custom which, by comparison, is static. This is due to the fact that fashion is based fundamentally on differentiation and emulation. In a class society, the upper classes or so-called social elite, are not able to differentiate themselves by *fixed* symbols or badges. Hence the more external features of their life and behavior are likely to be imitated by classes immediately subjacent to them, who, in turn, are initiated by groups immediately below them in the social structure. This process gives to fashion a vertical descent. However, the elite class finds that it is no longer distinguishable, by reason of the imitation made by others, and hence is led to adopt new differentiating criteria, only to displace these as they in turn are imitated. It is primarily this feature that makes fashion into a movement and which has led one writer to remark that a fashion, once launched, marches to its doom.

As a movement, fashion shows little resemblance to any of the other movements which we have considered. While it occurs spontaneously and moves along in a characteristic cycle, it involves little in the way of crowd behavior and it is not dependent upon the discussion process and the resulting public opinion. It does not depend upon the mechanisms of which we have spoken. The participants are not recruited through agitation or proselyting. No *esprit de corps* or morale is built up among them. Nor does the fashion movement have, or require, an ideology. Further, since it does not have a leadership imparting conscious direction to the movement, it does not build up a set of tactics. People participate in the fashion movement voluntarily and in response to the interesting and powerful kind of control which fashion imposes on them.

Not only is the fashion movement unique in terms of its character, but it differs from other movements in that it does not develop into a society. It does not build up a social organization; it has no personnel or functionaries; it does not develop a division of labor among its participants with each being assigned a given status; it does not construct a set of symbols, myths, values, philosophy, or set of practices, and in this sense does not form a culture; and finally, it does not develop a set of loyalties or form a we-consciousness.

Nevertheless, the movement of fashion is an important form of collective behavior with very significant results for the social order. First, it should be noted that the fashion movement is a genuine expressive movement. It does not have a conscious goal which people are trying to reach through collective action, as is true in the case of the specific social movements. Nor does it represent the release of excitement and tension generated in a dancing crowd situation. It is expressive, however, of certain fundamental impulses and tendencies, such as an inclination toward novel experience, a desire for distinction, and an urge to conform. Fashion is important especially in providing a means for the expression of developing tastes and disposition; this feature establishes it as a form of expressive behavior.

The latter remark provides a cue for understanding the role of fashion and the way in which it contributes to the formation of a new social order. In a changing society, such as is necessarily presupposed for the operation of fashion, people are continually having their subjective lives upset; they experience new dispositions and tastes which, however, are vague and illdefined. It seems quite clear that fashion, by providing an opportunity for the expression of dispositions and tastes, serves to make them definite and to channelize them and, consequently, to fix and solidify them. To understand this, one should appreciate the fact that the movement and success of fashion are dependent upon the acceptance of the given style or pattern. In turn, this acceptance is based not merely upon the prestige attached to the style but also upon whether the style meets and answers to the dispositions and developing tastes of people. (The notorious failures that attend efforts to make styles fashionable upon the basis of mere prestige provide some support for this point.) From this point of view, we can regard fashion as arising and flourishing in response to new subjective demands. In providing means for the expression of these dispositions and tastes, fashion acts, as suggested before, to shape and crystallize these tastes. In the long run fashion aids, in this manner, to construct a *Zeitgeist* or a common subjective life, and in doing so, helps to lay the foundation for a new social order.

Source Excerpted from Blumer, H. Fashion movements. In R.E. Park (Ed.), *An outline of the principles of sociology*. New York: Barnes and Noble.

Biographical note Herbert Blumer was an American sociologist. He studied under George Mead and received his doctorate from the University of Chicago in 1928. He taught at the University of Chicago from 1928 to 1951, and at University of California-Berkeley from 1952 until 1967 when he retired. Blumer is considered the father of symbolic interactionism. In 1983, he received the American Sociological Association's highest recognition, The Award for a Career of Distinguished Scholarship.

Influence of Custom and Fashion upon our Notions of Beauty and Deformity

Fashion is different from custom, or rather is a particular species of it. That is not the fashion which every body wears, but which those wear who are of a high rank or character. The graceful, the easy, and commanding manners of the great, joined to the usual richness and magnificence of their dress, give a grace to the very form which they happen to bestow upon it. As long as they continue to use this form, it is connected in our imaginations with the idea of something that is genteel and magnificent, and though in itself it should be indifferent, it seems, on account of this relation, to have something about it that is genteel and magnificent too. As soon as they drop it, it loses all the grace which it had appeared to possess before, and being now used only by the inferior ranks of people, seems to have something of their meanness and awkwardness.

Dress and furniture are allowed by all the world to be entirely under the dominion of custom and fashion. The influence of those principles, however, is by no means confined to so narrow a sphere, but extends itself to whatever is in any respect the object of taste to music, to poetry, to architecture. The modes of dress and furniture are continually changing; and that fashion appearing ridiculous to-day which was admired five years ago, we are experimentally convinced that it owed its vogue chiefly or entirely to custom and fashion. Clothes and furniture are not made of very durable materials. A well-fancied coat is done in a twelvemonth, and cannot continue longer to propagate, as the fashion, that form according to which it was made. The modes of furniture change less rapidly than those of dress; because furniture is commonly more durable. In five or six years, however, it generally undergoes an entire revolution, and every man in his own time sees the fashion in this respect change many different ways. The productions of the other arts are much more lasting, and, when happily imagined, may continue to propagate the fashion of their make for a much longer time. A well contrived building may endure many centuries; a beautiful air may be delivered down, by a sort of tradition, through many successive generations; a well-written poem may last as long as the world; and all of them continue for ages together to give the vogue to that particular style, to that particular taste or manner, according to which each of them was composed. Few men have an opportunity of seeing in their own times the fashion in any of these arts change very considerably. Few men have so much experience and acquaintance with the different modes which have obtained in remote ages and nations, as to be thoroughly reconciled to them, or to judge with impartiality between them and what takes place in their own age and country. Few men, therefore, are willing to allow, that custom or fashion have much influence upon their judgments concerning what is beautiful, or otherwise, in the productions of any of those arts; but imagine that all the rules which they think ought to be observed in each of them are founded upon reason and nature, not upon habit or prejudice. A very little attention, however, may convince them of the contrary, and satisfy them that the influence of custom and fashion over dress and furniture is not more absolute than over architecture, poetry, and music.

Neither is it only over the productions of the arts that custom and fashion exert their dominion. They influence our judgments in the same manner with regard to the beauty of natural objects. What various and opposite forms are deemed beautiful in different species of things! The proportions which are admired in one animal are altogether different from those which are esteemed in another. Every class of things has its own peculiar conformation, which is approved of, and has a beauty of its own, distinct from that of every other species. It is upon this account that a learned Jesuit, Father Buffier, has determined that the beauty of every object consists in that form and colour, which is most usual among things of that particular sort to which it belongs. Thus in the human form the beauty of each feature lies in a certain middle, equally removed from a variety of other forms that are ugly. A beautiful nose, for example, is one that is neither very long nor very short, neither very straight nor very crooked, but a sort of middle among all those extremes, and less different from any one of them than all of them are from one another. It is the form which Nature seems to have aimed at in them all, which, however, she deviates from in a great variety of ways, and very seldom hits exactly; but to which all those deviations still bear a very strong resemblance. When a number of drawings are made after one pattern, though they may all miss it in some respects, yet they will all resemble it more than they resemble one another; the general character of the pattern will run through them all; the most singular and odd will be those which are most wide of it; and though very few will copy it exactly, yet the most accurate delineations will bear a greater resemblance to the most careless, than the careless ones will bear to one another. In the same manner, in each species of creatures, what is most beautiful bears the strongest characters of the general fabric of the species, and has the strongest resemblance to the greater part of the individuals with which it is classed. Monsters, on the contrary, or what is perfectly deformed, are always most singular and odd, and have the least resemblance to the generality of that species to which they belong. And thus the beauty of each species, though in one sense the rarest of all things, because few individuals hit this middle form exactly, yet in another is the most common, because all the deviations from it resemble it more than they resemble one another. The most customary form therefore is, in each species of things, according to him, the most beautiful. And hence it is that a certain practice and experience in contemplating each species of objects is requisite, before we can judge of its beauty, or know wherein the middle and most usual form consists. The nicest judgment concerning the beauty of the human species will not help us to judge of that of flowers or horses, or any other species of things.

Economic Theory of Woman's Dress

The line of progress during the initial stage of the evolution of apparel was from the simple concept of adornment of the person by supplementary accessions from without, to the complex concept of an adornment that should render the person pleasing, or of an enviable presence, and at the same time serve to indicate the possession of other virtues than that of a well-favored person only. In this latter direction lies what was to evolve into dress. By the time dress emerged from the primitive efforts of the savage to beautify himself with gaudy additions to his person, it was already an economic factor of some importance. The change from a purely aesthetic character (ornament) to a mixture of the aesthetic and economic took place before the progress had been achieved from pigments and trinkets to what is commonly understood by apparel. Ornament is not properly an economic category, although the trinkets which serve the purpose of ornament may also do duty as an economic factor, and in so far be assimilated to dress. What constitutes dress an economic fact, properly falling within the scope of economic theory, is its function as an index of the wealth of its wearer or, to be more precise, of its owner, for the wearer and owner are not necessarily the same person. It will hold with respect to more than one half the values currently recognized as "dress," especially that portion with which this paper is immediately concerned - woman's dress that the wearer and the owner are different persons. But while they need not be united in the same person, they must be organic members of the same economic unit; and the dress is the index of the wealth of the economic unit which the wearer represents.

Under the patriarchal organization of society, where the social unit was the man (with his dependents), the dress of the women was an exponent of the wealth of the man whose chattels they were. In modern society, where the unit is the household, the woman's dress sets forth the wealth of the household to which she belongs. Still, even to-day, in spite of the nominal and somewhat celebrated demise of the patriarchal idea, there is that about the dress of women which suggests that the wearer is something in the nature of a chattel; indeed, the theory of woman's dress quite plainly involves the implication that the woman is a chattel. In this respect the dress of women differs from that of men. With this exception, which is not of first-rate importance, the essential principles of woman's dress are not different from those which govern the dress of men; but even apart from this added characteristic the element of dress is to be seen in a more unhampered development in the apparel of women. A discussion of the theory of dress in general will gain in brevity and conciseness by keeping in view the concrete facts of the highest manifestation of the principles with which it has to deal, and this highest manifestation of dress is unquestionably seen in the apparel of the women of the most advanced modern communities.

Woman, primarily, originally because she was herself a pecuniary possession, has become in a peculiar way the exponent of the pecuniary strength of her social group; and with the progress of specialization of functions in the social organism this duty tends to devolve more and more entirely upon the woman. The best, most advanced, most highly developed societies of our time have reached the point in their evolution where it has (ideally) become the great, peculiar, and almost the sole function of woman in the social system to put in evidence her economic unit's ability to pay. That is to say, woman's place (according to the ideal scheme of our social system) has come to be that of a means of conspicuously unproductive expenditure.

The admissible evidence of the woman's expensiveness has considerable range in respect of form and method, but in substance it is always the same. It may take the form of manners, breeding, and accomplishments that are, *prima facie,* impossible to acquire or maintain without such leisure as bespeaks a considerable and relatively long-continued possession of wealth. It may also express itself in a peculiar manner of life, on the same grounds and with much the same purpose. But the method in vogue always and everywhere, alone or in conjunction with other methods, is that of dress. "Dress," therefore, from the economic point of view, comes pretty near being synonymous with "display of wasteful expenditure."

It is not that the wearers or the buyers of these wasteful goods desire the waste. They desire to make manifest their ability to pay. What is sought is not the *de facto* waste, but the appearance of waste. Hence there is a constant effort on the part of the consumers of these goods to obtain them at as good a bargain as may be; and hence also a constant effort on the part of the producers of these goods to lower the cost of their production, and consequently to lower the price. But as fast as the price of the goods declines to such a figure that their consumption is no longer *prima facie* evidence of a considerable ability to pay, the particular goods in question fall out of favor, and consumption is diverted to something which more adequately manifests the wearer's ability to afford wasteful consumption.

Dress as an Expression of the Pecuniary Culture

It will be in place, by way of illustration, to show in some detail how the economic principles so far set forth apply to everyday facts in some one direction of the life process. For this purpose no line of consumption affords a more apt illustration than expenditure on dress. It is especially the rule of the conspicuous waste of goods that finds expression in dress, although the other, related principles of pecuniary repute are also exemplified in the same contrivances. Other methods of putting one's pecuniary standing in evidence serve their end effectually, and other methods are in vogue always and everywhere; but expenditure on dress has this advantage over most other methods, that our apparel is always in evidence and affords an indication of our pecuniary standing to all observers at the first glance. It is also true that admitted expenditure for display is more obviously present, and is, perhaps, more universally practised in the matter of dress than in any other line of consumption. No one finds difficulty in assenting to the commonplace that the greater part of the expenditure incurred by all classes for apparel is incurred for the sake of a respectable appearance rather than for the protection of the person. And probably at no other point is the sense of shabbiness so keenly felt as it is if we fall short of the standard set by social usage in this matter of dress. It is true of dress in even a higher degree than of most other items of consumption, that people will undergo a very considerable degree of privation in the comforts or the necessaries of life in order to afford what is considered a decent amount of wasteful consumption; so that it is by no means an uncommon occurrence, in an inclement climate, for people to go ill clad in order to appear well dressed. And the commercial value of the goods used for clothing in any modern community is made up to a much larger extent of the fashionableness, the reputability of the goods than of the mechanical service which they render in clothing the person of the wearer. The need of dress is eminently a "higher" or spiritual need.

This spiritual need of dress is not wholly, nor even chiefly, a nai've propensity for display of expenditure. The law of conspicuous waste guides consumption in apparel, as in other things, chiefly at the second remove, by shaping the canons of taste and decency. In the common run of cases the conscious motive of the wearer or purchaser of conspicuously wasteful apparel is the need of conforming to established usage, and of living up to the accredited standard of taste and reputability. It is not only that one must be guided by the code of proprieties in dress in order to avoid the mortification that comes of unfavorable notice and comment, though that motive in itself counts for a great deal; but besides that, the requirement of expensiveness is so ingrained into our habits of thought in matters of dress that any other than expensive apparel is instinctively odious to us. Without reflection or analysis, we feet that what is inexpensive is unworthy. "A cheap coat makes a cheap man." "Cheap and nasty" is recognized to hold true in dress with even less mitigation than in other lines of consumption. On the ground both of taste and of serviceability, an inexpensive article of apparel is held to be inferior, under the maxim "cheap and nasty." We find things beautiful, as well as serviceable, somewhat in proportion as they are costly. With few and inconsequential exceptions, we all find a costly hand-wrought article of apparel much preferable, in point of beauty and of serviceability, to a less expensive imitation of it, however cleverly the spurious article may imitate the costly original; and what offends our sensibilities in the spurious article is not that it falls short in form or color, or, indeed, in visual effect in any way. The offensive object, may be so close an imitation as to defy any but the closest scrutiny; and yet so soon as the counterfeit is detected, its aesthetic value, and its commercial value as well, declines precipitately. Not only that, but it may be asserted with but small risk of contradiction that the aesthetic value of a detected counterfeit in dress declines somewhat in the same proportion as the counterfeit is cheaper than its original. It loses caste aesthetically because it falls to a lower pecuniary grade.

But the function of dress as an evidence of ability to pay does not end with simply showing that the wearer consumes valuable goods in excess of what is required for physical comfort. Simple conspicuous waste of goods is effective and gratifying as far as it goes; it is good *prima facie* evidence of pecuniary success, and consequently *prima facie* evidence of social worth. But dress has subtler and more far-reaching possibilities than this crude, first-hand evidence of wasteful consumption only. If, in addition to showing that the wearer can afford to consume freely and uneconomically, it can also be shown in the same stroke that he or she is not under the necessity of earning a livelihood, the evidence of social worth is enhanced in a very considerable degree. Our dress, therefore, in order to serve its purpose effectually, should not only be expensive, but it should also make plain to all observers that the wearer is not engaged in any kind of productive labor. In the evolutionary process by which our system of dress has been elaborated into its present admirably perfect adaptation to its purpose, this subsidiary line of evidence has received due attention. A detailed examination of what passes in popular apprehension for elegant apparel will show that it is contrived at every point to convey the impression that the wearer does not habitually put forth any useful effort. It goes without saying that no apparel can be considered elegant, or even decent, if it shows the effect of manual labor on the part of the wearer, in the way of soil or wear. The pleasing effect of neat and spotless garments is chiefly, if not altogether, due to their carrying the suggestion of leisure exemption from personal contact with industrial processes of any kind. Much of the charm that invests the patent-leather shoe, the stainless linen, the lustrous cylindrical hat, and the walking-stick, which so greatly enhance the native dignity of a gentleman, comes of their pointedly suggesting that the wearer cannot when so attired bear a hand in any employment that is directly and immediately of any human use. Elegant dress serves its purpose of elegance not only in that it is expensive, but also because it is the insignia of leisure. It not only shows that the wearer is able to consume a relatively large value, but it argues at the same time that he consumes without producing.

The dress of women goes even farther than that of men in the way of demonstrating the wearer's abstinence from productive employment. It needs no argument to enforce the generalization that the more elegant styles of feminine bonnets go even farther towards making work impossible than does the man's high hat. The woman's shoe adds the so-called French heel to the evidence of enforced leisure afforded by its polish; because this high heel obviously makes any, even the simplest and most necessary manual work extremely difficult. The like is true even in a higher degree of the skirt and the rest of the drapery which characterizes woman's dress. The substantial reason for our tenacious attachment to the skirt is just this: it is expensive and it hampers the wearer at every turn and incapacitates her for all useful exertion. The like is true of the feminine custom of wearing the hair excessively long.

But the woman's apparel not only goes beyond that of the modern man in the degree in which it argues exemption from labor;

it also adds a peculiar and highly characteristic feature which differs in kind from anything habitually practised by the men. This feature is the class of contrivances of which the corset is the typical example. The corset is, in economic theory, substantially a mutilation, undergone for the purpose of lowering the subject's vitality and rendering her permanently and obviously unfit for work. It is true, the corset impairs the personal attractions of the wearer, but the loss suffered on that score is offset by the gain in reputability which comes of her visibly increased expensiveness and infirmity. It may broadly be set down that the womanliness of woman's apparel resolves itself, in point of substantial fact, into the more effective hindrance to useful exertion offered by the garments peculiar to women. This difference between masculine and feminine apparel is here simply pointed out as a characteristic feature. The ground of its occurrence will be discussed presently.

So far, then, we have, as the great and dominant norm of dress, the broad principle of conspicuous waste. Subsidiary to this principle, and as a corollary under it, we get as a second norm the principle of conspicuous leisure. In dress construction this norm works out in the shape of divers contrivances going to show that the wearer does not and, as far as it may conveniently be shown, cannot engage in productive labor. Beyond these two principles there is a third of scarcely less constraining force, which will occur to any one who reflects at all on the subject. Dress must not only be conspicuously expensive and inconvenient; it must at the same time be up to date. No explanation at all satisfactory has hitherto been offered of the phenomenon of changing fashions. The imperative requirement of dressing in the latest accredited manner, as well as the fact that this accredited fashion constantly changes from season to season, is sufficiently familiar to every one, but the theory of this flux and change has not been worked out. We may of course say, with perfect consistency and truthfulness, that this principle of novelty is another corollary under the law of conspicuous waste. Obviously, if each garment is permitted to serve for but a brief term, and if none of last season's apparel is carried over and made further use of during the present season, the wasteful expenditure on dress is greatly increased. This is good as far as it goes, but it is negative only. Pretty much all that this consideration warrants us in saying is that the norm of conspicuous waste exercises a controlling surveillance in all matters of dress, so that any change in the fashions must conform to the requirement of wastefulness; it leaves unanswered the question as to the motive for making and accepting a change in the prevailing styles, and it also fails to explain why conformity to a given style at a given time is so imperatively necessary as we know it to be.

Psychological Analysis of Fashion Motivation

The psychology of choice is one of the most fundamental problems in applied social psychology. It is essentially the study of motivation, of attitudes and desires functioning as "coercive" and directive energies leading to acceptancerejection responses.

It is the purpose of this investigation to study the practical problems of choice in the selection of women's clothes. For the sake of concreteness and comparability of data only the selection of the "daytime frock," a garment of general utility, is considered. This study is concerned with the complex of numerous varied factors in such selection, their relative potencies, their interrelationships and their conflicting and congruent effects on the resultant activity of choice.

The choice of a dress is a major social activity. A study of this selective activity involves not only a consideration of the cultural pattern but of the individual as an element in the pattern. It involves also a consideration of the individual's awareness of the self as an entity, a Gestalt, within the total configuration.

The problem is concerned with such questions as: To what extent does the awareness of self involve self-analysis? How cognizant is the individual of the qualities and characteristics of the physical I and the I that is called personality? If self-analysis leads to awareness of the qualities that contribute to the total Gestalt, the prevalent mode determines the standard of beauty by which these qualities are judged acceptable or unacceptable. Clothes attitudes may be analyzed down to awareness of self, self-analysis, recognition of defects and the creation of an "ideal" self. Clothes are not only part of the self, but they are the means for expressing those traits which seem desirable. They are at once the instrument of self-expression and of conformity to an ideal. If a woman chooses clothes to present a certain picture of herself, the choice depends not only on a knowledge of self, but also on the perception of certain basic elements of design of the garment. Thus the desire for conformity, desire for self-expression and aesthetic preferences and judgements exert their influences on the selection of the dress, which is both an end and a means. Fashion is sometimes compared to or contrasted with "custom" which, of course, has greater stability as well as wider scope. In general, fashion is defined as the "mode" in chôices within a group; mode in a statistical sense. But, besides its connotations of conformity, popularity, prevalence and majority opinion, it is also recognized as being characterized by change often described as "cyclic," but not necessarily associated with progress. The modal elements might be considered centripetal and the cyclic elements centrifugal in their influences. Suggestibility, imitativeness, desire to conform, desire for companionship and fear of social disapproval are some of the individual tendencies most often mentioned to account for this group modality in choices. Desire for the new, progress, desire for economic and social prestige and desire for leadership and self-assertion are some of the urges usually associated with change in fashion. Commercial interests and fashion experts are included among the factors which make for style change and style adoption.

Relative Importance of Group Attitudes

Of the fundamental attitudes involved in the psychology of choice of dress, the following are found to be among the more significant:

1. Desire to conform is the most diffuse of the desires measured; is more effective as a motive in determining the time of buying than desire for economy, and varies in intensity with the technical or professional interest of the group.
2. Desire for comfort with respect to temperature and tactual sensations is very important.
3. Modesty, though a significant factor, is not a very important motive for resisting a new fashion (brassiere bathing suit).

Desire for comfort (freedom of movement), aesthetic standards, awareness of physical style defects, desire for conformity, are other factors creating resistance.

4. Desire for economy is very widespread as an attitude but as a motive in determining time of buying is less effective than the desire to conform.
5. The aesthetic impulse is very important in the choice of a dress and functions in conjunction with the desire to be beautiful and the desire for conformity.

Of the constellation of fundamental attitudes related to the desire for selfexpression:

1. Awareness of the physical self is very important in the choice of clothes.
2. Desire to be beautiful is important and operates in conjunction with the desire to conform.
3. The expression of different personality traits through the choice of a dress is of variable importance:

Desire to express "personality" is of more than moderate importance. Desire to appear distinctive is of moderate importance. Desire to appear dignified or youthful is of barely moderate importance. Desire to appear competent is of less than moderate importance. Desire to appear prosperous is of very little importance.

The most important factor determining the place of purchase is direct experience or experimental investigation rather than advertisements or recommendation. Sources of style knowledge are of variable importance to the different groups. Reading sources are on the average, among the more important; social sources are among the less important.

Fashion knowledge is approximately commensurate with reading habits and technical interest in fashion.

Summary

The following conclusions are drawn from the results of this investigation: The really fundamental attitudes in the choice of clothes those associated with the desire to conform, desire for comfort, desire for economy, the artistic impulse, and with self expression through sex and femininity occur so positively and so widely diffused as to seem to be "universal." They cut across differences in educational backgrounds, in economic status, in reading habits, in amount of technical fashion knowledge and in professional interest in fashion.

Most differences in attitudes involve differences in the intensity of the desire to be in fashion and in the more specific and practical expression of the fundamental attitudes. Awareness of the physical Gestalt and a definite desire to attain to ideals of slenderness and tallness, particularly by those who deviate most from the standards of beauty set by fashion, are keen. Attitudes are naturally very closely interwoven and interact functionally on each other. The choice of particular design elements in a dress may at once express the individual's ideas of what is beautiful, the desire to conform to the prevailing mode and the desire to be beautiful through creating the illusion of beauty of form and through enhancing personal coloring with clothes colors.

The desire to be beautiful is evidenced by the choice of design elements of dress effective in creating the illusion of beauty of form and by the choice of colors to enhance the tones of the physical self. The desire to express personality is very widely diffused, although such individual personality characteristics as distinctiveness, youthfulness and dignity seem to be of barely moderate importance as objectives in the choice of a dress. Expression of the economic or social traits the desire to appear competent or affluent seems to be definitely negative as motivating factors.

The attitudes involved in the expression of the self do not differ significantly as between different groups. An index of the importance which the choice of a dress assumes in the mind of the consumer is the amount of time and effort expended in windowshopping and shopping around, which more often than advertisements or recommendation directly determine the place where to buy.

Advertising seems to be more potent as a source of fashion ideas than as a direct stimulus to buying. Discrepancies in advertising practice and consumer attitudes may account in part, though not entirely, for this loss in effectiveness.

❑❑❑

3

Fashion, Dress Reform and the New Women

Introduction

The mid-nineteenth century to the early years of the twentieth century there were plainly many advocates of reform dress striving to move toward what they perceived to be more comfortable, healthful, and beautiful clothing. Between the turn of the century and the end of the First World Waress than twenty years many changes took place in women's dress. Some of them reflect the efforts of the reformers. The move toward rationality continued in the twentieth century, with the strongest voices coming from the arts communities, especially from the reformers who advocated applying the principles of art to dress.

This impact of the reformers in "making fashion rational" in the twentieth century. It considers the impact of each reform style trousers, underwear, and artistic dress on future fashion and the reasons for the eventual acceptance of these styles. It also addresses the connection of high-fashion designers to reform efforts, particularly the efforts of avantgarde designers Paul Poiret and Mariano Fortuny, who are often credited, wrongly perhaps, with freeing women from constricting clothing. This chapter also incorporates the voices of early-twentieth-century women in the form of reports on the progress reformers thought they had made toward improving women's dress. Finally, this chapter addresses the legacy these reformers left for women and their impact on styles of clothing worn during the remainder of the twentieth century.

Became of the Reform Styles

In many respects, fashion capitulated to the efforts of the reformers well before the First World War. Indeed, after each reform style was introduced, it took on a life of its own. Bloomers, or some form of bifurcated garment, were worn for classes in physical education and all sorts of outdoor activities. Indeed, for sports women needed comfortable clothing, which they often devised themselves. Women denounced heavy and restrictive undergarments, and many of them refined and reduced the number of undergarments they wore, adopting the reform style universally until central heating relieved many women of the need for extra warmth. The very stiff steel and whalebone corset became passé, although many women did wear lighter corsets, some in a reform style; yet others wore no corset at all. Ultimately, the philosophy of the aesthetes took hold. The lighter-weight medieval and classically inspired gowns of the artistic reformers gained support with the makers of fashion. This support allowed artistic reform dress to become an acceptable fashion.

Trousers

The problem with women's dress, as argued by reformers in the mid-nineteenth century, was that it was harmful to women's health women's outer clothes were too voluminous, heavy, and bulky; skirts and trains were too long and dragged on the ground; and the weight was distributed unevenly on the body. The underclothes were too heavy, women wore too many petticoats and other layers, and the corset was worn much too tight. In addition, underwear provided no warmth in winter and was too hot in summer. In short, many women felt encumbered by fashion. Feminists added the complaint that their cumbersome clothes were politically at fault because the burden of fashion prevented women from partaking in the public world of politics, business, and commerce. In order to eliminate these problems, both health reformers and feminists adopted loose trousers worn under short skirts, a style that came to be called the Bloomer costume.

Although reformers promoted trousers as street wear for women throughout the second half of the nineteenth century, their efforts to make trousers an alternative to fashion were successful only in the area of active sports and then largely for events that occurred away from public view mountaineering, hiking, and bicycling. However, women did have a choice of skirt, trousers, or a skirt worn over trousers for these activities. As more leisure time gave women the opportunity to engage in these and other sports, they could experience wearing trousers. Of course, in colleges many young women were required to wear a bifurcated gymnasium suit. Indeed, the gymnasium outfit, which served as inspiration for the Bloomer, continued to be worn for calisthenics and physicaleducation classes in schools well into the twentieth century, sometimes with a skirt attached. Apparently women's wearing trousers in public places went against strong gender roles and ideas of propriety or etiquette in dress. Pants were not considered feminine and hence were deemed unattractive on women. Cultural expectations of women definitely placed restrictions on their wearing trousers. Acceptance occurred only when trousers seemed a truly practical and logical choice for a specific activity.

Reform Underwear

In the early 1870s, when health reformers decided to solve women's clothing problems by devising lighter-weight and less restrictive underwear and promoting the abolition of the corset, they were more successful than they had been with trousers. Underwear reform had a broader base of activists and greater acceptance in part because it was more subtly subversive; the changes could not be seen. The idea of returning women's bodies from the distortions caused by heavy, stiff, and rigid underwear to a more natural human shape was a desire of the artistic reformers as well as of the feminists, physicians, and hygienists. Reformers with an artistic perspective were some of the most ardent supporters, and many developed underwear systems of their own. The new underwear systems offered many improvements even distribution of the weight of the clothing, fewer undergarments, and the demise of the corset.

Reform underwear promoted by these reformers became popular, although it was difficult to convince women to leave off their corsets. Some women adopted simple bust supporters that looked very much like tightly fitting, yet boneless and cordless under bodices, or a reform-style corset that was softer and had less stiffening than fashionable corsets, something similar to Annie Jenness-Miller's "model bodice." Others chose to replace the corset with an early form of the brassiere, or what they also called a bust supporter, a garment that fitted over the breasts and not over the upper torso as a "bodice" would fit. Of course, as the outer dress became simplified, less rigid and cumbersome, underwear styles conformed to it. The introduction of central heating in homes also eliminated the need for excess underwear. These new systems of underwear clearly solved some of the problems of unhygienic clothing. Nonetheless, problems remained the tightness, weight, and length of the outer garment.

Artistic Dress

In Europe and America artistic reformers argued that beauty was apparent only in a body that had not been misshapen by the fashionable corset. In many instances they recommended a return to earlier forms of dress, designs based on classical Greek or medieval dress. The aesthetic concept of fitness to purpose was a dominant theme, one that supported the idea that dress should correspond to the individual woman. Yet these reformers believed that the body as it appears in nature could be improved through exercise and enhanced by making choices of clothing styles and colors based on the principles of art.

The princess and Empire-style garments that Liberty advocated in London and that Annie Jenness-Miller promoted in America in the 1880s and 1890s were advertised as acceptable "fashionable dress" in "the reform style" in Europe after 1905. Most of all, major fashion designers discovered that the simplicity of antique classical dress would enhance the natural beauty of the female form. When fashion designers began to copy the simple, artistic reform styles and recreated a new Empire or Directoire look in 1907, referring to it as the new reform style, the New Woman of the twentieth century quickly adopted it. How many women actually went without a corset under these garments is not known. Images in magazines are misleading, for fashion illustrators of the period often made women fit a corseted fashionable ideal that was even more unnatural than the effect of the corset in normal circumstances; photographs would provide more accurate examples.

Offering "A New Philosophy of Fashion" in 1900, Helen G. Ecob stated the case clearly for the artistic reformers, observing that the problem with "contemporary dress" was that it "attempts to conform the human figure to the prevailing fashion." Her solution was to draw on science and art to force fashion to conform to the human figure. "Intelligence, " she declared, "must be applied to dress." Her thoughts were clearly in accord with the artists of Europe and America when she stated that "the science of dress" was based on two basiç laws. The first was the law of necessity wherein the means were adapted to the ends. In her view, "Every ornament must have a purpose." The second law was "the demand of the aesthetic nature of beauty." The first aim of scientific dress was to set up a standard of beauty for the feminine form based on the study of nature. "Dress, " she believed, "must adapt itself to the laws of the human body."

Ecob argued that the tyranny of the trade was a serious obstacle and "their despotism will cease only when women combine to demand stability and intelligence in design." Furthermore, she suggested, "We must learn to distinguish between good and bad fashions through the application of art criticism, just as we learn the worth of literature, or feel the laws of literary art." In order to accomplish this, Ecob proposed a school of design that would assume that dress is "a philosophical study that raises the profession to a dignity becoming so serious a subject." Dress, she stated, is related to economics, medicine, art, social questions, and ethics. The school would provide systematic and comprehensive training in "this difficult branch of decorative art" and be a sort of bureau of intelligence open to the average woman. The curriculum would include: anatomy and physiology, art anatomy and drawing, physical training, color theory, historic art and the history of dress, principles of ornamentation and tex tile design, sewing and drafting, cutting and fitting, designing, and the economics and ethics of dress.

Most of all, Ecob argued, "Woman's new relations to the industrial world call for the evolution of clothing suited to her new activities. As men and women cooperate in comradeship in the work place, comfort and good taste must replace attraction as the emphasis of dress."

Impact of Reform: Sum is Greater than its Parts

Efforts toward improving women's dress were, of course, related. The artistic reformers would have worn a trousered outfit for mountaineering, hiking, and similar outdoor activities, and they quite enthusiastically adopted union suits and favored shaped under bodices and bust supporters in place of a corset. Annie Jenness-Miller's nonradical "improvements" for women confirm this. For not only were her dress designs largely artistic, in that she acted on the belief that clothing designs should be based on art principles, she was also an advocate for women's wearing reform undergarments and she promoted comfortable trousered garments for outings and other outdoor activities. To dress correctly, women would have to wear her artistically designed dresses with her system of reform ("correct") underwear, which replaced the corset with her model bodice if needed. These dresses were meant for all occasions, for use both at home and in public. Her most radical suggestion was the "business suit" for women that consisted of a short skirt worn with gaiters. Her success centered on her ability to work within and around existing ideas of propriety and appropriateness and, of course, in concealing her methods.

Fashion Business and Reform Garments

The extent to which women adopted trousers, improved their undergarments, and wore artistic dress reveals the distaste that advocates of clothing reform had for fashionable dress. Yet little has been said about how the fashion industry felt about these promoters of anti-fashion. The producers of fashion dressmakers and department stores, and indeed the *haute couture* were not immune to the efforts of the reformers. Some supported their efforts. Since they needed to maintain their client base in order to survive, the professionals had to produce clothing that fit the requirements of their customers. They could not ignore the needs of the public, and clearly women's needs changed from the mid-nineteenth century to the early decades of the twentieth century. Not only was there a growth in population and more wealth but women's roles were changing. Manymore women were employed outside of the home and attending universities and colleges.

As observed by Helen Ecob, the new women needed clothing appropriate to their new public activities. They wanted clothing that emphasized practicality rather than femininity. Women also had more time to pursue leisure activities that required activity-specific, comfortable, and appropriate clothing.

Reform Efforts of the Haute Couture

Dress-reform efforts within the world of the *haute couture* actually occurred as early as the mid-nineteenth century. Although many may not view the creation of the cage crinoline as "reform," in many respects it was an improvement. It lightened the overall weight of the clothing worn by women by reducing the number of petticoats they needed. When Charles Frederick Worth altered the shape of the crinoline after it had reached enormous proportions in the mid1860s, this, too, could be viewed as an improvement. Furthermore, while they were not ready to give up the corset, or suggest trousers for everyday, many high-fashion designers agreed with the reformers when it came to the creation of artistic dresses (tea gowns) and clothing for sporting activities. Although couturiers such as Charles Frederick Worth and his sons made their reputations on elaborate court gowns and ball gowns, their elite customers also needed clothing for other occasions. In fact, their clients were often the first women to take up preoccupations that required special clothing for example, elaborate entertaining at home, bicycling, yachting, and shooting. Dresses worn for other daytime activities or for evening pursuits would not do, nor would a gymnasium costume or a bathing suit. Clients of the *haute couture* included not only women of the aristocracy but also the wealthy bourgeoisie, actresses, dancers, and opera singers. Among them were newsworthy women such as the dancers Eleanora Duse and Isadora Duncan, socialite Peggy Guggenheim, and member of the aristocracy Queen Marie of Romania.

Designers often made up special gowns for these women to wear when posing for their portraits. Apparently the tea gown was a favorite for informal portraits. Diana DeMarly believes that the timeless quality of tea gowns, based as they were on historical style, made them appropriate selections for portraits. Sitters for the artist M. Dagnan-Boureret, for instance, often wore "timeless" gowns designed by Jean Phillipe Worth.

There are a number of examples of couture involvement in reform efforts. The London branch set up a booth at the 1883 Rational Dress Association Exhibition held in Prince's Hall, London, with designs suggested by the Rational Dress Association. Worth et Cie., entered the competition with garments for a variety of occasions and competed for first prize in the evening-dress category. Worth even went so far as to produce a "Dress of the Future" for Mrs. E. M. King, the sponsor of the exhibition. Her futurist garment had no skirt and included short knickerbocker trousers in a vaguely seventeenth-century man's style. Worth et Cie., received a silver award for the artistic design of their evening dress. Worth evening gown with trousers, shown at the Rational Dress Association Exhibition in Prince's Hall, 1883.

Impact of Aesthetic Reform on Couturiers

Of all the dress-reform efforts, it is clear that the artistic-dress reformers had the most influence on fashion. The clothing created by artistic reform-minded artists and designers became accessible to the fashion world not through advertising as we know it today but rather by a more informal means. Communication about artistic dress occurred at an individual level through the women who wore it. Wider publicity would have come, however, through favorable commentary by art critics and journalists who gave vivid accounts of clothing worn by aesthete women to art exhibitions and from their reports on reform gowns shown at arts and crafts and fashion exhibitions. Such favorable coverage was in stark contrast to the reaction of the press toward women's wearing trousers in public in the mid-nineteenth century.

The public was made aware of artistic dress promoted by the Liberty Company through magazines such the *Queen,* Liberty's own sales catalogs, and the expansion of its shops and depots throughout Europe and America between the mid-1880s and the early twentieth century. As noted in chapters 5 and 6, artistic ideas for dress spread quickly throughout Europe. In Italy the reform dress took the name of "style liberty." Efforts were aided by art magazines such as *Dekorative Kunst* and *Deutsche Kunst und Dekoration,* whose writers commented very favorably on artistic styles. Frequent exhibitions of artistic dress also communicated the reformers' efforts in promoting the new aesthetic ideal for women's dress.

Artists and designers involved in the modern movement were receptive to exotic new ideas from abroad. Aesthetic ideas and design forms from Japan, Turkey, and the Near East all became sources for new ideas and expressions of taste. These new aesthetic ideas were often incorporated into the clothing designs of artistic reformers, along with the romantic, historical expressions influenced by classical Greece, the Middle Ages, and the Renaissance. It would have been practically impossible for designers of couture clothing to have no contact with these artistic efforts, especially when, as was frequently the case, the designers themselves were interested in the modern movement in the arts and looking for ideas to express this new-found modernity through fashion design.

In 1913 the *Independent* commented on the influence of the artistic reformers on fashion, noting that "the women of Germany and France, in their recent dress reform movements, developed designs that satisfied the artistic sense as well as the desire for comfort, and their influence has had a great deal to do with shaping new styles."

Although a number of designers were clearly sympathetic to the reformers' efforts, the two most often linked with artistic reform of dress are the earlytwentieth-century avant-garde designers, Paul Poiret and Mariano Fortuny. Both were in tune with the efforts of the artistic-dress reformers in Germany and Austria, yet there were obvious differences in their approach. Poiret worked from inside the couture business; Fortuny created his designs as an extension of his art enterprises, which included theatrical design.

Paul Poiret. Artistic dress promoted in the 1880s generally did not include constricting undergarments. The gowns were meant to free the body and allow it to retain its natural shape. Women were advised to wear reform undergarments with them, which meant, of course, that no corsets, bustles, or constrictions of any kind would be worn. Yet in the early twentieth century, Paul Poiret claimed that it was he who freed women from the corset. From the previous discussion of artistic-reform dress in Britain and Europe, it should be clear that women had many opportunities to free themselves of the corset long before Paul Poiret came on the fashion scene.

Although previous scholars have pointed out that Poiret was not solely responsible for freeing women from corsets, there has been little recognition of the reciprocal influence between Poiret and the designers of artistic dress in Germany and Austria or of the possible influence on him of the classical styles promoted by the Liberty Company. Poiret also claimed to have invented the brassiere, but we know, of course, that the reformers of underwear had long been promoting a similar garment, a bust supporter, as a reform undergarment. Wearing it allowed women to discard the corset.

Garments that Poiret designed in 1908 (and later) that were very much in keeping with the artistic reformers' philosophy included his "pantaloon skirts, " a two-piece garment with a tunic-like dress worn over long trousers and his Directoire gowns. After his marriage in 1904, Poiret traveled continuously in Europe, discovering new movements in the decorative arts and meeting artists and architects. He met Emilie Flöge, Gustav Klimt, and Josef Hoffmann in Vienna. Poiret was aware, therefore, of the reform dress being promoted within the artistic community, and certainly he would have been aware of the artistic gowns offered by the Liberty Company, which, in fact, opened a shop in Paris beginning in 1890. Paul Poiret clearly was not the first designer to adopt the Directoire high-waisted style. His own high-waisted "Directoire" dresses are not that much different from the Liberty offerings of a much earlier date. It is ironic, perhaps, that by the 1920s, Poiret was creating dress designs for Liberty's.

There was considerable interaction between Paul Poiret and the Wiener Werkstätte. Poiret was especially impressed with their hand-painted silks. He later used examples created by Wiener Werkstätte designer Dogobert Peche. In fact, the head of the Wiener Werkstätte fashion department, Edward Joseph WimmerWisgrill, emphasized that Paul Poiret had picked up the general reform elements of artistic dress and adopted them "for the whole civilized world."

The influence, however, was no doubt reciprocal, for Otto Lendecke, who began to work for the Wiener Werkstätte in 1911, had worked for Poiret in Paris prior to his arrival in Vienna. Lendecke produced many fashion designs, dresses, textiles, stage designs, and ballet costumes. In 1917 Lendecke established the magazine *Die Damenwelt*, a short-lived but beautiful fashion paper formulated in an artistic manner rather than as a fashion periodical.

Paul Poiret saw the Wiener Werkstätte exhibit in Rome in 1911 and became so fascinated with Hoffmann's pavilion and Klimt's paintings that he immediately set off for Vienna. It was not until 1912, however, that Poiret was able to visit Hoffmann's famous pavilion, the Palais Stoclet in Brussels. As noted by Werner J. Schweiger, Poiret purchased many Wiener Werkstätte products in Vienna: "He bought so much that the products of the WW, the Austrian interior decorating industry and the Kunstgewerbeschule came to exert a very strong influence on Paris fashion in 1912."

In writing about the fashions of the Wiener Werkstätte, Jane Kallir described the line as incorporating two basic trends: the "Reformkleid" (reform dress) and its re-interpretation by "the French designer Poiret." When Kallir states that Poiret's contribution was the revival of the classical style, she was apparently unaware of the efforts of the artistic reformers in producing classical styles, as well as other historically inspired designs, especially the medieval and Renaissance silhouettes. Certainly, the styles promoted by the German and some Austrian artistic designers in the first decade of the twentieth century reveal a propensity for a high "Empire" or classical Greek waistline.

Another element that appears in both Wiener Werkstätte designs and those of Poiret is the influence of what has been called Orientalism. Both the Werkstätte and Poiret produced pleated, Middle Eastern inspired harem pants. Poiret's harem pants predate the brightly colored costume designs of León Bakst for the Ballet Russes, which were appearing on stage all over Europe. The exotic colors and styles were new and exciting, and they were greatly admired not only by the artistic community but by their general audiences as well. The popularity of the ballet in turn helped sales of harem pants. Interestingly enough, Mariano Fortuny also produced pleated trousers. All of these designers created the harem trousers as lounging pajamas, not as street wear.

Mariano Fortuny. Mariano Fortuny y Madrazo was a painter who created clothes. His ideas were largely divorced from fashion, yet his clothes were worn by many fashionable women. Although born in Granada, Spain, Mariano Fortuny spent his formative years in Paris and then settled in Venice, where he became an accomplished artist, theatrical designer, photographer, and architect. Yet today he is perhaps best known for his textiles and the design of the finely pleated "Delphos Robe" (dress), which he patented.

Fortuny used pleated silk for the Delphos dress, which was cut narrow and straight to hang loosely from the shoulders. Sometimes it was gathered in at the waist or just under the breast "as in the manner of Directoire or Empire gowns." The style of Fortuny dresses relates to the artistic reform dress of the period in that they both freed women from constraints of the corset and other restrictive undergarments. As Guillermo De Osma has argued, the real reformers were the artists and aesthetes who, like Fortuny, wanted to create a new style of dress, one that would "liberate the body, allow for complete freedom of movement, provide comfort and warmth, and, above all, be beautiful."

As in the case of Poiret, Fortuny traveled widely, especially in England and France. He had contact with the artistic community and the artists and designers in the modern movement. One objective of the European modern design movement was to break down the barriers of traditional art. Fortuny shared this view, believing that sculpture, paintings, etchings, photographs, and dresses were of equal artistic value.

Fortuny was familiar with the work of Arthur Lasenby Liberty, Walter Crane, Henry van de Velde, Peter Behrens, Gustav Klimt, Josef Hoffmann, and Koloman Moser, all of whom in one way or another aided the development of artistic dress in Europe. Fortuny also would have been knowledgeable about the Greek classicism found in the paintings of Albert Moore, Frederick Leighton, Sir Lawrence Alma-Tadema, and William Godward, who had exhibited their works in the Beinnale in Venice. Another source of influence on Fortuny's designs was his personal experience with Asian and Arabic art, which he gained from his father, who had been an accomplished painter. As noted by De Osma, painting, particularly Venetian painting, was also a main source of inspiration. Fortuny was able to incorporate ancient Greek, Venetian, and exotic elements into his work.

Fortuny, as De Osma argued, was greatly influenced by all elements of the artistic world, by art and artistic dress, critics, patrons, and the *literati*. He was well prepared to create garments that glorified the human body in the way that the clothing worn in ancient Greece had done. From De Osma's point of view, Fortuny in a very personal and quiet manner forced reform dress to become acceptable fashion.

There was a degree of escapism or theatricality found in many types of reform dress, including the tea gowns of the British aesthetes, the Empire and princess styles of the artistic reformers, and the Greek styles of Liberty, Poiret, and Fortuny. Many styles had historical elements that were for the most part unrelated to fashion. The extent to which reform styles differed from fashion placed them in a sphere that went beyond fashion, and thus by wearing these new reform styles women could feel that they were indeed escaping from the constraints of fashion. In its ability to transport the wearer beyond reality, to a new level of personal awareness, artistic reform dress actually aided in the eventual modification of that reality. De Osma has observed that this quality to transcend is usually the function of great art; but then the designers thought of their dresses as art.

Promotion of Artistic Dress: The Poiret and Fortuny Methods
Fortuny's success in promoting his designs owes in part to his clientele. Unlike Poiret, who made larger-than-life public gestures to gain attention for his creations, Fortuny gathered around him devoted

friends and clients who appreciated the quality and timelessness of his dresses and textiles. Fortuny's supporters included the writers Gabriele D'Annunzio and Marcel Proust, entertainers Eleanora Duse and Isadora Duncan, Queen Marie of Romania, and many socialites and aristocrats in Europe as well as wealthy Americans. Peggy Guggenheim maintained a palace in Venice and was a great admirer of Fortuny. By wearing the Delphos dress, or through making references to Fortuny's works of art, his friends provided a link between Fortuny's Venice and the world at large.

While Fortuny's gowns were at first usually worn only in the home, women in the visual and performing-arts fields often wore them on stage and even in public. Ruth St. Denis wore Fortuny's Knossis scarves for performances of Indian dances in Berlin in 1907. Isadora Duncan, who revived Greek dance, and who performed frequently throughout Europe, also was an admirer of Fortuny. Duncan frequently wore classically inspired Greek dress, both on and off the stage. She considered herself to be a dress reformer. Her clothing allowed her to dance in a style far removed from the stiffness of the traditional ballet. In many respects Duncan reformed the dance and paved the way for the later innovations of Shawn, Duse, and Martha Graham. Duncan's performances revealed dance full of movement and expression. The director of the Ballet Russes, Sergei Diaghilev, and the designer Bakst had seen Duncan perform in Russia during her tour in 1906. Bakst, in particular, reinterpreted her dress for such ballets as *Narcisse* (1911), *Daphnis et Chloe* (1912), and *Après-Midi d'un Faune* (1912).

Fortuny's influence on women's clothing reform cannot be denied. Yet it can be said that the popularity of the Ballet Russes largely created the demand for Fortuny's dresses and cloaks with their exotic names. Clearly, there was a mutual impact. Even Poiret admired and copied Fortuny's work, creating his own version of the Delphos dress in the 1910s and selling Fortuny's tunics as early as 1908. Fortuny's influence on reformers in the United States became a reality after his gowns were exhibited in New York in 1914. Two years later, Belle Armstrong Whitney used Fortuny gowns to illustrate "ideal dress" in *What to Wear, a Book for Women*. Whitney believed that Fortuny's gowns fulfilled all her conditions for the ideal dress, which should be above fashion and change: "efficiency, simplicity, personality, quality materials and a high standard of workmanship and artistry."

Other artists who followed Fortuny's lead include several Italian dressmakers. One was Maria Monaci Gallenga, who also had been a painter. Madame Babani opened a shop in Paris in 1919 selling her own Fortuny-like designs, as well as Liberty fabrics and Fortuny's garments and materials. A third dressmaker who relied heavily on the Ballet Russes and Fortuny designs was Madame Bertillon. While these women created dresses in the genre of Fortuny, none of their work is considered to be as refined as Fortuny's. Nonetheless, they were expanding the possibilities for women to wear a "reform style."

Poiret's method of promoting both his Paris fashion house and his interiordesign workshops was different from what couturiers like Worth had been doing. Indeed, his flamboyant approach was such a departure from the rather subdued tactics of most couture houses that Worth admonished him for it. Poiret was not like other couturiers he thrived on promotion and flaunted his successes. Illustrations of Poiret's gowns appeared in many fashion publications. The first of these were the albums devoted exclusively to Poiret designs. The initial album, *Les Robes de Paul Poiret racontées par Paul Iribe,* appeared in 1908; the second, *Les Choses de Paul Poiret vues par Georges Lepape,* came out in 1911.

Two new fashion magazines devoted to Art Deco, *Gazette du Bon Ton* and *Journal des Dames et des Modes,* featured Poiret fashions on a regular basis and greatly improved spreading fashion news to the public. Illustration was likewise important in *Les Modes, Vogue,* and other publications. The exposure raised fashion illustration to an art form and communicated fashion ideas to the public. Another aspect of the theater that aided the dissemination of fashion ideas was the publication *Comoedia Illustre,* which devoted many pages to *haute couture* between 1908 and 1912. The illustrators for these magazines Paul Iribe, Georges Lepape, Georges Barbier, and Roman de Tirtoff, better known as Erté helped to place new couture designs well within the context of Art Deco, thus establishing for the art of illustration a distinction unknown to previous artists of the genre.

Poiret was the first couturier to make a fashion tour of major European cities. He would show his latest fashions, using fashion models, and give lectures, appearing in Berlin, Vienna, Brussels, Moscow, St. Petersburg, and Munich. He also took his entourage to the United States, where he was lauded by the women of fashion and denounced by moralists and ministers. Poiret had his models attend the races at Longchamps, where they could parade around in his new styles with ease.

Both Poiret and Fortuny designed costumes for the ballet and theater, where members of the audience could easily spot a new creation and later order a similar gown or cloak. It is quite clear, then, that all the performing arts dance, opera, theater, ballet shared the designing talents of the couturiers for the creation of sets and costumes and that notable dancers, actresses, and opera singers were capable of communicating the latest styles both on and off the stage. Through early-twentieth-century promotion of artistic reform styles in fashion magazines such as the *Wiener Mode* and the *Queen,* and through the efforts of artists and avant-garde designers such as Fortuny and Poiret, reform dress became a more viable choice. Indeed, this promotion of reform styles as a fashion choice made these styles more accessible and hence gave the idea of wearing reform dress greater agency for women who, perhaps, had previously thought they could not be comfortable wearing styles that might be considered *outré.* Promotion was a key to their success. The Wiener Werkstätte also made the new styles acceptable to the public through distribution of postcards. The styles would seem fresh and appropriate to a new generation seeking change.

Contemporary Reports on the Progress of Reform Dress

It is safe to say that the movement to improve women's dress that emphasized artistic and healthy principles certainly benefited from the successful promotional efforts of Poiret and Fortuny, whose gowns nearly replicated the efforts of the artistic reformers. But these successes were largely at the high end of fashion. What were middle-class reformers saying about the progress they had made in improving their dress? What were designers of women's artistic dress saying about progress? Early-twentieth-century magazines published women's reactions to changes in dress styles. These commentaries report on the progress made in dress reform and reveal individual, personal feelings about the success of the movement in general.

Writing in 1903, Elizabeth Dryden observed that "the dress reformer, or physical culturist attired in her eccentric garbs, has lived to see her dreams realized: strangely enough the tabooed theories have been gradually adopted, but vanity, and not common sense won the day." She continued: "The tight waist was given up grudgingly ... and proof of its decline is seen in the pathetic appearance among us of a provincial creature gorgeously arrayed and sticking to her eighteen-inch waist." Indeed, Dryden argued, "It took a smart bicycle, golf or walking suit on a healthy, good looking woman, to show how comfort, neatness, and style might be combined; and to make the least natural of us feel ridiculous." Of course, she declared, reformers had an obligation to the athletic woman, for one could not golf or fence in a corset. She goes on to note that women who engaged in athletics learned to "stand tall, " which gave them the physique they needed to discard the laced waist, the corset.

Although women were very aware of the changes and improvements that had been made in their clothing, they were not satisfied. Many of them did not believe that reform ideas had been totally successful. For instance, Anna G. Noyes wrote in the *Independent* that while progress had been made in the elimination of the hoop skirt, the reduction in weight and number of petticoats, and the acceptance of the one-piece undergarment worn next to the skin, for the most part she wanted to see improvement, not simply change. "Clothes don't get better, " she said. "They are just different."

In an article titled, "Hygiene, Dress and Dress Reform, " Dr. Dudley A. Sargent, writing in the*Journal of Home Economics* in 1910, observed that "some evils have gone, some are on the wane or disguised, while some are still boldly displayed.Those who urge reform now do so on authority of scientific research and physiological laws." Obviously, progress had been made: the economic conditions of women's lives had changed, making the return to medieval, classical, or Asian styles unlikely. Yet, Sargent noted, women had to work out their dress reform in relation to the demands of living. He argued that women had a "moral obligation" to adopt "the light weight walking skirt and shirtwaist and the lightweight one piece dress, provided the undergarments, especially corsets, if worn, are properly made." He lamented that the high-waisted dress (worn in the previous year), which could have freed women from constraints of corsets, suffered in the hands of the caricaturists. Instead of accepting the soft lines down from the raised waist, women were wearing tightly fitting undergarments to maintain "the figure" and more often than not, the outer skirt had the same tightness, necessitating the long corset. Sargent argued that women should train their muscles so that they did not need corrective corsets.

Writing in 1914, Marguerite Wilkinson observed that "in our present period of development women's clothing does not express the personality of the individual woman." Women, she wrote, were still prey to absurdities in fashion. They still lived their lives in obedience to conventions. True individuality and appropriateness in clothing would come naturally, she believed, after women had their own life, work, interests, burdens, responsibilities, and "she will gradually find her own proper clothing to go with them that which is essentially suitable." Echoing the words of many artistic reformers who drew on aesthetic arguments, Wilkinson continued, declaring that the beauty of garments lies in their possessing "wholesome appropriateness and suitability to the uses for which they are made their essential simplicity and sincerity."

In 1913 an article in the *Independent* noted that progress had been made in a variety of ways. After recognizing the influence of the Germans and French regarding artistic dress, the article observed that there were now more choices of clothing styles that allowed greater scope for individual expression and taste. The new colors and color harmonies and soft, rich fabrics (the journal was referring no doubt to Liberty's) meant that clothing could fall into the "graceful lines of a Tanagra figurine." In addition, the article continued, there was no wasp waist of a corset: "The weight of women's clothing as a whole is only half or a third of what it used to be." Four dresses, the author observed, could be packed in the space that was formerly filled by one. One-piece dresses allowed the weight of the clothing to be supported from the shoulders, hips had fewer and lighter skirts to hold up, and the skirt no longer trailed behind. A thirty-two-inch waist was now permissible where formerly a twenty-inch waist was thought proper. And, although some women still wore the corset, it was worn lower and was softened through the use of rubber webbing in place of steel and whalebone.

Yet for all these positive comments regarding the demise of the corset, in 1915 the corset makers were still successful in turning fashion toward their products. Writing on corsets in the *Ladies Home Journal,* Edith M. Burtis argued, "The day of the corsetless figure is gone, and if you would be in fashion you must be corseted." The corsets, she believed, met the reformers' needs: comfort, hygiene, but also grace and charm never before obtained in corsetry. The article claimed that much harm had been done by the "no-corset" fad. The new corsets, it maintained, "support the abdomen and the bust and allow freedom over the diaphragm," and, harking back to arguments from centuries past, Burtis continued by saying that the corsets "brace the spine and force the body to stand in an erect, natural position."

By 1922, Jane Barr took notice of the progress made in improving women's dress: corsets had been discarded, heels and collars lowered, and one-piece dresses were the rule. However, reformers were still looking for improvement; now they wanted to have the freedom to wear knickerbockers (Bloomers) instead of skirts for sports.

In commenting on the influence of painting on the art of dress in 1927, Sonia DeLaunay observed that it was some time before the First World War that fashion began to free itself from the stranglehold of fashion; "It got rid of the corset, the high collar, all those elements of women's dress demanded by the aesthetics of fashion but which were contrary to hygiene and freedom of movement." DeLaunay attributed the improvement to "the change in women's lives [which] has provided the revolution. Women are increasingly active."

Legacy of Reform

In the early twentieth century, as each new generation came along, fewer and fewer young women were exposed to the corset and other restrictive garments; so it was not surprising that they would naturally accept trousers for specific activities; lighter, less restrictive underwear; and the new softer, less restrictive outer garments promoted by the fashion industry as the "reform style." As noted by several of the American commentators on the progress of reform, a number of events and cultural shifts aided the change in attitude about reform dress. Yet clearly women's clothing reform came about through evolution rather than revolution, a process that makes it difficult to assess the success of the various efforts.

Our judgment of what constitutes reform in women's dress from the 1850s to the 1920s is, unfortunately, clouded by our own experiences with clothing. We have difficulty comprehending that shortening a skirt to two inches above the floor would be viewed by women in the nineteenth century as a significant improvement. Mary E. Tillotson's reaction upon seeing the Bloomer after altering her clothing to improve her health is enlightening she went home and immediately started cutting away more of her own costume. Her piecemeal reaction to change suggests the hesitancy of women to make any alterations that were too blatant, even when they felt that their clothing was endangering their lives.

Many women worked at making fashion rational by altering their garments in ways that appear to us as subtle, but for them were not shortening skirts, reducing layers of underwear, supporting garments from the shoulders rather than from the waist. For us these changes may seem trivial because we have no understanding of what their clothes felt like. Nineteenth-century women wore heavy and restrictive clothing compared to ours; for them these alterations were significant efforts toward reform. Annie Jenness-Miller's efforts were most profound in this regard and obviously reflect the attitudes of many women, who wanted change but in an unobtrusive way.

Each type of garment introduced as a reform dress remained as a "style" possibility for a considerable amount of time. Some garments introduced as "reform" were already classic styles; some became classics. Trousers were perhaps the most problematic garment even the bifurcated "leglettes, " an undergarment sold by Annie Jenness-Miller, came under scrutiny for being somewhat *outré* for the times though loose full trousers and leggings were acceptable for sports activities. It is curious that in the development of women's clothing for sports, although the Bloomers or knickerbockers were worn for certain activities (especially mountaineering and bicycling), the skirted gymnasium suit was the normal costume for school physical education classes, and shortened skirts became the standard costume for sports played by women tennis, bowling, ice skating, croquet, and golf. Skirts for sports activities are vestiges left over from when women were expected to wear skirts in public. Indeed, women often had a skirt to match their sporting attire, so they could be appropriately dressed after climbing a mountain. Some of these traditions remain today: women still wear tennis dresses and skirts, golfing skirts, and skating dresses; for field hockey, tradition demands akilted skirt. It is curious that the shortened skirt became shorter, rather than being replaced by shorts, for there are no rules prohibiting shorts or trousers for these activities, except perhaps in some educational institutions.

While trousers for leisure activities gained in popularity over the years, especially with the advent and popularity of slacks and jeans, and later Bermuda shorts and short shorts, these were very feminized garments. They did not have the cut of men's trousers. It may surprise us to realize that it took until the women's movement of the 1970s for women to be "allowed" to wear trousers for whitecollar jobs and for teaching, and then it was a struggle. Until then, trousers were deemed inappropriate for women to wear for these jobs. The patriarchy refused to give up trousers as a symbol of male supremacy in the workplace, except for menial positions, of course, where some type of "work clothes" uniform was, and is to this day, usually worn. Even at the turn of the twenty-first century, young women are advised to forego the trousered suit for job interviews.

Perhaps the most effective way in which women made fashion rational was through the adoption of reform undergarments. Some of these reform styles, like the drop-seat knit union suit, remain as practical, warm, undergarments for winter wear. The soft knit undershirts are similar to the warm wool knit under vests promoted by Jaeger. Even undergarments similar to Jenness Miller's leglettes have been offered in place of a half-slip. And we are thankful to the designer of nineteenth-century equestrian tights for our standard winter wear of footed nylon tights. The nineteenth-century reform garment called the bust supporter, now given its French name of "brassiere," gained eminence as the garment of choice for the support of the breasts. The corset eventually gave way to a girdle only to be revived for a period as a "Merry Widow" undergarment, which, although introduced in the 1940s, became popular in the 1950s as an appropriate undergarment to wear with strapless evening gowns. Then in the 1980s, the corset was revived again by Gaultier as "the bustier, " a garment popularized by Madonna and then worn as either a "showy" undergarment or, sometimes, an outer garment worn discreetly, or not, under a jacket. (Indeed, in the late twentieth century, beginning in the 1960s, many earlier underwear items besides the corset corset covers, chemises, and petticoats that could be found in vintage clothing markets, became acceptable as outer wear.)

Simplicity in dress evolved in the 1910s, in part owing to the artistic reformers but also, perhaps, because the increasing number of women in the workforce needed simple, serious clothing for the business environment and for ease of travel to and from work. Historicism in fashion has seen the revival of many earlier styles that were promoted as reform dress. Artistic styles have been popular. The neoclassical style the Empire and Directoire derived from the classical Greek chiton has remained as a standard, often being revived by designers who want the look of simplicity and associations with the classical world. There was almost no decade in the twentieth century when the style was not present.

The high-waisted Greek chiton became a reform style in the first decade of the century, and it continued as inspiration for fashionable garments designed by the couture into the teens by Poiret, Lucile, the notable English designer who became Lady Duff Gordon, and many others. The tubular, slim styles in the 1920s were as simple as any Greek chiton, and the 1930s saw the bias-cut body-hugging creations of Madame Grès and Madeline Vionnet. Designers continued to draw on the classical silhouette in the 1940s and 1950s. The style clearly became a classic for lingerie, formal wear, and bridal gowns. It was not surprising to see it reappear in earnest in the 1996 collections of Givenchy.

The princess line has also remained as a classic style, occasionally revived as a dominant look, as in the 1960s when Jackie

Kennedy helped to make it popular. With historicism in fashion so prevalent in the later years of the twentieth century, it was not surprising to see a princess-style revival in the 1980s and 1990s. The obviously comfortable Mother Hubbard style is another classic used for intimate apparel, and it still appears in nightgowns, bathrobes, maternity clothing, and housecoats. Even the more elaborate styles of tea gowns based on vaguely medieval and Renaissance styles are apparent in wedding dresses, which often draw on historical styles for inspiration.

The legacy of reform is also seen in education. Indeed, the philosophical principles and arguments remain intact. It may be no surprise that the principles of art are still applied to dress and taught in college and university courses in fashion design, with consideration given to individuality. When the ideas moved into the realm of popular culture, we saw publications such as *Color Me Beautiful* and, interestingly at virtually the same time, the literature on how to dress for success. The progression toward modernity that provided women new options for dressing trousers, reform underwear, and comfortable artistic dresses in many ways paralleled the evolution in women's roles. As observed above, these new forms of dress eventually were transformed into the comfortable styles that we wear today.

4

Making Fashion Rational and Dress System

Introduction

The adoption of trousers clearly eliminated the need for petticoats and reduced the problem of skirts dragging on the ground, not all women were comfortable wearing what they perceived to be a radical form of dress. Except for athletic endeavors, many women felt that trousers were *outré,* too extreme for everyday dress. There was, nonetheless, a large number of dressreform enthusiasts who promoted a change in women's clothing that was both hygienic and rational but that did not greatly alter their outward, fashionable appearance. Such changes might be termed the "invisibles." These changes were a subtle if not subversive means of letting women appear "as usual," that is, in outer clothing considered fashionable and appropriate. Some advocates, such as Annie Jenness-Miller, saw improvements in women's dress as evolutionary, not revolutionary.

This new look was not associated with men's clothing and did not expose the body or create an uncomfortable situation by drawing unwanted attention to the wearer. Some promoters of more healthful clothing for women wanted to "make fashion rational" through subtle changes, such as shortening the shirt and loosening corsets. However, most women achieved this rational and invisible reform of their clothing by altering the way in which their gowns were supported on the body and through changes in the style and amount of underclothing. Thus, one of the essential features of making fashion rational was the new underwear, which, while it released women from the bonds of the corset and heavy petticoats, could not be seen. Since many objections to fashionable dress were directly related to abuses caused by undergarments, it is not remarkable that reformers found a way to alter them. Fashionable women of the nineteenth century generally wore too much underwear; it restricted them and weighed them down. It could be too hot in the summer and not warm enough in the winter. Certainly, the hoop of the 1860s allowed air to blow around a woman's legs. The corset often was worn too tight. The many skirt layers created excess bulk at the waist, which in turn encouraged women to resort to tight lacing, a practice that many believed greatly damaged women's internal organs and caused disease.

The creators of reform underclothing devised new styles of undergarments to replace the heavy and bulky combination of corsets, corset covers, petticoats, bustles, and other paraphernalia worn under fashionable dress. They also desired to eliminate problems of uneven distribution of the weight of the clothing on the body. Some promoters of reform devised what they termed "dress systems," whole sets of rational underclothing, which reduced the number of garments worn. Many completely eliminated the corset. Health and hygiene were an underlying concern that continued to generate improvements in dress. The new underwear was meant to be worn over a body that had been revitalized through appropriate exercise.

America

One of the earliest writers to offer a rational, invisible alternative to trousers was Mrs. M. M. Jones. At the World's Health Convention in New York in 1864, Mrs. Jones, who also lectured on health and dress reform, suggested that health reformers achieve their goals by:

"making the long dress hygienic." Jones advised women to "let out your dresses and never wear a tight dress again. Make all your waists bodices precisely as you would for the reform dress, leaving them a little looser and shorten your skirts till they swing free entirely from the floor." More significantly, in the matter of underwear, she advised women to wear drawers instead of petticoats under their hoops, and reformstyle "underdrawers" underneath the drawers, two for extra warmth if needed. To support their skirts, Mrs. Jones suggested wearing suspenders.

In a speech before the New England Women's Club in 1873, Elizabeth Stuart Phelps argued for a change in current women's fashion, which she thought debilitating. "Something of the nature of the American costume the gymnasium dress, the beach suit, the Bloomer, call it what you will must take the place of our present style of dress, before the higher life moral, intellectual, political, social, or domestic can ever begin for women." However, she went on to note that "we cannot at one fell swoop impose such a style of dress upon the prejudices of the public. Here, I fancy, has been our most serious mistake." Phelps offered one more way to make fashion rational. She suggested that women begin first by shortening skirts to a regulation distance of from four to six inches from the ground; that "we dispense with the biassed [*sic*] waist and corset, and retain the plaited gamp, or little jacket that we hang every thing from the shoulders; and that we set ourselves humbly to study the grammar of ornament.'"

In her discussion of how she would dress a young woman Phelps added that she "would also reduce the number of skirts to two the dress and underskirt, and these should be of as light material as possible." She suggested that women could gradually loosen the corset until they no longer needed it. Without the corset, the appearance of the outer dress might become sloppy. To eliminate the problem, Phelps suggested a style change: "make the gown with a loose front, " tied in with a belt. To reduce the amount of material, she suggested removing folds and plaits and "clumsy frills." The gown would be reduced to the simplicity of the smooth surface of the fabric.

Phelps saw further reform needed in underwear and referenced the designs of several water-cure establishments. "Valuable suggestions [for patterns of hygienic underwear], " she advised, "may be obtained from New-England Hygeian Home, Concord, VT." She noted that "there is also Health Home in Dansville, N.Y., I think where patterns of the American costume can be found. Some similar garment is imposed on the lady patients in almost all such institutions." She was careful to remark that petticoats also should be suspended from the shoulders.

For practicality, Phelps suggested that women "acquire thick, double soled boots, a loosely fitting sack [coat] or cape, and a broad brimmed full crowned hat to equip [themselves] for the street." Parasols would no longer be required. She noted that gaiters made of waterproof cloth were essential for rainy days. A pattern was available from *Demorest's Monthly Magazine.* In the end, recognizing the amount of extra work entailed in making fashion rational, Phelps suggested that "women hire a seamstress to make the changes earn, borrow or beg the money."

If a change were to take place, Phelps argued, it would need support from a great number of influential men and women in a group action. Directing herself to the audience, Phelps observed that "a body of ladies for instance the New England Club should call into council with itself one hundred ladies" of social influence from a number of American cities. They could decide on what needed to be done by first asking such questions as: What of women's attire needed to be retained? What could be dispensed with immediately? What could be dropped ultimately? What were the essentials of modesty? If they all agreed on changes in their dress and gained the support of the government; the leaders of the fashion industry, such as Madame Demorest; and dispensers of the fashion news, such as *Godey's*, then things might change for the better. "Suppose, in short, by one subtle, strong *coup d'état,* the thinking women of America could make it *fashionable* to dress like rational creatures?"

The result of Phelps's inspirational talk on "What to Wear" was that the members of the New England Women's Club established a dress-reform committee. The Boston committee, headed by Abba Goold Woolson, a teacher, lecturer, and popular literary essayist, sponsored a series of lectures on the hazards of fashionable dress by four eminent female physicians (Mrs. Woolson contributed a fifth lecture). In 1874 Woolson published the series of lectures under the title *Dress Reform.*

One of the first reform undergarments to be promoted in America was the "emancipation union under flannel" patented in 1868. This union suit combined a knit flannel waist (shirt) and drawers in one. The concept of a one-piece under garment apparently was not new, for in 1905 *Textile World* published a note titled "The First Union Suit" that made reference to a letter written in August 1843 by Thomas Carlyle, in which the English author made a reference to a "uniondress, a women's spenser and drawers all in one, which women wore in winter time."

Various knitwear companies and reformers in America continuously worked at improving the combination, as the union suit was often called. One early designer of a union undergarment was the reformer Dr. Mary Walker, who often wore a man's frock coat and trousers. On several occasions she was arrested for appearing in public wearing "unproper apparel." Dr. Walker devoted her energy to freeing women "from the bondage of all that is oppressive, " but in the 1870s she infuriated her colleagues in the women's movement by adopting tailored masculine-style trousers. It did not matter that she won the Medal of Honor for her service in Civil War hospitals. Dr. Walker's practical solution to "cruel corsets, tight garters and other underpinnings" was a garment she designed herself and called a "dress reform undersuit." She was convinced that her invention improved female health and discouraged seduction and even rape. Susan Taylor Converse of Woburn, Massachusetts, designed an improved version of the union suit in 1875. She named her version the Emancipation Suit.

Since this suit was actually a corset and corset cover all in one, it reduced the number of undergarments. It had a gathered section across the bodice that freed the breasts from compression and had sets of buttons at the waist and hips for suspending several layers of skirts. The Emancipation Suit also could be purchased as two separate parts that buttoned together at the hips.

The dress-reform committee of the New England Women's Club held an exhibition of reform garments in 1874 and then gave a seal of approval to those garments, particularly the undergarments, that met their standards. It was here that Converse first displayed her Emancipation Suit, which had the official endorsement of the New England Women's Club. Many of the approved undergarments were manufactured by George Frost and Co., of Boston. The club also offered patterns and set up its own shop in Boston, presided over by Mrs. H. S. Hutchinson and Mrs. E. R. Horton, where they sold patterns of their chemiloon (a union suit), gabrielle skirt, and other approved garments for twenty-five cents each. It was not long before other shops offering reform garments appeared in large cities across the country.

At the Centennial Exhibition in Philadelphia there were many exhibits of hygienic undergarments for women that were meant to improve health and comfort. Manufacturers also marketed these through advertisements in newspapers and magazines. Although the Bloomer costume was not to be seen at the Exhibition, the movement for dress reform was very much in evidence. Prominent among the innovators was Mrs. H. S. Hutchinson, who had moved to New York from Boston. Her rooms in New York City served as national headquarters for the wholesale and retail trade of garments approved by the dressreform committee of the New England Women's Club. These garments were constructed on four basic hygienic principles: no ligatures, uniform temperature, lightness of weight, and suspension from the shoulders.

At the exposition, Madame Demorest, who with her husband ran one of the most successful fashion houses in America, received commendation for her corsets, stocking suspenders, and skirt supporters. The centennial judges praised their "`utility, form and fashion, and high degree of excellence in workmanship.'" It was not surprising that the Demorests received such awards, for Ellen Demorest and Jane C. Croly ("Jennie June"), editor of *Demorest's Monthly Magazine,* supported the dress-reform movement in New York. Both were founding members of Sorosis, the women's club of New York City, and were equally active in a number of feminist causes. *Demorest's Monthly Magazine* insisted that the only way that American women could achieve beauty was to preserve their health. These women did not condemn corsets; indeed, they believed corsets were absolutely essential during many periods of a woman's life.

However, they did insist on health corsets, especially the Demorest designs, which, they stated, were constructed on scientific principles.

By the 1870s hygienic principles had been clearly defined, encouraged, and taught in public schools. Therefore, designers and manufacturers all over America quickly began marketing a great variety of healthful garments. At the Centennial Miss Emmeline Philbrook showed her patented "Equipoise Waist." The Worcester Corset Company won an award for Madame Griswold's abdominal skirt supporting corsets, which were covered by patents awarded to Catherine A. Griswold of New York. Olivia P. Flynt of Boston who had been designing, patenting, and selling reform undergarments long before the dress-reform committee took up the cause won an award for improved underwear for women and children.

In a very real sense, the reformers did succeed in raising public consciousness. After the 1876 exhibition, corset advertising almost invariably stressed comfort and health even though many of the garments did not always live up to their promise. Almost twenty years later, the judges of corsets at the Columbian Exposition in 1893 noted the great progress made in improving undergarments, pointing out that "every woman if she so desires can have a good form and be comfortable." The reform elements of the Ferris-patented "good sense" corset included "button fronts instead of clasps, cords instead of bones [leaving the corset pliable], adjustable shoulder straps which support the skirt and stockings from the shoulders, and shaping to conform to the natural figure, not made after `French Patterns.'" Other corset manufacturers making sincere claims regarding the reform aspects of their corsets still used whalebone.

Dress Systems

The cause of underwear reform gained much impetus from the commitment of the New England Women's Club, particularly through the efforts of Abba Goold Woolson. While promoting new designs for improvements in underwear, they made it clear exactly what should be worn. Indeed, the appendix to Woolson's *Dress Reform* offers an underwear system for improving women's health and illustrates it as well. One of the most prolific reformers of the late nineteenth century was Annie Jenness-Miller, who clearly supported the efforts of the New England Women's Club. Indeed, Jenness-Miller also developed an underwear "dress system" and became one of the best-known promoters of hygienic dressing. Jenness-Miller was a lecturer, author of several advice books, including *Physical Beauty, How to Obtain and How to Preserve It,* and publisher of *Dress,* a journal that focused on educating women about the need for correct dress and physical culture. As Jenness-Miller stated in the first issue, the magazine was to become the "authority on the subject of healthful, beautiful clothing for women and children" and to "secure health and beauty to the race." In its first years (1887 – 88) she referred to the magazine as *Dress, a Monthly Magazine.* By volume 2 it became *Dress, The Jenness Miller Magazine.* By 1893 it was known as the *Jenness Miller Monthly,* and in 1896 it became the *Woman's World and Jenness Miller Monthly,* then in 1898 the title changed to *Gentlewoman,* with a declining emphasis on correct dress and physical culture until it reached its final year of publication in 1900.

The term "dress reform" was not acceptable to Jenness-Miller, who preferred to use the term "correct dress." She stressed that their object was the adaptation of healthful and artistic principles to life and dress:

Accepting the human figure in its divine beauty and purity, it will be and remain our idea to so adapt essential clothing as to preserve the unity of the whole figure, and not call attention to the details of anatomy, as fashion is so prone to do. We shall lead so gently that the sting of sarcasm directed against our efforts as a "dress-reform" work will necessarily recoil upon the author and glance harmless from off our armor. Freedom from pressure, weight, and deformity will be our aim dresses adapted to the natural body undefiled by the appliances of death that compress the vital organs and paralyze mental and bodily energy; freedom for the exercise of all God-given faculties; the right to the use of every member unimpeded by dress respected; life and health exalted above all considerations of fashion and sacrificed never to the mandates of ignorant customs which defy physical law.

In both *Physical Beauty* and her journal *Dress* Jenness-Miller promoted the ideas of physical culture and the Greek ideal promoted by François Delsarte, a French singing teacher who invented a system of expressive body movements and offered readers articles on the aesthetic effect of fabrics and colors. Editorial policy was clear in that there were persistent instructions to readers on how to go at the work of "emancipating themselves from the discomforts, dangers, and crudities of fashions which have no other reason for challenging popular favor than daring and novelty." Jenness-Miller invited correspondence on the subject of "How, What, When, and Where" regarding dress and offered the following advice concerning the aesthetics of clothing: "The question of what to wear can be answered by the analysis of what constitutes art and utility with beauty."

More important, the magazine featured the Jenness-Miller System of Dress. This system included a variety of undergarments for women that were to be worn in place of fashionable chemise and drawers, corset, corset cover, and petticoats. As first described and illustrated in *Dress,* in 1887, the system of undergarments included beginning with, first, a "union suit" worn next to the body; second, a "bosom support, " or stiffer, and more supportive "model bodice"; third, a combination of cotton or linen called a "chemilette, " which was a perfect substitute for corset cover, drawers, and chemise; and fourth, the replacement for the petticoat, the "leglettes, " straight-legged or in the full Turkish style. The outer dress would be formed over a foundation called the "gown form, " which served as the lining for the skirt. As further described by JennessMiller the garments were:

Union Suit. A jersey-fitting garment of woolen or silk. Annie Jenness-Miller often suggested the Ypsilanti Union Suit made in Michigan or those made by Mrs. Converse in Massachusetts.

Chemilette. A combination garment of cotton or linen worn over the union suit. This garment, like the woolen union suit, put no pressure on the body.

Leglettes. These took the place of petticoats and were worn over the chemilette. Leglettes garment caused the most alarm because they were most like trousers. But unlike the divided skirt promoted by the English reformers in the Rational Dress Society, leglettes were not meant to be seen.

Gown Form. The gown form was a foundation dress on which all drapery could be designed. It was a waist (bodice) and skirt combined, fitting the body smoothly.

Bosom Support or Model Bodice. The bosom support was available for stout women who needed more support. It was not recommended unless necessary. This garment most resembled the corset but without the objectionable features. The model bodice was a boned version of the bosom support and meant to be worn in place of a corset.

The system itself was available as patterns that could be purchased through the Jenness-Miller offices in New York City or through their *Pattern Illustrator*, a separate publication. Prices for patterns ranged from $.20 to $.30 each. Patternsalso were available at various "dress reform depots," which were retail agents, usually dressmakers or stores, which purchased patterns wholesale from the Jenness-Miller System Co., East Orange, New Jersey. Although it was not an undergarment per se, the "gown form" promoted by Jenness-Miller (and later by J. H. Kellogg) was crucial to her system and the new "invisible" reform, or as Jenness-Miller would state, "correct dress." The Jenness-Miller gown form was cut in the princess style and served to replace the lining of a fashionable bodice and skirt. The outer "dress" would be formed over this "lining." Jenness-Miller boasted that the gown form would distribute weight equally over the body and thus avoid the pressure of heavy skirts. It eliminated "tie backs" and had no constricting band at the waist.

In an article titled "What Others Are Doing for Improved Dress," published in 1887 Jenness-Miller reviewed the dress-reform activities in other American cities, noting especially that "Boston took the lead in [the] so-called `dressreform' movement... and it may be said that it boasts at present more establishments devoted to this branch than any one other city." The best known, perhaps, was George Frost and Co., at 287 Devonshire Street. However, as Jenness-Miller observed, "Mrs. Flynt and Miss Fogg the former at 319 Columbus Avenue, the latter on Hamilton Place," both "have extended reputations for good and faithful service in the cause of improved underwear. Mrs. Flynt has pushed her business until it reaches every State in the Union. She has the good fortune to have been the originator of a very desirable nursing and extension waist. Holmes & Co., at 17 Kingston Street, hold a patent on a union suit which is simply perfect in quality, workmanship, and price." Jenness-Miller continued noting that "outside of Boston, at Woburn, Mass., can be found the veteran union-suit maker, Mrs. Susan Converse, whose combination garment was the first to attract public attention. Here in New York, besides ourselves can be found the old stand, at 6 East Fourteenth Street, of Mrs. A. Fletcher, whose long and faithful efforts in behalf of healthful dress have given her a national reputation." Jenness-Miller went on to note the flourishing establishment in Philadelphia managed by Madame Smith on Walnut Street and farther west, in Battle Creek, Michigan, the Sanitary and Electrical Supply Co., doing a very large business in hygienic goods, both as manufacturers and retailers. She recognized the efforts of an enthusiastic worker, Mrs. Rosinah H. Tonge, 8 Clayton Block in Denver, Colorado; Mrs. Ober, of 332 Sutter Street in San Francisco had built up an enviable business and reputation in the line of improved dress specialties.

Another reformer who promoted a dress system was one of America's bestknown health advocates, J. H. Kellogg. Kellogg argued that the common mode of dress produced widespread and marked physical deterioration of women and frequently lectured on the subject before the Michigan State Medical Society. While he was the director, the Battle Creek Sanitarium developed a "Dress System" which was "practical, healthful and artistic." The fundamental point of this system, like that of Jenness-Miller, was to avoid any appreciable sense of weight on the hips, shoulders, or any other part of the body. According to the general plan for the "system" included 1) union underwear, 2) tights, for cold weather, 3) combination suit to replace the drawers and chemise, and 4) a divided skirt with attached or detachable freedom waist. While not an undergarment, a gown form would provide a lining for the outer dress. Fashionably styled draperies placed over the gown form could be made to suit the individual tastes of the wearer. According to the pamphlet, corsets and tight waists (bodices) were meant to be discarded so that perfect freedom could be obtained.

Possibilities with the Battle Creek system were endless. In addition to the gown form, there was a princess dress and varieties of waists (bodices, without whalebone) and jackets. Although this system appears to be more practical than aesthetic, the classical ideal of beauty was adopted as a standard by the sanitarium. The pamphlet that described the system offered advice to women on how to correct the faults created by corset wearing. Kellogg believed that any young woman who had not permanently ruined her body by badly constructed apparel could learn to stand like the Venus Genetrix.

The ideas promoted by Jenness-Miller and Kellogg concerning rational underwear, hygiene, and exercise for women became popular, and they appear in advice books written in the 1890s by Frances Mary Steele and Elizabeth Livingston Steele Adams, Helen G. Ecob, and Frances Parker. They all offer systems for underwear reform, but, in fact, their goal, like Jenness-Miller's, was to return the body to its natural form. They promoted exercises for women that would allow them to achieve a more natural body, and they recommended replacing restrictive undergarments with new, loose-fitting, lightweight underwear. They believed that women could reach true ideal beauty by following their advice.

In *Beauty of Form and Grace of Vesture*, Frances Mary Steele and Elizabeth Livingston Steele Adams were largely concerned with the application of the principles of art to dress. Yet they also observed the importance of bathing, exercise, and proper diet, and they expanded on the necessity of discarding the corset. Foremost, they focused on the importance of the condition of the physical body and good health in general, advocating physical conditioning to attain body symmetry. This they noted could be obtained at a gymnasium, which would prescribe proper general exercise. The whole physique could then be further beautified using Delsarte principles of expression. The result would be grace and elegance through the achievement of harmony of mind and body. They also recommend "health-lifts," rowing machines, and other devices. Their goal was the beauty of classic models rather than the protuberances of the athlete. They saw exercise as a way of reducing fat, believing that corpulence destroys beauty of form and grace of motion. They recommended Mr. Edwin Checkley's *A Natural System of Physical Culture*. One good year of exercise, they believed, would "do more for a woman's good looks than all the cosmetics that were ever invented."

They also recommended a healthful diet of grains, fruits, and vegetables and frequent bathing. In addition to the above, Steele and Adams professed that in order to achieve the "ideal body," a woman should immediately procure health ful underwear. "Not an hour should be spent in the faulty garments." A suitable garment would be aunion suit: "one piece from neck to foot, hung from the shoulders, without whalebones or bands, and loose enough to allow the fullest breathing." The union suit was the first garment in their system of rational underwear. They also suggested a good bust supporter that was light, adjustable, elastic, with no horizontal bands around the body; it "is a most valuable adjunct to underwear for women" desiring to discard corsets. It could be worn with a corset cover over it or a knitted vest underneath. The next item they recommended was a waist, with or without an attached petticoat, and with no whalebones. They advised against health waists, which "are as pernicious as any corset, " and recommended only the Equipoise Waist or Mrs. Flynt's True Corset, suggesting changes to each. Equestrian tights (footless knit leggings) are the next item suggested in silk, wool, or cotton. Finally, they suggested a petticoat with attached waist. They offered an illustration of what they thought would be appropriate.

In *The Well-Dressed Woman: A Study in the Practical Application to Dress of the Laws of Health, Art and Morals*, Helen Gilbert Ecob also discussed the problem with heavy skirts and petticoats, corsets, and the so-called health waists. As with the efforts of these other reformers, her system of underwear tried to eliminate all of the weight hanging from the shoulders, which was a departure from the stance taken by the earlier reformers such as Oscar Wilde and Mrs. M. M. Jones. The garments Ecob suggested would distribute the weight evenly, "by having nether garments continuous with upper garments." Therefore, in addition to the reform union underwear, she stated, when "the need for firmer support was felt we have the Flynt, Bates, Equipoise, and Emancipation Waists, " all to be worn without whalebones. Other women, Ecob observed, wore the combination waist and drawers, either the Bates "chemiloon" or the Jenness-Miller "chemilette." For apetticoat, Ecob recommended adivided skirt. Other suggestions were to adopt the Jenness-Miller "gown form, " a lining consisting of a skirt attached to a sleeveless bodice (waist). All of these garments, Ecob declared, should be made from a lightweight material, and the outer dress should be one piece; otherwise the outer skirt should be sewn to a sleeveless lining.

The Chicagoan Frances Stuart Parker was active in establishing a dressreform club called the Chicago Society for the Promotion of Physical Culture and Correct Dress. She stated that Annie Jenness-Miller had influenced her own efforts, and, like her mentor, she promoted physical exercise as provided by the Delsartean system of physical culture, a method of French gymnastics. In her book *Dress, and How to Improve It*, she also provided information on correct undergarments. Frances Parker was an active lecturer and spoke on the subject of dress at Chautauqua programs, a popular lecture circuit. In order to show the advantages of reform garments, she illustrated the number of undergarments normally worn as part of "fashion" and contrasted them with drawings of reform garments.

Parker's underwear system included a combination garment like those manufactured by the Jaros Company and the Ypsilanti Manufacturing Company. For warmth in winter she recommended equestrian tights (which were as warm as "two additional underskirts"). Over this Parker recommended that women wear a thin silk, cotton, or linen underdress, with a petticoat attached to a waist. She suggested making one by cutting off an under shirt just below the waist and gathering to it five breadths of material to form a skirt. For large-breasted women she felt a bust supporter would be needed and suggested Mrs. Newell's Perfection Bust Supporter. In order to reform their dress, she observed, all women needed were two combination suits, "two pairs of tights, three pairs of socks, three under vests, two pairs of equestrian tights, and two silk petticoats (made with a waist), one black, one white."

The new reform underwear systems that included union suits, knit chemises and drawers, and even corsets with a few whalebones and elastic inserts (such as the Flynt and Ferris waists), and especially the Kellogg and Jenness-Miller boneless bodices would have given women more comfort. Eliminating the excessive bulk and weight of fashionable undergarments and the heavily boned corset allowed more ease of movement. The divided underskirt, worn in place of the petticoat, the union suit, and the equestrian tights provided needed warmth. All these reform undergarments no doubt could be worn without being readily noticed, and from a reformer's point of view were a great improvement over the more fashionable heavy, bulky, and body-distorting undergarments. The bust supporter recommended for heavily endowed or stout women is similar to a brassiere, thus giving the modern bra the status of being one of the earliest of reform garments. Women wore the bust supporter under the simple boneless bodice (waist), gown form, or vest.

For most underwear reformers, the idea was to return the body to its natural shape unfettered and undeformed by constrictions caused by tight corsets or appliances such as bustles. The care of the body through good hygiene and exercise was essential to their ideas of how women could achieve beauty. In *Physical Beauty* Jenness-Miller includes chapters on the care of skin, eyes, teeth, hair, and hands, as well as one on food, sleep, and the effects of fabric.

While a large number of women worked at reforming their dress in the 1890s, fashion still retained a hold on many women. *Needlecraft* magazine offers insight into undergarments worn in 1911 when the ideal fashionable style was one based on the natural figure. Despite the "naturalness" of the look, fashion still called for women to wear a corset, one that "molds the hips, flattens the abdomen and raises the bust, while all the time preserving the natural lines." (In the summer months women had the option of wearing only hip confiners of ribbon elastic sometimes worn with a brassiere or bust supporter if one were heavily built above the waist.) Underwear did follow the reformers' suggestions about combinations of corset covers and drawers, with drawers taking the place of petticoats. As it happened, these styles worked best with the slim silhouette.

Underwear Reform

Advocates for the reformation of women's dress in England also believed that fashionable dress could be made to conform to hygienic principles, and, indeed, many reformers were adamant that the outer dress should not differ from what was in fashion. The idea to improve undergarments had many supporters in England and was greatly encouraged by health and hygiene reformers whose theories had taken hold in Britain. The success of numerous health exhibits that took place in the early 1880s in South Kensington attests to a growing public interest and awareness in personal hygiene and health at that time.

Even Wilde, while perhaps best known in this respect for his promotion of artistic dress while on an American tour, held a health promoter's view of the problems with women's dress. He was concerned about the proper cut of garments as well as the harmful effect of corsets. For Wilde, the ideal dress should be "shaped more or less to the figure, but in no case should it be confined at the waist by any straight band or belt. It should fall from the shoulder in fine curves and vertical lines, giving more freedom and consequently more grace." Remarks by Wilde that appeared in the *Pall Mall Gazette* in 1884 clearly reveal his attitude regarding the corset and other articles of dress prescribed by fashion. "Indeed all the most ungainly and uncomfortable articles of dress that fashion has ever in her folly prescribed, not the tight corset merely, but the farthingale, the *vertugard*, the hoop, the crinoline, and the modern monstrosity, the so-called 'dress improver' also, all of them have owed their origin to the same error, the error of not seeing that it is from the shoulders that all garments should be hung."

Dora de Blaquière expressed the reformers' point of view in an essay titled "Modern Dress Reformers," which appeared in the magazine *Leisure Hour*. She observed that the true evil that needed to be rectified was not the "outward dress but the faults of the underclothing, and weight." As is clear from reading mid-nineteenth-century British magazines and journals, the English also considered tight lacing of the corset to be an evil supported by "Dame Fashion." As was the case in America, many English producers of corsets advertised somewhat false claims for their "health corsets"; nonetheless, real efforts were made to design more healthy corsets. For example, in response to a need to develop a corset that would not distort the body and be ruinous to health, W. Thomas and Brothers of London offered a "rational corset" made of India rubber, a corset that was "made for la dame, not, as hitherto, la dame for the corset." The medical journal *Lancet*, recommended this new elastic corset, which, it noted, would "obviate and supersede the close armor of the ordinary stay, and would do away with tight lacing."

While individual corset and underwear manufacturers in England developed "new" reform undergarments corsets and knit union suits, it was the dress-reform associations that effectively promoted reform of clothing as part of the general physiological and hygienic movements. These associations drew on arguments that took on a "scientific air" and were clearly distinguishable from the rhetoric of artists and individuals swept up in the aesthetic movement of the 1870s and 1880s.

Indeed, in a letter in response to the many comments on women's use of corsets and clothing reform that appeared in *Knowledge,* Richmond Leigh recommended the Rational Dress Association to every intelligent lady "to combat the stupid vagaries of fashion, to show how to dress rationally, and to restore the pristine beauty of the human figure." "Reason and science, he optimistically noted must eventually succeed."

One of the requirements of dressing rationally was the need to have hygienic dress made so that it appeared to be fashionable but in fact be designed so it gave freedom to the wearer. This point was made in print by leaders of the rational dress movement on many occasions. Indeed, in an essay titled "Principles of Dress Reform," which appeared in *Knowledge,* Mrs. E. M. King, who along with Lady F. W. Harberton led the society, offered readers the requirements for the perfect dress. These requirements became the motto of King's new association, the Rational Dress Association, and were used as criteria in judging reform garments at their exhibition in 1883. King's fifth requirement, upon which she "specially desired to write," was that reform wear must not depart too conspicuously from the ordinary dress of the time. She later noted that this fifth requirement meant that "we must depart a little conspicuously." King observed that two things are necessary reform of the individual and reform of the social medium in which the individual lived. The latter might put the reformer out of harmony with her surroundings. It was King's hope, since dress appeals to the eye, that society would become accustomed to rational dress just as they became adjusted to the more tasteless forays of fashion. Her reasons for having an exhibition were valid.

The exhibition of the Rational Dress Association in 1883 included some reform undergarments. In some cases explanations of outer reform garments state specifically that they should be "worn without a corset." Some descriptions mention a union suit, a "flannel combination for extra warmth," as part of the reform dress. Mr. G. Patten exhibited two quilted bodices "designed to replace the ordinary corset, and the skirt must be suspended from them." He noted also that they were "admirably adapted for tricycling, lawn-tennis, and other out-door amusements." Mrs. J. Wright showed "boneless stays, " and Worth et Cie., "Boneless corsets constructed so as not to give undue pressure to any part of the body." There were also knitted vests, working dresses, hygienic boots, and hosiery.

The Rational Dress Society is clear about the need for altering undergarments. The title page of their *Gazette* reads, "The maximum weight of underclothing (without shoes), approved of by the Rational Dress Society, does not exceed seven pounds." The society was aware of efforts made in America: they include a quotation from Mary Tillotson in the first number of the *Gazette* in April 1888. The *Gazette* was full of commentary on the need for reform and the progress being made in England and America. It reported on events of interest to society members such as a lecture by Mrs. Oscar Wilde titled "Clothed and in Our Right Minds, " presented at the Somerville Club, chaired by the honorary secretary of the society, Lady Harberton. Most important the society maintained a depot where they sold patterns for their system of underwear reform.

The society's "A Rational System of Underclothing" included several garments: "Vest and drawers (or combinations) of wool, silk, or the material called `Cellular cloth'"; a bodice of some firm material cut high to the throat, to support the breasts and also enable "such garments as fasten round the waist to be buttoned to it"; a chemise of their own design (sometimes called the "Survival"); and a "divided skirt made in whatever shape or material the individual may prefer. The ordinary dress is worn over this." They noted that as "the common dress skirt is indefensible on any grounds of common sense, it should be regarded as mere concession to an ignorant public, and be as light and short as possible. It should never weigh more than two pounds, all needful warmth being supplied by the underclothing." Apparently the original divided skirt, initially worn as a garment to be seen, such as the Bloomer, began to be worn in place of a petticoat under long dresses. In 1889 the *Gazette* reported on atennis costume designed for ayoung woman who planned to spend the summer at Newport. It noted that she planned to wear it with a divided skirt, which the *Gazette* considered a replacement for a petticoat. The outfit consisted of a gray-green silk divided petticoat with ruffles up to the waist, worn with a little low-necked silk bodice. The tennis dress proper was gray-green serge embroidered with buttercups about the hem. The skirt was cut full and hung to just below the ankles, and there was a Garibaldi loose blouse of white serge. A yellow silk sash and silk scarf completed the outfit. A green serge sleeveless jacket was worn over it. It is interesting that just one year earlier, in 1888, the *Gazette* had observed: "Though they may not yet see their way to have their over skirts made dual, the time is not very far off when dressmakers will drape dual foundations instead of single ones."

Ada S. Ballin

Ada S. Ballin, lecturer to the National Health Society, was perhaps one of the few women to publish a book on the subject of dress reform in England. She thought that the majority of books on the subject of dress in relation to health had indifferent success because, as she believed, "they have been written for women by men." Her views on the subject of beauty of the human figure is immediately apparent in the frontispiece of her work, *The Science of Dress in Theory and Practice,* which has an illustration of a normal female figure with no distortions caused by tight lacing or stays. Ballin observed that "what we want is reform, not revolution. We want in dress to obtain the maximum of health with the maximum of beauty." Drawing on classical standards of beauty and art, she further declared, "If our girls were taught the laws of health and a few of the principles of art as known to the ancient Greeks, they would soon see `what a reformed thief this fashion is.'" Continuing her argument, Ballin stated that if everyone were so educated they would "laugh at the squeezed-in waist, the crinolette, and the foot mangled and crushed by the high-heeled and pointed boots of recent times."

Ballin further noted that "Fashion's sins against health are well understood by sanitarians." She had much to say about underwear and surprisingly did not totally denounce the corset. In chapters titled "The Use and Abuse of Corsets" and "A New System of Dress for Women," she discussed the abuses of the corset and substitutions for it that would be healthful, beautiful, and fashionable. Furthermore, in her conclusion she offered broad principles. Many of her arguments and suggestions reflect the beliefs of the Rational Dress Society, which supported the trousered dress, or divided skirt as the society euphemistically called it, as an alternate to fashionable dress.

Ballin argued that women should teach their children the principles of dress reform so they would become accustomed to dressing rationally. She came to this conclusion after realizing that men and women could not understand the contentions of the reformers because they were so accustomed to the painful effect of fashionable dress that it no longer registered as an inconvenience or pain.

Many authors of reform literature liked to illustrate the "evil" and detrimental effect of tight lacing on the female body, and Ballin was no exception. She illustrates not just the effect on the ribs but displacement of organs of the body when women laced the corsets too tight .While she abhorred corsets, she did not denounce them completely. She thought women who were stout needed stays, and she designed a corset made of woven fabric, woolen preferably, with full-length elasticized inserts along each side, as few bones as possible, and only a thin, narrow busk placed down the center front. Ballin recommended the new method of lacing that used pulleys, which was an awardwinning invention at the International Health Exhibition in 1884.

Ballin likewise recommended the "Girton stays" sold by the Rational Dress Society for women who tended toward corpulence. It was believed that the stiffer, tighter stays could help check an increase in fat. Her opinion regarding corsetwearing was that the need for stays was peculiar to each individual: some needed no stays, others a light corset, and still others those of a more substantial kind.

She also thought that the chemise could be wholly dispensed with. Many people, Ballin noted, quit the chemise because it was bulky, not for sanitary reasons. Chemises should not be worn, she thought, because they were made from cotton or linen, both of which, compared to wool, were good conductors of heat, bad absorbers of moisture, and bad ventilators. When it was wet, she observed, wool might feel dry or merely damp, whereas cotton would be wringing wet. Ballin also objected to chemises because they were poorly cut: armholes were cut round, and the sleeves were cut in one piece with the garment itself, preventing arms from being raised. According to most reformers, any garment that impaired free movement was objectionable because such movement is necessary for development of the chest. Ballin recommended that chemises be made of thin materials with an open weave so they could ventilate, with gussets added at the armpit to ensure movement.

Ballin also urged the use of woolen combinations. To the question, "What garments ought to be worn over these?" her answer was, "as few as possible." Knit combinations would be stretchy and so would fit quite close to the body and reveal the symmetry of the figure. Combinations, she noted, helped support the outer garments. For when stays were not worn it became more difficult to hold up the clothing so that the weight would be distributed evenly. The union undergarment or other combination suits could be fastened to separate outer skirts and bodices, or the skirt and drawers could be fastened to the bodice. Braces, Ballin concluded, were objectionable because they supported clothing only from the shoulders, weighing them down and causing women to stoop.

Ballin's system for rational dress included the following: A high-necked and long-sleeved woolen combination vest and drawers should be worn next to the skin. Over this women should wear a closely fitting flannel bodice, on to which the suspenders of the stockings should be buttoned and to which the drawers could be fastened if made separate from the vest. The divided skirt also should fasten onto the bodice. (When worn as an outer garment, these loose trousers should be made of the material of the dress, the bottom of each leg being finished with a kilting.) These garments then form the whole of the underclothing, although in very cold weather an extra pair of woolen drawers might be worn under the divided skirt. The advantages of this system of dress, Ballin observed, were manifold. The system clothed every part of the body evenly and warmly, permitted perfect freedom of movement, gave the maximum of warmth with the minimum of weight, and, as none of the garments fastened round the waist, avoided injurious pressure on the abdominal and pelvic organs. Besides the advantage to health in adopting this plan, as the thickness of the clothing was removed from the waist, its natural outline was shown; and if the figure was beautiful, "its light is not hidden under a bushel, as in the former case." Ballin's recommendations for using knits and wool fibers for reform underclothing reflects the influence of German health reformers who promoted new clothing for better health. One of the best-known reformers of underwear was the German Dr. Gustav Jaeger, who in his writings on dress and health advocated wearing wool next to the skin. Jaeger's knit union suits were particularly popular with reformers in England after they were featured at the International Health Exhibition in 1884. A depot also was set up on Fore Street in London for its sale. In an essay in *Leisure Hour* de Blaquière included a description of Jaeger's "normal" clothing and briefly discussed the scientific dress movement in Germany.

Undergarments and Health Waists

Dr. Jaeger, a professor at the Royal Polytechnic School of Stuttgart, was one of the most prominent health reformers in Europe. He began his investigations in 1872 and reached the conclusion that health was dependent on the materials and the form of clothing. His theories were widely accepted in England; in Germany they supposedly revolutionized trade, and many leading men, Count Van Moltke and others, adopted his clothing. Jaeger's reform clothing was also sold in the Swiss cities of Berne, Lucerne, and Vevy. Jaeger's reform for "normal clothing" consisted of using wool that was specially arranged to keep the front midsection of the body warm. "The general object is to prevent accumulation of fat and water in the system; the author's leading principle being that the greater the specific gravity of the human body the more it is able to resist epidemic diseases."

Professor Jaeger made acurious addition to the well-known properties of wool. He desired to prove that there are certain volatile gaseous substances *Dufstoffe* (odorous substances) that we expel in the acts of breathing and perspiring, which have important relations to our mental state. He distinguished two distinct groups: those of *Lust* and *Unlust Stoffe* (substances of pleasure and disliking). The first group is exhaled during a joyful and pleasant state of mind and produces a state with heightened vitality if inhaled. The second group has the opposite effect. It may be readily verified, Jaeger argued, that during joy and happiness the odor of perspiration is not disagreeable, while during anguish and great nervous excitement the odor is offensive. The substances of disliking must then have bad odors and in an atmosphere full of them the vitality is lowered. Therefore, in a state of anguish and fear the body is more susceptible to contagious diseases. Professor Jaeger believed that sheep's wool attracts the substances of pleasure while clothing made of plant-fiber favors the accumulation of the offensive substances. He gathered a large amount of experimental evidence in support of these views. He claimed that the many persons who adopted his "normal" clothing, both for summer and for winter, had a very satisfactory experience.

The clothing recommended for women was not too different from that advised for men. The night dress was the same, except for a slight trimming of lace at the neck. The union, or "combination," garment, a pair of woolen stays (corset), and apetticoat of knitted dyed wool, with another, if desired, of woven stockinette, constitute all the clothing needed in addition to the outward dress, which also should be made of wool, high in the neck. By living in a more "normal" environment of animal fibers, Dr. Jaeger believed people would have improved immunity from disease.

Prior to Dr. Jaeger's scientific studies becoming well known, the need for clothing reform in Germany was presented to the public by Dr. Max Pettenkofer, Professor of Hygiene at the University of Munich. At the request of the crown princess of Saxony, Pettenkofer gave several popular lectures on the "relations of the air to the clothes we wear, the houses we live in, and the soil we dwell on."

In writing about the development of dress reform in Germany, Brigitte Stamm observed that the movement was part of a "life reform, " a social reform that occurred after the first phase of industrialization in the mid-nineteenth century. Lifereform advocated by numerous physicians embraced nudist culture and "natural healing" methods that excluded medication and instead embraced watermassage and exercise treatment, air and light cures, and, most important, a rational way of dressing. Private natural healing centers were very popular and had increasing numbers of visitors. Healing experiments started around 1820 and continued in popularity for much of the century.

Heinrich Lahmann was one of the early promoters of life reform and director of a natural healing center. Like Gustav Jaeger, he attempted to provide a scientific foundation for women's dress. Lahmann, however, promoted linen and cotton rather than wool. He saw the revolution in female dress as a significant liberation for women because "the fashion-stage is useless for the resurrection of mankind." He was, perhaps, expressing views shared by many American advocates of hydropathic therapy.

It is not surprising that the German dress-reform movement also was connected to the feminist movement. The German women's liberation movement started in 1848 1849 as a liberal association for women through the effort of Louise Otto-Peters. The movement was largely concerned with women's right to work and gain an education. Clothing reform was not greatly discussed until the first International Congress for Women's Work and Women's Endeavors held in Berlin in 1896. Delegates at that gathering came to realize the need for clothing reform for working women. They needed clothing "which would not affect [their] health nor be too tight fitting." The congress drew seventeen hundred people from Germany, America, Belgium, Denmark, England, Finland, Russia, Sweden, Switzerland, and Hungary. Dr. Spener, a well-known advocate of clothing reform, was the main speaker on the need to dispense with harmful fashions for practical and health reasons.

Following the congress, the Club for the Improvement of Women's Clothing came into being in Berlin in February 1897. The Berlin club soon published an informative booklet, held workshops, and organized exhibitions of reform clothes. The first exhibition was held April 11 24, 1897, with thirty-five firms taking part and eighty-five hundred visitors in attendance. A second exhibit was held in 1898. Its concern was to develop women's clothing that was healthy, practical, and beautiful at the same time, and its booklet noted that the club detested any kind of uniformity. They welcomed cooperation from doctors and artists. Most of the designs were improvements in undergarments, the use of a combination garment, and an improved corset. The movement for reforming undergarments was effective, for Stamm found thirty-four establishments offering rational undergarments in Germany.

The Berlin organization for improving women's clothing had branches in several other German cities, but both Dresden and Düsseldorf formed their own distinct societies. In 1902 the Berlin organization joined with the German Organization for Popular Hygiene. These organizations existed largely to publish magazines devoted to reform dress and health. However, in 1906 the Dresden organization joined forces with the artists in putting on a dress-reform exhibition of fourteen reform dresses, Liberty and Co., of London "art" fabrics, reform underwear, and accessories. By 1912 the organizations all merged into one, the German Association for New Female Dress and Female Culture, with a publication titled *New Female Dress and Female Culture.*

In 1907, Minna Cauer observed that the corset was on the "black list"; even with many new and improved models, manufacturers were complaining that their profits were falling off. In Paris, she noted, designers were inventing new styles to do away with the old rigid lines. Cauer thought that the medical profession did not support the dress-reform movement as it should. The exception, of course, was the sensible dress prescribed for women during visits to health resorts. Hygienic underclothing, however, had a tremendous following with women. Women were able to reduce the number of petticoats by wearing lightweight tights or Bloomers in their place.

Cauer noted that the early development of women's dress reform in Germany was practical and utilitarian, more attention being paid to the mandates of health than to the dictates of form. She commented on the invention of the Mother Hubbard dress, which she observed, "transformed the average woman" into a "human caricature of a marsupial." The style, she noted, was transitory and was later improved. Cauer did not object to the style noting that "if the material is soft and hangs well and the figure well proportioned and slender, this style of gown may be made most attractive."

Minna Cauer edited a German paper titled *Die Frauenbewegung* (*The Women's Movement*), the best paper in Germany for the education of women in the fields of politics, business, and the home. Cauer was a leader in the so-called *Party of the Left,* in the woman's suffrage movement in Germany. The aim of the party was the practical advancement of the cause of women in all its various forms.

Cauer concluded that "it must be admitted that reform dress is more suited to the house than to the street." She further observed, "I think I have never yet seen a successful walking gown on the reform plan. The most suitable are simply straight-cut English tailor suits worn without a corset." Cauer believed that the reform dresses only fulfilled hygienic and practical demands and that the reform movement lost many adherents and prestige owing to what she termed its ugly and clumsy creations that failed to appeal to popular taste. Many women had a horror of reform dress, regarding it as nothing more than a flabby, badly fitting bag made of cheap material and depriving the wearer of the very last vestige of gracefulness and elegance. The reform of the "invisibles" was more successful.

Sweden

In 1887 Oscara von Sydow, secretary for the Reform Dress Society of Sweden, apparently corresponded with Annie Jenness-Miller, editor of *Dress,* the American clothing reform magazine. In an extract of the correspondence Von Sydow commented on the advances made in reforming women's and children's clothing, especially that of schoolgirls. She noted that the Swedish reform society sent circulars to schools and physicians that included a drawing of a hygienic costume for girls. The garments, illustrated in *Dress,* included a jersey knit union suit, a bodice to which a skirt could be buttoned, and a pair of leglettes or knickerbockers that came just below the knee. The outer dress was a simple sailor dress with a natural waist and short, pleated skirt. The society also established a museum of hygienic clothing and a shop, and it set up exhibits throughout the country. Von Sydow noted that dress reform had spread from the society to Denmark, Norway, and Finland.

In commenting about the Swedish efforts toward clothing reform, the author, probably Jenness-Miller, declared that however different in detail the hygienic garments may be, generous waist proportions and freedom for the vital organs were recognized as essential to health by thinking people and students of anatomy everywhere.

In her discussion of dress reform in Scandinavia, Brigitte Stamm noted the efforts of Christine Dahl, who had studied reform dress worn in America. Dahl's reform dress focused on placing the weight of the dress on the shoulders. The basic style that she promoted was the princess line. She designed dresses so that the dress lay on the outer curve of the hips. Dahl patented the pattern for this dress and sold it through the company Steen & Stromm in Christiana, Sweden. A doctor from Copenhagen wore this dress in 1896 to the International Congress for Women's Work and Women's Endeavors in Berlin.

The efforts toward underwear reform carried out throughout Europe and America were persuasive. The early "scientific" studies by Lahmann and Jaeger had great appeal, especially in England. The systems of underwear devised by Americans in the late 1880s and 1890s were practical and easily achieved, with the invisibles being an accepted way to reform women's clothing. The most practical garment, however the Mother Hubbard was viewed by many as comfortable but unattractive on most women and unsuitable to wear in public. Seeing the need for a more attractive, yet comfortable alternative fashion, it was not surprising that artists and designers involved with the modern design movement created what we now come to know as aesthetic dress or that they, like the reformers Jenness-Miller, Mary Haweis (an important writer on artistic dress), Wilde, and Steele, promoted the idea that art principles should be applied to dress.

❑❑❑

5

Artistic Dress in Visions of Beauty and Health

Introduction

Highly decorative fashionable clothes made of stiff fabrics and worn with corsets obviously were not in accord with new concepts of design promoted by artists, architects, and designers associated with Art Nouveau, Jugenstil, or Secessionstil in Germany, Austria, and other parts of Europe. These modernists shared the American and English moral aesthetic argument for reform that equated good health and the natural body with beauty unique to each individual. An especially prominent idea was the aesthetic concept that beauty lies in the fitness of an object to its purpose. Other aesthetic arguments also provided strong motives for reform. These architects and designers saw the need to create forms and objects for living. For them all objects the house, its furnishings, and the people in it should be in aesthetic accord. That is, the clothes should correspond to the interior of the house, as well as to the personality of the individual who lived there. All objects should work together to create a personalized beauty reflective of the individual.

Influences from Abroad

Artistic dress did not suddenly emerge unannounced on the continent of Europe. Artists, designers, and architects were very aware of the earlier artistic developments in improving women's clothing that had occurred in Britain and America. The Liberty Company based in London had been supplying fabrics in Europe since the 1880s. Their shop opened in Paris in 1889 and they had several branches in other cities as well. Most artists sensitive to the issues of modernity in the late nineteenth century were aware of the philosophies of John Ruskin and William Morris, on which the modern design movement was founded. While the British and Americans tended to adopt a historical approach, the Germans and Austrians were more futurist and accepting of new technology.

The Japanese influence was widespread in the modern movement, and elements of an Asian aesthetic are apparent in a substantial amount of the new art and design. Leonie von Wilckens observed that Asian influence occurred in technique, symbolism, choice of motif, and color. Japanese motifs the wave, fish, flowers, and birds became apparent in almost all expressive arts: the fine and decorative arts, as well as theater and ballet.

British influence had occurred early with the establishment in 1864 of the Austrian Museum for Art and Industry (Osterreichisches Museum für Kunst und Industrie) on the model of London's South Kensington Museum (renamed the Victoria and Albert Museum). In many respects the Vienna institution and its adjoining school provided the setting for the revival of arts and crafts in Austria. However, the British influence on the Continent, especially in Austria, had its first real impact on modern art when the Glasgow School of Art, represented by Charles Rennie Macintosh and his wife, Margaret Macdonald, exhibited their assemblage of furniture and textiles in 1900 at the Eighth International Exhibition in Vienna. The Glasgow School also exhibited at Turin in 1900; therefore, it is clear that the Continent was well acquainted with modern British style.

The Glasgow artists drew on design elements that were applied geometric forms, which in later developments became integrated into the form of the object. This was especially true with the

Macintoshes and became apparent in Vienna with Koloman Moser's and Josef Hoffmann's work for the Wiener Werkstätte (see below). The black and white color scheme used for the Glasgow exhibit also, no doubt, had an impact on Gustav Klimt, on the early work of Moser, and on the designs of other artists working in the Wiener Werkstätte. While it is clear that the artistic communities on the Continent were influenced by artists and designers from abroad, their interpretations of the new concepts were strictly their own.

Modern Design Movement Dress Reform

Artistic reform of women's dress in Germany, as elsewhere, gained impetus from architects, designers, and artists who were in the forefront of the modern design movement that brought profound changes to architecture and the decorative arts and crafts. *Jugenstil* is the term usually used to describe this movement in Germany. The name *Jugenstil* is from the Munich journal *Der Jugend,* established in 1895 to publish works of avant-garde artists and writers. Indeed, Munich was the first center for the German version of Art Nouveau.

The artistic-dress reform movement in Germany, although influenced by the earlier aesthetic reform in Britain and America, had its own character, both in the manner it was introduced to the public and in the creation of specific styles of dress. The movement had several components. Starting with Krefeld, Germany, in 1900, there were exhibitions of artistic dress in a number of cities.

These were reviewed in newspapers and art journals. Several books by artists and physicians provided theoretical bases for the movement. Schools and programs of study in the applied arts embraced the idea that artistic clothing was an art form. Eventually, department stores and fashion magazines promoted the new concept of artistic reform dress.

In 1907 Minna Cauer, a prominent women's-dress reformer, summarized the theoretical basis of the movement. Cauer observed that the question of dress reform would never be settled until women took it upon themselves to assert their independence and strike out for themselves on commercial and professional lines, at the same time asserting their right to dress as they pleased and refusing to conform to the dictates of tailors and manufacturers. In reflecting on artistic reform, she, too, declared that individuality must be carried out in a woman's gown, so that it and its wearer would be one harmonious whole. Furthermore, she wrote, true reform in dress must combine utility and beauty and health; that is, beauty of fitness and the beauty of form. Embracing the precepts of artistic reformers throughout the West, Mrs. Cauer argued that women must think for themselves in regard to their homes and personal adornment and bring these both into harmony with their new individuality.

The German modern design movement had its roots in Munich. Indeed, an early illustration of reform dress can be found in Bruno Paul's 1897 drawing *The Fountain of Youth,* which appeared in the Munich paper *Simplicissimus,* as well as in a tapestry designed by Otto Eckmann, titled *The Arrival of Spring,* circa 1897. Yet it was a Belgian, Henry van de Velde, who was the most ardent promoter of artistic dress reform in Germany. Indeed, van de Velde was one of the earliest and best-known activists in the modern design movement on the Continent. He lived and taught in Germany from 1900 until the outbreak of the First World War. Although most prominent as an architect and designer, he created women's reform dress, planned reform-dress exhibitions, lectured frequently on the subject, and presented his theories in a number of publications devoted to modern design.

In *Deustche Kunst und Dekoration,* van de Velde put forth his "New Art Principles in Modern Women's Clothing." He believed that the earlier hygienic (anti-corset) movement for dress reform failed because beauty was not a consideration with these reformers. However, Van de Velde also felt that women were indeed the victims of the fashion profession, which had a primary interest in profits and little real interest in beauty.

In support of a new artistic dress, van de Velde also noted that they (architects) had finally found out that women's dress must be as sensible and homogeneous as a piece of furniture or carpet. This was a new decorative idea and one that made dress immediately a piece of art. Like other artistic reformers, van de Velde further suggested that clothing should express a woman's individuality but that this individuality should be suppressed in street wear because the clothing should be defined by place and circumstances; that is, clothing should adapt to private, general, or ceremonial spheres. Regarding the specifics of dress, he supported the aesthetic concept that everything should be fit to purpose and that each material has its own beauty, "an expression of its life." He felt that the artists' task was to awaken this life of give life to the cloth. Van de Velde denounced the revival of historical styles and called for a new modern style using new forms, new materials, and new techniques. Functionalism for van de Velde was essential to the beauty in all objects, not only clothing. Any ornament had to be abstract and organic.

Exhibitions of Reformkleid

Van de Velde was perhaps repeating the text of a talk he gave at the first German exhibition of artist-designed reform dress, which was held at the town hall in Krefeld in April 1900. Dr. Deneken, director of the Kaiser Wilhelm Museum in Krefeld, had asked several well-known architects, artists, and designers to create "Reformkleid" for this event, which was held in conjunction with a tailors' exhibition. The artists who exhibited were indeed well known and included van de Velde himself. The other artists in the exhibition also aspired to bring modernity to the world of art and raise the level of respect for the applied arts. They included Alfred Mohrbutter and Curt Hermann of Berlin; Richard Riemerschmid, Bernard Pankok, Otto Krüger, and Margarethe von Brauchitsch from Munich; and Paul Schultze-Naumburg.

The exhibition had an impact on those who visited and on those who were informed of it by newspapers and through the publication of an *Album* with a forward by Mrs. Maria van de Velde. In critiquing the Krefeld exhibition, Maria van de Velde mentioned two mistakes. First, she noted, the quality of construction was imperfect, but second, and even more neglectful, the artistic garments did not approach the idea of reform decisively enough in the cut and composition of the dresses. The central idea, she argued, was to invent more logical, healthier, and beautiful clothing than fashion can manage.

Maria van de Velde commented further on the decisive gap between real innovators and those content with "artistic interference only in the ornaments." Designs that fell into the latter category were those of Schultze-Naumburg, Curt Hermann, and Alfred

Mohrbutter, although van de Velde thought Mohrbutter showed tendencies toward liberation. She placed her husband, Henry van de Velde; Richard Riemerschmid; and Margarethe von Brauchitsch among the innovators.

Styles of Artistic Reform Dresses

The types of gowns presented by the artists varied in style, amount of ornamentation, and in intended use. Where the gown would be worn, that is, its intended use, determined the style and decoration. There were ball gowns, house gowns, and tea gowns, as well as dresses for concerts, walking, visiting, parties, and gardening. The cut of the Krefeld dresses reveal that the corseted small waist was not considered beautiful by any of the designers. In terms of style, The fullness of this gown by Alfred Mohrbutter suggests the Mother Hubbard style; it also mimics the "blouse dress" or jumper style. From Mohrbutter, *Das Kleid der Frau.* most were a variation of a princess cut with variety in fullness, sleeve type, and jacket length. The gowns could be quite loose or barely skimming the body. Some gowns were a modified princess style with a waistline defined just below the breasts. Another popular style was similar to the Mother Hubbard, with a set-in yoke placed just above the breasts and a gathered skirt falling from the breast line or just above it. Sleeves frequently had fullness from arm's eye to the elbow, or wrist to elbow in imitation of the medieval styles that appeared frequently in British and American aesthetic dress

Gown descriptions include a wide range of fabric types, with light silks used most often for society dresses and heavier silk or wool for street dresses. Velvets often were used for tea gowns. Street dresses, of course, were plainer and simpler than society dresses. Pleating to contain fullness and add an organic decorative effect was placed on upper sleeves, bodices, and vertically on the skirt (Brauchitsch). Other dresses had applied ornamentation. Gowns designed by van de Velde and Mohrbutter often incorporated embroidery and appliqué of curvilinear motifs usually associated with the Art Nouveau style .Henry van de Velde apparently preferred Liberty silks for his Krefeld dresses. However, since he was involved in the design of silks manufactured in Krefeld, he also incorporated these in having dresses made up for his wife and her younger friends.

The success of the Krefeld exhibit generated exhibits of artist-designed reform dress in other cities as well Leipzig, Dresden, Wiesbaden, Darmstadt, and Berlin. The Leipzig exhibition took place in autumn 1901 under the guidance of Adolf Thiele. That year a special division for artistic clothing also was set up in Dresden in conjunction with the Exhibition of Art and Industry. Clothing was also shown at the exhibition center in Darmstadt in 1901. Although artists and architects took credit for designing artistic dresses, most dresses were made by someone other than the artists. Peter Behrens's designs, for instance, were made up by Klar Blay of Darmstadt.

Peter Behrens, architect, designer, and founding member of the Munich Secession in 1892, along with his wife, Lilli, designed artistic clothing for women. While there are few records of Lilli's designs, those of Peter Behrens are well documented. His designs for the Leipzig exhibition of artistic reform dress are very severe and have little ornamentation. Behrens's style contrasted sharply with the styles of van de Velde and Mohrbutter, which had soft flowing lines and decorative applications. Leonie von Wilckens noted that contemporary critics thought Behrens's designs were too cold and masculine. His wellpublished society dress, however, was better received, in part, no doubt, because it did have flowing ornamentation at the hemline. Behrens's designs for a two-piece walking dress reflect the later commentary by Schultze-Naumburg that one alternative for a street dress is a skirt and jacket. In their simplicity, Behrens's designs were more like those of fellow architect Richard Riemerschmid, who had exhibited in Krefeld in 1900. However, while Riemerschmid's style is simple and stark with no ornamentation, most of his designs do have a defined waist, an element that would not be appreciated by many dress reformers unless worn without a corset.

The Berlin exhibit focused on two of the best-known supporters of women's reform dress in Germany, the artists Paul Schultze-Naumburg and Else Schultze-Naumburg's designs in this exhibition included several dresses with an Empire-styled high waist; all of these were society gowns. In writing about a suitable style for artistic reform dress, Schultze-Naumburg thought that three designs were appropriate: a loose dress falling freely from shoulder to heel or held in by a belt fastened just under the breasts or at the hips; a two-piece close-fitting costume made of a skirt and jacket; and the "blouse dress," which was a blouse with a sleeveless gown worn over it with waistline under the breasts or at hips. This garment is much like the late-twentieth-century American jumper. An example of a blouse dress designed by Else Oppler-Legbaud is a walking dress, a practical, functional garment that would contrast greatly with the more highly embellished society dresses that were made by various professional firms such as Herrmann Gersen in Berlin.

Of the professional dressmakers who exhibited reform clothing in Berlin, the most influential was Else Oppler-Legbaud, who had studied under van de Velde in Berlin. In 1903 she took charge of the reform-dress department in Wertheim's, a large department store in Berlin. She was a versatile artist, for her designs for interiors earned her silver and gold medals at art exhibitions held in Leipzig and Turin.

At about the same time as the Berlin exhibition, the Wiesbaden Society for Fine Art arranged an exhibition for women's clothing in which Peter Behrens, Alfred Mohrbutter, and Schultze-Naumburg took part. In writing about the Wiesbaden exhibit in *Dekorative Kunst,* Oscar Ollendorf offered his theoretical opinions, saying that dresses should conform to artistic laws and that artists were particularly equipped to design women's dresses not only because of their knowledge of drawing a woman's body and the functions of ornament but also for their sensitivity to color and, above all, their sense of fantasy and awareness of the effect of the homogeneous whole.

As noted by Leonie von Wilckens, Else Oppler-Legbaud organized an exhibition of artistic clothing in 1904. For this exhibition, Anna Muthesius spoke on the progress made in artistic reform dress, noting improvement in construction, color, materials, and in the individual fit and suitability to the wearer. Anna Muthesius was one of several Germans who, after 1901, gave extra support to the artisticdress reform movement by publishing theoretical work on the subject. Muthesius used the term *Eigenkleid* (proper or personal clothing) to define the new artistic dress. For her the concept of dressing to express individuality was imperative; the dress should conform to the needs of the individual and express the unique creativity of the artist. She also designed many of her own dresses.

Reform Publications

Henry van de Velde, Anna Muthesius, and Paul Schultze-Naumburg were joined in their efforts by others writing on the need for artistic dress reform. These authors also provided ethical and aesthetic arguments for reforming women's clothing. They included Alfred Mohrbutter, Heinrich Pudor, and Adolf Thiele.

In his text on women's dress, *Das Kleid der Frau*, Alfred Mohrbutter repeated observations made by Henry van de Velde and Anna Muthesius, stating that women think they dress individually when, in fact, they continue to be the slaves of fashion. Like van de Velde, Mohrbutter believed that cloth alone could make a good dress, through the beauty of its pleats, which allow for movement, which in turn enhances the fabric. He, too, believed that the choice of fabric and color depends on the destination of the dress. In *Das Kleid der Frau* Mohrbutter included illustrations of several gowns and sketches for gowns of his own design, as well as designs by several women who had reform-dress salons in various German cities. Dress-reform artists represented in Mohrbutter's text included Anna Muthesius, a house dress (Hauskleid); Marie Hartmann, a society dress; P. A. Winker, a street dress, summer dresses, house dress, and society dress; E. Friling, a visiting dress; Else Oppler-Legbaud, a visiting dress, theater dress, street dress (blouse dress), and festival dress; Dr. Elly B., a visiting dress; Fia Wille, a summer afternoon dress; and Clara Müller, a society dress.

In 1903 two publications from Leipzig appeared to further the cause of artistic reform. The art critic Heinrich Pudor published *Women's Reform Clothing,* in which he championed the notion that women's clothing should follow beautiful forms. Adolf Thiele, author of *Toward a Philosophy of New Women's Dress,* put his words to action by directing the exhibition for artistic clothing in Leipzig. In *Women's Clothing,* in a chapter titled "Improvements in Women's Clothing, " C. H. Stratz observed that improvements had been made in women's clothing for recreation, but he stressed the point that, until women improved their bodies and quit depending on corsets (even reform corsets), there would be no true reform of women's clothing. He suggested that women adopt the Japanese kimono for use in the home, noting that Dutch and Indian women had substituted it for the house dress.

The media supported efforts of artistic-dress reformers, which, of course, was crucial to the communication of the new style. Franz Lipperheide's Illustrat*ed Women's Newspaper* regularly reported on the exhibitions and included illustrations of many so-called reform dresses that were not designed by artists but rather came from leading ateliers who wanted to follow the times. The journals of the Jugenstil promoted the new style. Both *Dekorative Kunst,* published in Munich, and *Deutsche Kunst und Dekoration,* published in Darmstadt, reported on artistic-dress exhibitions held between 1900 and 1904. Publications of the women's associations featured artistic dress as well. These included *The New Female Clothing* and *Healthy Women*.

Women's Clubs

The various women's organizations that early on were most concerned about the hygienic and practical needs of women's dress held several exhibitions where artistic dress was featured. Von Wilckens stated that the Club for the Improvement of Clothing and the Club for People's Hygiene united to organize a ReformClothing Festival in Berlin in December 1902. All of the participants at the festival wore clothing of the new style. Brigitte Stamm noted that in 1906 the Free Association for Improvement of Female Dress worked with the Third German Art and Craft Exhibition in Dresden. This exhibition featured fourteen reform dresses, Liberty fabrics, underwear, and accessories.

Writing on the German dress-reform movement in the *Independent* in 1905, Else Oppler-Legbaud noted that we "enter the fray with ethical, hygienic and esthetic arguments." In writing, she summarized the artistic theory regarding dress, stressing the idea that the beauty of the natural human form should be appreciated and that the new artistic reform dress actually offered individuality, not a uniformity of dress. And, again, she declared that the form of the dress should depend on its intended use. She applauded

Mohrbutter for designing a reasonable, practical street dress along artistic lines a dress that, in her mind, was most difficult to make artistic. Her own designs, for which she also used soft drapable Liberty silks, reveal a fitness to purpose as well. That is, a street dress was simple compared to a more diaphanous and decorated society dress, ball gown, and festival dress.

Regarding the form of artistic dress, Oppler-Legbaud noted that the reform dress was "never allowed to fit so closely to the body as French fashion requires." When a belt was worn, the dress was fastened either directly under the breasts or rested on the hips, in order to avoid the wide, loose dress, which was neither practical nor aesthetic. The form of dress, she concluded, reiterating van de Velde's thoughts, depended on its use, whether to be worn "at home as a working dress, a street dress, or in society only."

Effectiveness of the Reformers' Crusade

In commenting on progress, Oppler-Legbaud observed that the practical street dress had caused the most difficulty. No bloomers were being worn; but skirts now were to the ankles, and the weight of garments was distributed from the shoulders, especially the dress (jumper) worn with shirtwaists, what SchultzeNaumburg termed a "blouse dress." Sometimes the garment was designed so the weight was distributed onto the hips. Oppler-Legbaud noted that at the time the reform dress was seen everywhere in society, at theaters, concerts, and in the streets, and it only depended on artists and tailoresses to impart variations and quality technique to dispel the last trace of prejudice in conservative quarters. The prejudice of tailoresses and dressmakers had been overcome. Those who lacked skill to make reform dress had at first refused to promote it in belief that it was in opposition to their interests, but after a few dared to make them, others quickly followed so that by 1905 every German town had a few artists producing reform clothing.

Austria

In Austria the Arts and Crafts Movement had its earliest impetus with the founding of the Wiener Secession in 1897 by a group of progressive artists, architects, and designers who defected from the more conservative association, the Künstlerhaus, which had been the only exhibition space for contemporary works. The group included Gustav Klimt, Josef Hoffmann, Joseph Maria Olbrich, Koloman Moser, and Carl Moll. Greatly influenced by the British Arts and Crafts Movement, they demanded new aesthetic forms of expression in keeping with modern life. The motto on their exhibition building, the Secessionhaus, completed in 1898, reads "Der Zeit ihre Kunst, der Kunst ihre Freiheit," or "To the Age its Art, to Art its Freedom." The title of the Secession magazine, *Ver Sacrum,* marked their direction toward a rebirth for art in Austria.

Although it is doubtful that women's dress was a consideration when they placed the motto on the building, it could be applied to dress: "to every age its dress, to dress its freedom." Several members of the Secession very clearly held this point of view. Koloman Moser designed many gowns for the women in his family. In 1902 a number of artists and authors associated with the new art movement Josef Hoffmann, Alfred Roller, and Hermann Bahr published their theories and opinions on why women's dresses needed to change in *Dokumente der Frauen.* Certainly the Wiener Werkstatte (Vienna Workshop), organized in 1903 by Moser, Hoffmann, and Fritz Wärndorfer, was receptive to reform in dress. The Wiener Werkstätte added a textiles department in 1909 and a fashion department in 1911 under the direction of designer Edward Joseph Wimmer-Wisgrill.

Gustav Klimt and Emilie Flöge

Gustav Klimt, a famous Viennese artist, no doubt believed in dress reform for women. In his portraits women are often clad in long, loose flowing garments that may have been of his own design. It has been said that Klimt collaborated with his close friend Emilie Flöge in designing reform dresses for her fashion salon in Vienna. Indeed, the modern reform dresses would have been appropriate to the interior of the salon itself, which was a Wiener Werkstätte commission designed by Moser and Hoffmann in 1904. Investigation into the source of Flöge's designs for an exhibition on Klimt and Flöge at the Vienna.

History Museum, in the late 1980s, was inconclusive about whether Klimt collaborated with Flöge. Some scholars believe that Flöge may have told her customers that her clothes were designed by Klimt because of his status as an artist. It is highly likely that the designs were Flöge's own. On the other hand, it is also possible that Klimt sketched out ideas for dresses that were then worked up by seamstresses in Flöge's workshop in Vienna. The Flöge gowns that appear in the art journal *Hohe Warte* (1905 1906) are similar to the very stark styles of the German reform artists, especially those of Peter Behrens. Emilie Flöge often wore reform-style gowns herself. She posed for the photographer D'ora wearing a loose, ruffled artistic gown, and on many occasions for Klimt.

Architectural historian Udo Kultermann believes that Flöge's gowns carry Klimt's imprint. He argues that the dress worn by Flöge in Klimt's 1902 portrait could only have been designed by Klimt. He observed that the geometric motifs (circles and squares) and flowing, shapeless style show exactly the reform ideas that were later to be seen in Wiener Werkstätte designs. In support of his argument for Klimt's impact on the design, Kultermann refers to a photograph of Flöge wearing a dress that also carries Klimt's characteristic style, exhibiting a mixture of geometric and floral motifs. The dress is similar to designs found in a collection of Klimt's drawings owned by Zamuel's Gallery in New York. The drawings, which date to 1903 1904, were studies for portraits. Regardless of who actually designed the dresses, one thing is certain: they were meant to be reform dresses.

Klimt remained true to his appreciation of the avant-garde reform style, for in 1916 one of his patrons and supporter of the Wiener Werkstätte, Fredericke Maria Beer, wore a Wiener Werkstätte harem outfit for her portrait by Klimt. Her niece commented in a letter that her aunt had all of her dresses made by the Wiener Werkstätte at that time. Beer later had the harem outfit made into a dress.

Photographs of Klimt lead us to believe that he thought that men, too, should have the option to be comfortable. He often wore a loose gown, even on occasions when other men wore suits. Of course, a loose, flowing smock was a privileged garment for an artist. Hermann Bahr, a poet, critic, and Klimt's supporter and friend, apparently also wore a similar gown, which may have been designed by Klimt to emulate a Japanese kimono. Such an exotic garment would be quite acceptable for these young artists who were infatuated with all Asian objects, a passion shared by many artists of the modern design movements.

Koloman Moser

Klimt was not alone in his dislike of fashionable dress. Many artists who became associated with the Secession, the School for Arts and Crafts (Kunstgewerbeschule) connected to the Austrian Museum of Art and Industry (Osterreichisches Museum fur Kunst und Industrie), and the Wiener Werkstätte also held a similar aversion for the dictates of Paris. Koloman Moser, painter, graphic artist, and designer, was one of the most active reformers in Vienna and a key figure in the Austrian modern design movement. Along with several other young artists, Moser was a founding member of the Vienna Secession. He provided the relief decorations for the building that housed the Secession artists, the Secessionhaus, designed by Joseph Maria Olbrich. Moser frequently exhibited with Josef Hoffmann at the Secessionhaus and contributed to their journal, *Ver Sacrum*. In 1898, Moser began teaching at the Kunstgewerbeschule. In 1903, he and Josef Hoffmann became artistic directors of the Wiener Werkstatte, with Fritz Warndorfer as administrator and financial director. They started small but soon became international leaders in the Arts and Crafts Movement. Their honest approach to design was applauded at exhibitions in Berlin, London, and Dresden. The taste for black and white executed in geometric precision suited the taste of the avant-garde in art. In 1907, Moser left the Wiener Werkstätte to pursue a career as a set designer, interior designer, and graphic artist.

Moser produced several dresses for his wife and sisters. These are now housed in the costume collection (*Mode Sammlung*) of the Vienna History Museum. All of the gowns would have hung from the shoulders and free the waist. The gown designed for Moser's wife, Data, is a society dress, *Gesellschaftkleid*, made of printed linen. The style is loose-fitting with no defined waistline. A matching long coat accompanies the dress, a copy of which is on display in Vienna at the museum. The gown of Moser's mother is made of black silk. It has no defined waist, trim along the seamlines, and pleats on the sleeves for added interest. Leopoldine had a dress dated 1900 1905 made in a similar style from A society dress designed by Koloman Moser for his wife, ca. 1905. Courtesy Historisches Museum, der Stadt Wien. A copy of the dress is on display in the city Museum; the original is housed in the museum's costume collection in Hertzendorf. These designs are similar to other reform gowns in the collection of the Vienna History Museum, one of which was designed in the style of Paul Schultze-Naumburg.

As noted by Daniele Baroni and Antonio D'Auria, Moser had already designed an entire collection of reform clothes in 1900. By the end of 1906, Moser turned out to be the most incisive in following the theoretical directions set forth by Schultze-Naumburg. The novelty of Moser's designs, they point out, consisted of a simplicity of line, sometimes resembling a kimono, and an absence of excessive trimmings such as lace, fringes, or a crinoline. Moser greatly influenced his students, especially Wimmer-Wisgrill, who later became head of the Wiener Werkstatte fashion department.

In 1895 Moser traveled to Munich and immersed himself in the local artistic circle, which included the avant-garde artists who were just beginning to publish their magazine *Der Jugend.* At this time Moser would have been aware of the artistic rumblings for dress reform that were coming from abroad. The idea of *Gesamtkunstwerk,* the integration of all visual design elements to create a total artwork, was by now well accepted. The need to have clothing be in harmony with the environment as well as with the uniqueness of each individual conformed with the concept of *Gesamtkunstwerk.*

From very early on, both Moser and Hoffmann adopted geometric forms, which became the hallmark of Wiener Werkstätte products. Clearly, such designs were a favorite of Klimt's. Delight in geometric forms created a split in the early years of the Secession. In the 1890s, according to Baroni and D'Auria, there was a shift toward an understanding of form based on an internal search, either for organic or for more geometric elements of an abstract nature. The line became the principal element a potent means of expression and abstraction. The works by British designers such as Walter Crane provided guidelines for this new approach to the decorative arts. Moser came into contact with Charles Rennie Macintosh, Crane, and others, and he studied Japanese art, particularly Katagami stencil techniques. Moser's studies of line and form led quickly to an emphasis on geometry. Moser, as Baroni and D'Auria attest, had such a mastery of expression geometric and chromatic interpretation, "use of typographic characters, references to Oriental emblems and kaleidoscopic fantasies" that he may rightly be considered one of the founders of modern graphic art.

Josef Hoffmann

While Moser concentrated on expressing his modern concepts of design and the need for clothing reform through the execution of various art projects, others focused more on writing about them. Josef Hoffmann, Moser's friend and colleague, accomplished both. Hoffmann frequently worked with Moser on projects, especially after the establishment of the Wiener Werkstätte in 1903. More important for this study, however, is that Hoffmann also designed reform gowns for women. Unfortunately, there are no extant Hoffmann-designed garments; only illustrations remain. Hoffmann's writings in *Die Wage* reveal his attitude and beliefs about the need to improve women's clothing. In an essay entitled "The Individual Dress" ("Das Individuelle Kleid"), he expressed his astonishment that in a time when everyone wants to be original and special, so few people appear really original. In their outer appearance they (women) subjugated themselves ostentatiously to fashion. He felt that individuals should express their uniqueness in their dress, "that we should be able to recognize them through their dress and how they wear it." For instance, Hoffmann continued, "the dandy should appear to be a dandy, the dignified, dignified, a modest girl should dress simply, a serious one in dark clothes, the energetic in clothes that do not hamper, an unpretentious person should wear plain clothing, " and so on. He believed that people should stand above the tailor so that the tyranny of fashion would be broken and the individual sense could achieve its rights. Hoffmann suggested specifically that clothes should be light and allow movement and that they should be made so they could be put on fast and easily without the help of a second person. Hoffmann's arguments clearly fall within the realm of the aesthetic principle of "fitness." His philosophy is expressed in his clothing designs.

Dokumente der Frauen: Roller, Bahr, and Loos

During the early years of the twentieth century, the condition of women's fashion became a topic of interest in the arts community in Vienna. In March 1902, *Dokumente der Frauen* offered the opinions of several Viennese artists, designers, architects, and doctors regarding women's clothing. Professor Alfred Roller, director of the Angewantekunstschule (the Vienna School of Arts and Crafts) and of the Vienna Opera, included his opinions in the form of a letter. Roller believed that women should not go to male artists for clothing designs of the future, but rather that more women and girls who had an understanding of their own particular clothing needs should be trained in the arts to solve the problem of dress. He believed that it was important for women who worked to have clothing that would facilitate the act of work and, like the new sports clothing, the function should create the form. For him, clothing should be seen as a facilitating tool, whether it was for work, climbing, mining, or deep-sea diving, or for a circus artist.

Roller noted that women in public had worn mainly ornate clothing unsuitable for work. He believed that the "fake" items of dress could be removed without being conspicuously absent "buttons that don't button, ribbons that don't tie, laces that don't lace, " and so on. He also felt that other hurdles needed to be removed. First, the tight waist (corset) had to go. Second, the decoration should be incorporated into the design. There was no need to mask stitches or pockets; they should become part of the ornament. Women must break with the lies of these fake items applied to dress fabrics, skirts, sleeves, hems, pockets, and collars.

Of the other writers in *Dokumente der Frauen,* Hermann Bahr is perhaps in most agreement with Hoffmann and Roller, for he declares that a dress is beautiful if it is a perfect skin of a person and it has no deception (no fake ribbons or sleeves). Furthermore, he believed that reform dress should be distinctive for each individual person and that it could change with age, body changes, and set of mind. For him, to be elegant was to be natural.

The well-known architect Adolf Loos, a prolific essayist who feared no subject, was not a member of the Secession or involved with the Wiener Werkstätte. It is not surprising that his comments on women's fashion are far from bland: "Lady's Fashion, you horrible chapter of cultural history. You tell hidden lusts to mankind. If one turns your pages, the soul is shaky in view of the terrible aberrations and incredible vices." Writing initially in 1898, the sensible, if frequently contentious, Loos believed that women's clothing forced them to achieve equality with men through the power of the clothing to appeal to man's licentious nature, to his pathological sensuousness (forced on him by the culture of his time, of course). In the future, he believed, equality would no longer be achieved by sensuousness but rather by the economic and spiritual independence of woman gained through her work. This, perhaps, is one of the most accurate futurist appraisals of the period.

Wiener Werkstatte

Both Koloman Moser and Josef Hoffmann could publicize and propagate their ideas for modern design in Vienna through exhibitions at the Secession and teaching in the Kunstgewerbeschule. What they needed, however, was a place for the production and sale of objects based on their principles. In 1903, with financial backing from Fritz Warndorfer, the Wiener Werkstätte came into being to fill this need.

From the beginning, the designers and the craftspeople, the ones who actually built the objects, had equal billing. The operation allowed patrons to deal directly with artists, which was the usual Austrian method for selling art. Few dealers in art were very successful. Indeed, many Austrian artists, Oskar Kokoschka in particular, lived in Germany to be closer to dealers who offered a friendly reception for their works. However, as Jane Kallir has observed, in many respects the rise and fall of the Wiener Werkstatte reflects an inherent difficulty in the marriage between creators of art and dealers or sellers of art. The Wiener Werkstätte was a business enterprise handicapped by artistic principles, just as the Secession was an artists' organization with commercial problems.

There were several foreign models for the Wiener Werkstätte enterprise. The first was Ashbee's British Guild of Handicrafts, which Hoffmann visited in 1902. Others were two German organizations: The United Workshops for Artand Crafts, founded in 1897, to which

Peter Behrens and Hermann Obrist belonged, and the Dresden Crafts Workshop, founded in 1898. The philosophy of the Wiener Werkstätte echoed that of Ruskin and Morris, the earlier Secessionists, and the English and German modernists. In their work program for the Wiener Werkstatte, Moser and Hoffmann declared, "The work of the art craftsman is to be measured by the same yardstick as that of the painter and the sculptor!" If our cities, houses, rooms, furniture, clothes, jewelry, language, and feelings fail to reflect the spirit of our times, "in a simple and beautiful way, we shall be infinitely behind our ancestors!" They clearly evoked the spirit of the German *Gesamtkunstwerk*.

Like the earlier Secessionist artists, the Wiener Werkstatte received good publicity from the start, particularly from the Munich journal *Deutsche Kunst und Dekoration* as well as from Hermann Bahr and the art critic Bertha Zuckerkandl. One of the first major commissions was for the Stocket mansion in Brussels, designed by Hoffmann, which to this day remains one of the best known and admired Werkstätte creations. The Werkstätte contributed to a number of European art exhibitions as well as to international trade exhibitions. Its members established sales branches in Vienna, most notably on the Graben, the most fashionable street in the center of the city.

The Wiener Werkstatte produced a variety of decorative objects, furniture, jewelry, and textiles. In 1905 it established a textile workshop to produce handprinted and hand-painted silk designs. Werkstätte members designed and manufactured large amounts of fabrics designed by the leading artists: Moser, Hoffmann, and others. The textile department thus had some control of the fabrics used in the interior of buildings and houses as well as those for garments then possibly worn by people who lived in them. The textile workshop was another step on the way toward integration of the arts.

Beginning in 1907, artists in the Wiener Werkstätte began designing costumes for the Cabaret Fledermaus, a cafe with lighthearted music, dance performances, and other theatrical productions. However, it was not until 1910, under the able direction of Wimmer-Wisgrill, that fashion was first introduced, and then it occurred at the Karlsbad branch, not in Vienna. Vienna did not see a fashion sales room until the following year, when a fashion shop was opened next to the salesroom on the Graben. Finally, in 1914 the Werkstätte established a separate "factory" for fashion production and then opened more showrooms in 1916 and 1917. Branches were opened in other cities, including Marienbad, Zurich, New York, and Berlin. By 1928, in its twenty-fifth year, the Wiener Werkstätte was producing objects such as silver work; gold work; metal work; sheet-metal work; leatherwork; bookbindings; knitwear; beadwork; embroidery; woven, printed, and painted fabrics; ceramics; carpets; wallpaper; and lacework.

Kallir interprets the Wiener Werkstätte line as incorporating two basic trends: that of the loose fitting reform dress created by Flöge, Klimt, and Moser, and its reinterpretation as an Empire mode by the French designer Paul Poiret. Bertha Zuckerkandl referred to the reform dress as a "flour sack," so she must have been thinking of the gowns designed by Klimt and Moser, which were very full and loose-fitting with no defined waist at all. Attributing the first reform style to Flöge, Klimt, and Moser, however, neglects the very real possibility of its having origins closer to home, that is, in the creations of the German reformers previously discussed in this chapter. It also neglects to give credit to the classical and medieval models promulgated by the Liberty Co. These designs had been available since 1884 in Liberty catalogs and through many depots and shops in Europe, including Paris.

In the early years of the Wiener Werkstätte, until about 1914, the textile and fashion department experimented with many ideas. In fact, there was an attempt to assimilate many design sources the Empire waist, reform ideas, and Asian touches. Harem pants, which may have come from Poiret, appear to have had some success, for they survived into the twenties. Harem pants and other such styles were viewed as exotic or "artistic" dress, not really fashion (and indeed, only really wealthy, artistically inclined women purchased these clothes in the early years). During the First World War, patriotism placed fashions from France in a bad light. Many designers began to express an Austrian aesthetic with an emphasis on historical styles such as Biedermeier, which echoed French

Empire forms. The Wiener Werkstätte began to design low-key clothing that reflected the somber tone of the war. After the war the fashion department emerged as a respected institution, showing fashions abroad on a regular basis in the late teens and twenties. It gained extra prestige by being the "shop" for many actresses. It is ironic that the textile and fashion department grew during the twenties, while the Werkstätte itself began a steady decline, finally closing its doors in 1932.

Since fashion photography was used so little in Austria, the Wiener Werkstätte "line" was presented to potential mail-order customers through small watercolor sketches with fabric swatches attached to mail orders. The drawings, however, except for the first line executed by Mela Köhler, an artist in the fashion department, were little more than vague representations of the actual garments. Kallir notes that they evoke a Werkstätte feeling rather than the exact style. Two sets of fashion prints, *Wiener Mode* (*Viennese Fashions*) and *Das Leben eine Dame* (*The Life of a Lady*) were executed and published in 1914 1915 and 1916, respectively. Although created outside the Werkstätte, they do depict accurate designs, since the drawings were made by Hoffmann's former students or former employees of the Werkstätte. The published portfolios reveal all the prevailing fashion trends of these periods the Empire style, the harem pants, and the Biedermeier historical revival.

Fashion in the Reform Style

During the years 1902 1903, *Wiener Mode,* the leading conservative "Viennese Fashion" magazine, also available in Germany and other European cities, included variations of the new modern style of artistic dress and reported on exhibitions of artistic reform dress held in cities throughout Europe in the early years of the century. Terms used in *Wiener Mode* to define artistic dress were "reform dress," "new style," "Liberty style," "princess style," and even several references to "bride's reform dress". The reform models were interspersed with illustrations of high fashion. *Wiener Mode* also included advertisements for reform underwear.

Artistic Reform Dress in the Netherlands and Scandinavia

Through promotional efforts at arts and crafts exhibitions, fashion shows, portfolios, and feminist advocacy, knowledge of artistic reform dress made its way to other parts of Europe. In Sweden, Norway, and the Netherlands there was increasing interest in reform in women's clothing. Although this interest included reform of undergarments, the solution often fell into the artistic range of reform garments. The Wiener Werkstätte style was undoubtedly much appreciated.

The Netherlands

The dress-reform movement in the Netherlands began in earnest with the establishment in 1899 of the new Dutch Society for the Improvement of Women's Dress. Impetus for the organization came from knowledge of a similar German society established in 1896 and of an exhibition of women's work in The Hague in 1898, where a competition was held for the design of a reform costume for women who worked. The society published a monthly magazine with articles about improving health through improved underwear and hygiene. However, as noted by Carin Schnitger, "after 1903 the interest in artistic design grew." Membership in the organization increased to two thousand, and there were branches in several cities. The organization also held lectures, produced brochures, and held exhibitions of reform clothing with the cooperation of shopkeepers who regularly sold reform dress.

The new artistic dress and its relation to modern art drew the attention of women who were artistically inclined. The writers Marie Metz-Konig and Anna van GoghKaulbach wore artistic dress, as did musicians and singers Catharina van Rennes, Auke Schierbeek, Jeanette Molsbergen, and Alida Noorderweir-Reddingius. These women would have had no difficulty in finding examples of artistic dresses illustrated in the *Maandblad der Vereeniging voor Verbetering van Vrouwenkleeding*. These artistic gowns were all loose-fitting, cut full with a yoke or in the princess style.

For the most part, promoters and designers of artistic dress in the Netherlands relied on the publications and designs of Henry van de Velde, Alfred Mohrbutter, and Paul Schultze-Naumburg. Most of the styles made by Dutch artists were simple princess styles, more like the designs of Peter Behrens or an adaptation of the Directoire or Empire styles promoted by the Liberty Company. The Liberty Company had a dress department in the fashion firm of Metz and Company in Amsterdam. Examples from Liberty's 1905 catalog, *Dress and Decoration*, appeared in the Dutch artistic magazine *The Woman and Her Home* (*De Vrouw en haar Huis*).

Perhaps one of the best-known artistic-dress reformers was Madame de Vroye, who moved from Paris in 1901 to live in The Hague. She offered expensive, elegant reform dress in the princess style to the moderate women of the V.v.V.v.V. In 1903, she edited her own magazine, *Refome,* which catered to an audience that embraced the new art. At the Berlin exhibition of women's artistic reform dress, Die Neue Frauentracht, held in 1903, Madame de Vroye presented a group of gowns that were very favorably received for their elegance.

It is curious that few male artists in the Netherlands are credited with designing artistic dress. Carin Schnitger suggests that ideally women would have designed their own clothes since their garments in theory had to be an expression of the individual. Certainly this was a major thesis of many of the artisticdress reformers.

Yet, there is one well-known man who designed women's dress, the painter Jan Toorop. Toorop depicted reform styles of artistic dress in several lithographs, including *Arbeid voor de Vrouw*, 1899, and *Delftsche* Slaolie, 1894. The latter work depicts batik cloth, which would have been familiar to Toorop, who grew up in Java, where batik-designed fabric was the traditional decorative technique. Batik designs in cloth were familiar to the Dutch, who had been importing them as trade items for years. After an exhibition of batik fabrics in 1883, batik became a technique widely used in the Dutch new art movement in the 1890s, and the exotic nature of the fabric made it popular with modern designers everywhere.

Students at the newly established Trade School for the Improvement of Women's and Children's Dress in Amsterdam (established in 1909) were exposed to works by artists and architects of the Dutch new art movement, which had a preference for new geometrical forms usually associated with early Wiener Werkstätte design. In March 1917, the Wiener Werkstätte took part in a fashion show held in Amsterdam under the artistic direction of Otto Lendecke. Lendecke's fashion journal, Die Damenwelt, reported enthusiastically about positive comments by the Dutch press: "Among the exhibiting firms, the Wiener Werkstätte, so well known here by the individual character of its textiles, and the totally different style of its cutting and makeup. Its contribution struck me as a style of fashion in its own right!"

Scandinavia

Interest in reform dress in Sweden and Norway was spearheaded by Christine Dahl, who had studied reform dress in America. Dahl spoke regularly on the subject of the need for reforming women's dress; most of her suggestions were based on hygienic principles. In order to avoid wearing a corset and to have the support of clothing fall on shoulders, Dahl devised a princess-style dress. She patented her design, which was sold by the Steen & Strom Company in Christiana. Scandinavian efforts at reforming women's clothing became better known when a doctor from Copenhagen wore Dahl's princess dress during the 1896 International Congress for Women's Work and Women's Endeavors. This predated most of the German efforts toward artistic dress reform. Scandinavians had an opportunity to see Austrian crafts in Stockholm in April 1916, when the store Nordiska Kompaniet organized an arts and crafts exhibition in which the Wiener Werkstätte showed its latest clothing models, as well as leather, glass, jewelry, and tableware.

The relationship between reform dress worn in Britain and that adopted by women on the Continent may best be summed up by Margaret Swain's reflections on the personal relationships of individuals involved in these efforts. In an essay on Jessie Newbery, Swain refers to the close friendship between the Newburys from Scotland and the Muthesius family from Germany that lasted until the First World War. When Anna Muthesius published her book on dress reform, *Das Eigenkleid der Frau* (*The Proper Dress of Women*), photographs of the Newburys' two daughters and Anna's friends the Macdonald sisters are used as illustrations. Fra Newbery painted a portrait of Anna Muthesius in which she wears a dress made out of batik of either Dutch or Dutch Indies origin. The connections among the German, Dutch, and British artistic endeavors for reform were clearly cemented when the art magazineDer Jugend reproduced the portrait of Anna Muthesius for its cover in 1904.

❏❏❏

6

Commerce and Fashion Technology

Introduction

The government at the time controlled the art and fashion worlds, and periodic changes in desired appearance became sources of wealth and prestige. In a study of the court of the Spanish Hapsburgs, J. H. Elliott observed that the lesser rulers were the innovators in matters of display: the fifteenth-century dukes of Burgundy in ceremonial display, and the sixteenth-century Medicis in the art of court spectacle. It was only by compensatory effort of this kind that they could hold their own in a world of great powers. But the great powers followed at their own pace and convenience, conferring their own prestige on practices first developed in the lesser courts.

Emergence of Fashion

The court of Philip the Good, duke of Burgundy, is considered "the cradle" of fashion . Philip exploited the resources available in the territory he controlled to create new clothing styles. Until this time Paris had been the center of luxurious court dress. As mentioned, the International Gothic Style had been generated in Paris in about 1380, and attire in this style was worn in many of the courts in Europe, which were connected through a complex system of politics and marriage. After the beginning of the fifteenth century, however, Paris was eclipsed as the center of court dress by the court in the northern French duchy of Burgundy. This area lay along the spine of Europe, directly within the Mediterranean trade route for goods being transported to the North Sea and England. People, talent, and commodities flowed into its markets. Members of the court took increased interest in their clothes, adorning themselves with elaborate costumes to display wealth and an awareness of style.

In the painting *Hunting with Falcons at the Court of Philip the Good*, all participants are dressed in white as part of the theme of the festivities. Some wear attire in the International Gothic Style that came out of Paris. Others wear regional garments, including some from Bruges, Ghent, the Netherlands, and Germany. Some of the mantles, gowns, and hairstyles originated in Italy. The figures of the duke and duchess reveal a new fashion ideal, long and lean. The duke's short gown is belted around the hipline, with carefully arranged pleats in the front; his legs in full-length hose and his pattens, or pointy shoes, are exposed. His sleeves are moderately sized and end with a padded, furtrimmed cuff. Members of his household, courtiers, retainers, attendants, and musicians wear simpler versions of the same style (nonuniform uniforms). Most of the men wear no hats and their hair is in a bowl cut; the duke wears "a version of the turban." The duchess Isabella wears an ermine-lined long robe and a very sheer veil. A few of the women wear no headcovering at all.

The variety in appearance and the influx of new materials and ideas informed artistic endeavor, helping to develop and support local employment. In addition to its being an international trading center, however, Burgundy also became a fashion center. A sizable Italian community settled around Bruges, formed by Italian merchants who had escaped from Paris along with several Medici bankers during the English occupation. They helped turn the duchy into a cosmopolitan center with exposure to foreign styles and the use of readily available resources (fur and the black cloth manufactured in Flanders). The trade in fashion had begun. By the middle of the fifteenth century Burgundy had become the center of fashion. Fashion offered a level of prestige to the community that local culture could not. Moreover, aristocrats from the northern countries and other parts of Europe, such as Italy and Spain, copied the Burgundian style and the long, lean, and graceful silhouettes of the court of Philip the Good, thus establishing fashion as a distinct part of elite culture.

Fashion as an Economic Good

A more recent example of a monarch using fashion to stimulate growth of the economy while increasing national prestige is Louis-Napoléon. He used the Great Exhibitions of 1851 and 1855 in London and Paris to show that the French government was behind its fashion industry, encouraging new technology and the export of dress and ornament. The exhibits included the latest cloaks, gloves, hats, fans, and perfumes, which were displayed alongside the crown jewels and the dresses of Napoléon's wife, Empress Eugenie.

The emperor wanted to encourage the well-to-do members of the aristocracy to support the economy by spending money on clothes. There was no doubt that those who frequented the court were expected to dress up and change their costumes often. He also impressed upon Charles Frederick Worth, the court's couturier, that the production of fashion was essential for the well-being of the nation. He encouraged Worth to create a new fashion "each season because everything the Empress wore created a demand first among upper class women and then among the lower classes." He insisted that women who appeared before him be dressed in the latest fashion. Through his efforts, the French fashion industry revived, and it continues to be an important source of revenue for the country.

As Simmel observed, openness to social mobility is the social condition necessary for fashion to exist. He explained that there is no fashion in a hierarchical society where the boundaries between social classes are tightly shut and there is no possibility for mobility. The clothing of each class acts as a "uniform" that separates the classes and identifies rank. He noted that in Western society the aristocracy often had to compete with the rising middle class for social rewards, wealth, prestige, and power. To do so successfully the aristocracy had to maintain visual superiority. A new fashion was thus invented by members of the aristocracy as soon as their existing style was adopted by members of the middle class.

Fashion puts a premium on expense. It makes use of novel materials and design innovations, which by their nature are not readily available. Scarcity is the essential element limiting the kinds of fabrics fashionable people are interested in wearing. Fashion often reflects new ideas expressed in art and culture. To determine how to dress, fashionable people monitor what others are wearing so as to "be up to date."

The desire to make what was scarce more readily available encouraged innovation, as John Nef suggested. For example, the demand for calico like that brought to England from India in the eighteenth century stimulated the growth of the cotton industry. The expense and demand for calico, a light, sheer, soft fabric with bright floral patterns, encouraged scientists and practical inventors to concentrate their efforts on finding ways to improve bleaching and dyeing techniques that would facilitate fabric printing and yield washable colors.

Fashion and the Individual

Fashion, Simmel argued, encourages modification and adoption to individual needs. The wearing of fashionable attire enables individuals to separate themselves from their family, to develop a more distinct identity and a more unique sense of self, and yet to maintain an affiliation with the prestigious aggregate. Individuals can extricate themselves from a setting or a situation, scrutinize the image they present, and tailor it to the social response they desire.

Fashion enables individuals to deal with themselves as persons and as social objects. It makes possible both individuation and social connectedness. As Simmel observed: "There is no institution, no law, no estate of life which can uniformly satisfy the opposing principles of uniformity and individuality better than fashion," because it allows individuals to pursue competing desires for group identity and for individual expression. This separation or objectification allows one to correct the image if necessary to achieve the desired response, explained Simmet. By offering the opportunity for "trial and error," fashion encourages social and personal awareness.

❑❑❑

7

Gender Dressings in Fashion Technology

Introduction

The relationship between clothing and gender is the understanding that sexual characteristics at birth are the basis for the "script" identifying social expectations for sex-appropriate behavior. Recent research has shown that very early in life, before children are aware of sexual differences, they are alerted to differences in dress, and that as early as two years of age they classify people according to gender. Gender scripts help to create two social categories, the members of which deal with their bodies differently, as Goffman observed. Men are socialized to use their bodies in a straightforward manner; they learn to manipulate, grasp, and hold. Women learn to convey the feeling that their bodies are delicate and precious; they are supposed to caress objects and people.

Psychologist J. C. Flugel suggested that the basis for sex-specific attire is sexual *interdependence*. He noted that visual distinction between the sexes has been seen throughout history and in most places and in most parts of the world. Everyone assumes that people wear sex-specific attire because doing so follows "the natural order of things." Sex-specific attire was, and is, intended to alert an approaching individual about *suitability for sexual intercourse*. Even articles of clothing associated with a specific sex have the power to arouse passion in members of the other sex. The tie, jacket, trousers, and shoes of the male, for example, and the high heels, garter, and girdle associated with the female have been found to elicit sexual responses. Hence, the purpose of sex-specific attire is to spur interaction between the sexes. Survival of the species depends on such a distinction.

British costume historian James Laver suggested that sex-specific attire identifies the social spheres in which men and women function. The "hierarchy principle" underlies male dress: Men wear class-conscious attire that reflects their standing in the wider social sphere. Female attire is governed by the "seductive principle": It is designed to make women attractive to men and hence less significant. The meaning of appearance, thus, is closely tied to gender expectations for behavior.

Socialization to Gender

Clothing is used to create a gender distinction, as noted by Gregory P. Stone. He observed that dressing a newborn in blue begins a sequence of interaction that is different from the one experienced by a baby dressed in pink. The infant's appearance in clothing of a sex-specific color sets up expectations about how the child should act, think, and feel. Among other things, it is anticipated that a baby dressed in blue will be handsome, strong, and agile, whereas the pink-clad infant will be beautiful, sweet, and graceful. The color acts as a cue or stimulus that influences how people behave toward the child and how that child is expected to conduct himself or herself. It is the response of others to gender-specific attire that encourages gender-appropriate behavior, Stone concluded.

Norms governing gender-appropriate attire are so powerful, Stone pointed out, that male participants in a study he conducted were able to recall the revulsion they experienced when as children their mothers dressed them in "fussy" attire. They wanted to be clothed in what they had learned was "manly" attire. Sex-specific attire, Stone maintained, enhances the internalization of expectations for gender-specific behavior. Through subtle rewards and punishments, such as those given through tone of voice, parents encourage or discourage specific behavior, which leads to the development of a gender identity.

Gender-Specific Toys

In early childhood the clothing worn in play and the toys children play with may be important means of encouraging gender orientation. Girls are more likely than boys to play dress-up. Many also have fun creating ensembles for their dolls, coordinating the color and style of the doll clothes. Playing with Barbie, an extremely popular doll encourages awareness of textiles and fabrics. Barbie has kept up with the times and has been portrayed as an astronaut, a business executive, and a pilot, among other things. Her wardrobe, in appropriate colors and fabrics, covers everything from space travel to summit meetings. Playing with Barbie, however, requires staying close to home, limiting the opportunity to explore the outside world. Moreover, since Barbie's body was designed principally to look good in clothes, she is tall and the dimensions of her body, 36-18-33, are unrealistic. She embodies a standard that is almost impossible to achieve, and thus she encourages a sense of inadequacy.

The physical characteristics of the toy figures that boys carry around are often menacing. Batman, Superman, G. I. Joe, the Masters of the Universe, and the recent Killer Tomatoes are characters of power and action. Boys' toys are thus characterized by activity and toughness, even those played with indoors, like Nintendo. Functionality and goal-directed appearance inform boys' orientation to clothing.

Children's Picture Books

Children's storybooks also offer two distinct orientations to appearance. *Confluence* characterizes the portrayal of men, and *contrast* typifies that of women. In these books, the father is portrayed wearing form-following, body-concealing attire coordinated to create a unified whole. Dressed in a housedress or a skirt and blouse in contrasting colors, the mother is often depicted wearing an apron. Visually, these outfits cut the body in half, dwarfing the person and intimating a figure of less significance. The apron, moreover, has always been associated with physical labor, which is considered less important than "head work." It identifies people in service occupations who lack authority. From aprons to business suits, gender-specific attire varies along with the dimension of authority. Even when animals are used in place of humans, their identity is made visible through gender-stereotypical attire.

As they get older, children increasingly associate dress with stereotypical behavior patterns. They feel that "feminine" means a docile demeanor and that negative sanctions follow women who behave in gender-inappropriate ways. When young girls, ages seven through thirteen, were asked to select one of four clothing styles for a girl who is "bossy" bossy being a characteristic expected of a male 77 percent chose one of the two most extreme styles: jeans and a T-shirt (the most androgynous outfit) and a frilly dress (the most feminine). From the girls' comments, it became clear to the investigator that they viewed only two kinds of "scripts" leading to bossiness: a prissy, spoiled girl who is likely to wear frilly dresses, and a tough person, tomboy, or bully who is not afraid to get on the ground and get dirty. The respondents viewed "bossiness" as an attempt to exercise control, a negative female attribute.

The findings of this study bring to mind the fact that "tomboy" was coined in sixteenth-century England. It was used to describe a bold and immodest girl, one who violated society's expectation for meek behavior. That the phenomenon was recognized and given a name suggests that there were many young women at the time who engaged in such behavior. The word was coined during the reign of Elizabeth I, who inherited the throne and successfully ruled for over fifty years. When badgered by parliament to marry in order to assure succession, she publicly prayed to God "to continue me still in this mind to live out of the state of marriage."

Religious Injunctions

The church fathers have always insisted upon a visual distinction between the sexes and have submitted guidelines to the church for sex-appropriate appearance and behavior. Three beliefs have underlain their use of dress to establish gender distinction: that real differences exist between the sexes; that the male is the more superior being; and that women's social participation should be limited to reproduction. Saint Paul, for example, criticized the practice current during the first century of men and women wearing each other's clothing. He claimed that this habit violated the order of nature because each sex has its own place in the universe. He implored men and women to dress in a manner that demonstrated the superiority of men. Men, he said, must keep their heads uncovered when praying, whereas women must cover their heads as a sign of subservience to men:

> *Any man who prays or prophesies with his head covered dishonors his head, but any woman who prays or prophesies with her head unveiled dishonors her head it is the same as if her head were shaven. For if a woman will not veil herself, then she should cut off her hair: but if it is disgraceful for a woman to be shorn or shaven, let her wear a veil. For a man ought not cover his head, forasmuch as he is the image and glory of God; but woman is the glory of man. For man was not made from woman, but woman from man. Neither was man created for woman, but woman for man.*

Later he said:

> *As in all the churches of the saints, the women should keep silence in the churches. For they are not permitted to speak, but should be subordinate, even as the law says.*
>
> *If there is anything they desire to know, let them ask their husbands at home. For it is shameful for a woman to speak in church.*
>
> *And in Paul's Epistle to Timothy, he explicitly demanded women's submissiveness:*

Let a woman learn in silence with all submissiveness. I permit no woman to teach or to have authority over men; she is to keep silent. For Adam was formed first, then Eve; and Adam was not deceived, but the woman was deceived and became the Clement of Alexandria, a church father of the first century A.D., declared that beards were the badge of masculinity and that it was sacrilegious to trifle with them because they were a symbol of man's stronger nature. He claimed that "by God's decree hairiness is one of man's conspicuous qualities. Whatever smoothness or softness there was in him God took from him when he fashioned the delicate Eve from his side his characteristic is action; hers, passivity."

The Seven Deadly Sins were a set of guidelines for appropriate appearance and behavior. The sin of pride advocated humility and modesty in dress for both men and women. The prohibition against sloth, another of the deadly sins, supported the idea that males should play an active role in social life and was designed to encourage males to take part in the socioeconomic process. Medieval literature depicted idleness, or sloth, as the "feet of the devil that halt man in his tracks" and declared that it demonstrated a lack of feeling for the world, the people in it, and oneself. Church authorities in medieval times interpreted Saint Paul's dictum, "He who shall not work will not eat," as a universal injunction against the withdrawal from society. Monks were enjoined to remain in touch with secular matters in order to gain better control over "satanic forces."

Thomas Aquinas preached that work was essential for the survival of the individual and the community. Protestantism subsequently viewed labor as glorifying God and proclaimed it the moral duty of every man. Resistance to one's calling was considered blasphemy. *Rational piety* and *worldly engagement*, the expectations for male behavior, were supported by attire that conveyed obedience to the injunction to modesty and self-effacement.

Morality Tales

Prior to the sixteenth century (before the Protestant Reformation and printing), when most of the world's population was illiterate, paintings of religious themes warned men and women against the pursuit of sexual and other personal interests. One popular account portrayed in paintings was the story of Salome, which alerts men to female trickery and seduction and informs women of their power and their ability to get things they want despite disapproval and objection. For example, in the *Altarpiece of St. John the Baptist and St. John the Evangelist, 1479* by Hans Memling, King Herod and the soldiers are depicted in the attire of power. Salome is demure and tentative in manner, with eyes cast down, as she stands with a platter to accept the head of John the Baptist.

The cautionary tale of Saint Ursula directs young women to obey their fathers. The Saint Ursula Shrine, now in the Memlingmuseum in Bruges, Belgium, is a glittering miniature house of the late Gothic period. The shrine consists of small-scale sculpture and paintings that depict how Ursula went to Rome with ten thousand virgins to appeal to the pope to override her father's decision that she marry. Pope Cyriac is shown blessing Ursula, who is kneeling before him dressed in feminine attire and submissive in posture. He is giving her the Sacrament and bidding her to return home and obey her father's wishes. She complies, but on the way home the travelers are attacked by the Huns and Ursula is killed by an arrow. By disobeying her father she opened herself and her followers to misfortune.

Chivalry and Courtly Love

Between the tenth and fifteenth centuries, in the feudal courts of medieval Europe, gender expectations gradually changed. Female submission, male modesty, and self-effacement evolved into a new form: chivalry. Members of the nobility who acquired the title of knight acquired a new set of expectations for gender-appropriate behavior and appearance. These warriors on horseback viewed women as an inspiration to heroism. The code of chivalry, their rules of conduct, included a pledge to *protect* women. The initial phase of training entailed service in the house of the lord, where the aspiring young knight acquired more polished manners and an appreciation of the important part women played in his culture.

A different kind of relationship between the genders is seen in the courtly love ideal, which existed alongside chivalry. It consisted of the idea that love between a man and a woman is of supreme value to life on earth and that love uplifts and ennobles the lover. The courtly love ideal led to the elevation of women as objects of devotion. Today, the customary signs of deference toward women-holding the door for a woman, lighting her cigarette, and so on, are reflections of the code of chivalry and courtly love. Etiquette books continue to espouse these practices but in a somewhat diminished form.

To be a knight was a male privilege that had to be individually earned and personally given. Horsemanship and swordsmanship were part of the training. From early childhood on, male members of the nobility jousted, wrestled, and exercised to develop coordination and strength. Medieval jousts and tournaments pitted one man against another. Combative games were played during solemn occasions and social events, such as coronations and royal marriages, and physical prowess became a virtue. In his erect posture, with armor, shield, and sword, the knight conveyed an image of invulnerability.

In contrast, beauty was the desired characteristic for women. A woman was beautiful if she was small, well-rounded, slender, and graceful, "with a small willowy waist." Delicacy and refinement were the desired qualities of female attire in the feudal courts. Long hair was often braided with ribbons or enclosed in long tubes of silk or leather. Women adorned themselves with splendid necklaces. Dresses were made of wool, linen, and sometimes leather and were completed with embroidery, precious jewels, and fur. The floor-length jumperlike garment was the style of the time. It had a long, fitted bodice, low neckline, and very deep armholes. It was figure revealing. The generous open expanses around the neck suggested vulnerability. Thus, highly contrasting images of masculinity and femininity emerged from the feudal courts. Desired appearance and behavior for each gender diverged radically.

Masculine Physical Ideal

The erect posture, agility, and strength of the nobility became an ideal for the mercantile middle class during the Renaissance. Pope Pius II (1458-1464) recommended that schools adopt games and exercises to develop "the general carriage" of children. They should be trained to hold their heads upright and to look straight ahead, unafraid. Whether walking, standing, or sitting, children should bear themselves with dignity.

Male members of the royal courts exercised and played sports. The kings of England saw tennis as essential for developing agility, speed, and the kind of strategic thinking they believed would help them run the country. Henry VIII even had thin-soled shoes designed for himself to help improve his chances of winning.

In the United States the masculine ideal emanates from two sources. One is the need for simple physical strength. Among those making their way to the West, a strong physique symbolized the victory of man over nature. The election of President Andrew Jackson (1829-1837) represented the ascendancy of the brawny man, whose rough-and-tumble image diverged dramatically from the refined sensibility of the European aristocracy. Later, an interest in muscle power was brought to the country by new immigrants from Germany and Ireland, who competed physically among themselves or against others. Youths seeking to distance themselves from an older immigrant generation they considered sedentary seized the opportunity to engage in sports. They believed that to be successful in life they needed to develop a physically strong body.

The second source for the masculine ideal is the desire for agility and strength. A German professor at Harvard University, Charles Follen, a German immigrant, introduced his students to fitness. He met with them twice a week, on his own time, to do gymnastics. A formal physical education program was instituted in 1861. All students were required to appear at the newly constructed gym for half an hour four times a week. Erect posture, agility, physical strength, and competition were in this way incorporated into Ivy League education.

In the 1870s athletic clubs and baseball leagues were established in many American cities. In the 1880s football gained importance at American colleges, and working out with weights became a key part of programs at Young Men's Christian Associations (YMCAs). Famous weight lifter Eugene Sandow popularized bodybuilding among men. Those who relentlessly pursued muscle power and achieved their goal were admired for their "iron will."

Finally, connected with the masculine physical ideal in American society is a moral strand. Current actors like Clint Eastwood, Charles Bronson, Sylvester Stallone, and Arnold Schwarzenegger continue the medieval knightly tradition of righting wrongs. They often portray the idea that the male role entails competition and physical strength in the service of some higher ideal.

Female Images

The belief on the part of church fathers that men were unable to control sexual passion underlays their demand that women cover their bodies. The specific evil evoked by lust was its mastery over the whole man. Saint Augustine wrote:

> *This lust assumes power not only over the whole body and not only from the outside, but also internally; it disturbs the whole man, when the mental emotion combines and mingles with the physical craving resulting in pleasure surpassing all physical delights. So intense is the pleasure that when it reaches its climax there is an almost total extinction of mental alertness: the intellectual sentries, as it were, are overwhelmed.*

Christian thinkers argued that a man's affections should be expressed in the love of God. Shame was expected to accompany even the lawful practice of procreation. To help men remain pure and reach spirituality, women's attire had to obscure the body and be drab and colorless.

Although new opportunities were opened for the male in the medieval period, roles available to women seem to have decreased. Rules for female deportment during this period held that women's "eyes must be cast down, they must not glance left or right, ... they must neither look at nor address a man, and must not swing their arms when walking, or cross their legs when sitting, their hands must be hidden in their cloaks." These expectations for female deportment in effect limited women's involvement with society, according to M. von Boehn.

The rules for female deportment were reinforced in religious art, especially art depicting the Holy Family and Nativity scenes. In the Book of Hours, an illuminated prayer book that first appeared in the second half of the thirteenth century, women are shown in domestic settings, praying and reading the Scriptures, or working in the fields. The message conveyed is that women are pure, pious, and submissive. Often women are pictured holding babies. Spirituality, motherhood, and submission to those in higher authority were the characteristics of the ideal woman. The church's definition of modest attire that hides the female body was integrated into secular life. Even today, it continues to guide female role behavior.

The Secular Sphere

Female labor was essential in medieval times. In most social classes, men were dependent on their wives for doing household chores. Tasks assigned to wives varied from manor to manor, from region to region, and from countryside to city. Within a manor women always had control over the production of dairy, poultry, and vegetables. In the cities they were involved in the home brewing of beer and the making of cloth. Wives were dependent on a husband's protection and support. Men monopolized the more lucrative and rewarding trades and professions, leaving unattached women economically vulnerable. According to French historian Philip Aries, they were also physically vulnerable. Impoverished and with no family protection they were subject to rape. The community saw itself as a vast gathering of householders; living within a family context was the ideal. Departure from this ideal was unacceptable. For an unmarried woman living alone, a house of prostitution became a "safe harbor."

Clothing regulations recognized that to attract a husband women had to wear more frivolous attire than at other times. Women in the courting stage were allowed to make use of color and ornament different from what a wife could use. A woman remained under the jurisdiction of her father and was entitled to wear the attire of his rank until she married. Once married she was under the control and protection of her husband and wore the clothing of *his* rank.

Although women could not be party to a business contract, buy or sell land, or control significant amounts of money, they sometimes could do so through an inherited position. In the *"Wife of Bath,"* Chaucer (1342-1400) wrote about a widow, a merchant's wife, who took part in the pilgrimage to Canterbury. She carried on her husband's business after his death, "making cloth that bettered of Ypres and of Ghent." In company she loved to chat and laugh. She was skilled in love, having had five husbands, and knew how to take care of "love's mischances." Chaucer described her attire in this manner: Her kerchiefs were finely woven, her hose of the finest scarlet red, and her shoes soft and new. He concluded that her attire testified to her income. Yet she contrasted herself to those who decided to live in virginity, "as clean in body as in soul, and never mate. I'll make no boast about my own estate." The Wife of Bath clearly viewed the body as a source of sensual pleasure. This pleasure carried over to her joy of dressing and clothing herself in a manner that would attract male interest. Her resources, of course, made that possible.

Procreative Role

Throughout time women have been expected to marry and assume their biological role of procreation. In Indian art from prehistoric times, an emphasis on the hips, breasts, and belly alluded to women's biological ability to bear and nurture children. In the late Middle Ages, when plagues decimated the European population and an iconography of death was a popular subject in art, the prevailing style of dress focused on women's abdomens, simulating a "pregnant look." Breasts as "containers of nurturing" were a subject frequently portrayed in art. It was as if to remind women that bearing and nurturing children was their unique privilege and responsibility. After World War II, in the late 1940s and through the 1950s, fashion styles again alluded to pregnancy. Yves Saint Laurent's 1953 *"Trapeze line"* consisted of clothes that emphasized wide hips and called attention to the abdomen, glamorizing maternity and womanhood. The breasts assumed new importance. It was during this period that the large bosoms of Marilyn Monroe and Jayne Mansfield were celebrated. The exhortation by those in authority in the workplace that women return to the traditional female role, leaving the jobs to men, and the fact that men were back from the war resulted in the so-called baby boom.

The Wife's Role

With the advent of commerce and the growth of monarchies, it was no longer sufficient for a man to dress himself in attire that supported his claim for rank. To demonstrate his power and wealth a husband had to dress his wife and other members of the household well. The family members' appearance signified the consciousness of a "we." Their lavish attire was similar in style, texture, and color. To create dynasties, monarchs established the right to rule through birthright. The royal wife wore sumptuous garments and dazzling jewelry, supporting the king's claim to the monarchy and helping to create an image of stability, power, and wealth.

Female Authority Role

In the sixteenth century three women ascended the throne: Isabella of Aragon/ Castile, Catherine de Médicis in France, and Elizabeth I in England. They wore female attire – dresses, in a style that extended the body but de-emphasized the maternal and nurturing role. A high-necked masculine bodice flattened the chest and its V-shaped padded front resembled the armor of noblemen. The bodice extended over a voluminous skirt and was supported by a farthingale, a structure of stiff hoops. Like the high neck and skirt, puffed sleeves served to draw attention away from the body, thus forcing distance and creating a sense of amplification. The many gemstones the women wore provided the brilliance characteristic of male monarchs. Unlike male monarchs, they carried no arms, but they were surrounded by attendants who did.

Women of the nobility in other European courts also dressed within this new paradigm. The image they adopted was that of confluence: the breasts flattened, the waistline repudiated, their dress form-following, coming straight down and just touching the floor. A stiff white ruff effectively denied access to the expression of feelings.

Similarly, in the 1970s, women in managerial positions observed that a key to being considered professional was dressing in a manner that minimized the maternal, nurturing, and sexual dimensions of their appearance. A form-following jacket over a blouse concealed the contours of the female body and, like a shield, created distance. They felt that this distance strengthened their ability to give orders and the probability that they would be carried out.

Adopting Male Roles

Rejection of the traditional female role has usually been accompanied by a change in dress. For example, prior to the Renaissance the church allowed women who renounced their sexuality and publicly announced their virginity to wear male attire and to preach. The Acts of the Apostles, a text thought to have been written about A.D. 160, tells the story of Thecla, a beautiful young woman engaged to be married. One day, by chance, she heard Paul preach chastity. Enthralled, she rejected her suitor. When an attempt to burn Thecla at the stake failed, she appealed to Paul and was accepted as his student. After she completed her training, she went out to teach dressed in male attire.

Historian Marina Warner observed that there is ample evidence to suggest that many women who escaped arranged marriages cropped their hair in male fashion, donned male attire, and arrived at monastery gates disguised as men. Often their identity as women was not discovered until their death. Margaret of Antioch, bearing the name Brother Pelagius, lived quietly as a monk until she was accused by a young woman of fathering her child. Margaret suffered the accusation in silence and was condemned to solitary confinement for the rest of her life. With death at hand, she wrote a letter revealing her innocence. She was then recognized as a woman and honored as a saint for her suffering.

The most celebrated example of a woman who rejected female passivity is Joan of Arc. After proclaiming her virginity, and thus her right to wear male attire, she donned a knight's armor and led men into battle on a white horse. Because a woman bearing arms was not acceptable in the church's view, she was accused of immodesty. Refusing to the end to change into women's clothes, Joan was burned at the stake. It was not until World War I that women could formally wear military attire.

Decline of Passivity

At the beginning of the twentieth century, the expanding economy and increasing military needs in the United States encouraged women to move out of the home and into factories, offices, schools, hospitals, and shops. The Gibson girl attire signified the change. It consisted of a shirtwaist blouse and a tailored skirt. it was a practical style preferred by working women and women serious about sports. Artist Charles Dana Gibson popularized the style by portraying beautiful young women so dressed. Feminists at the time saw the Gibson girl as the prototype of the new woman-"braver, stronger, more beautiful, and more skillful and able and free, more human in all ways" than the traditional woman. According to the November 1911 issue of *The American Businesswoman* there were five million self-supporting women in the United States employed in 295 Occupations. Mass manufacture made shirtwaist blouses available for as little as $1.50 and suits for $10.00.

The movement of middle-class women into the full-time labor force has been increasing throughout the twentieth century. The 1970s women's movement and the civil rights acts made it possible for today's women to wear police and other uniforms that say that they have right to exercise force. The capacity of women to think rationally and make effective decisions was also recognized. The Puritan rejection of waste and its emphasis on individual determination, together with higher education, legitimated the movement of women into positions of authority. Arguing that national security was undermined by putting sex ahead of talent, the U.S. Senate voted on July 31, 1991, to remove the ban on women as combat pilots. Nearly five hundred years had passed since Joan of Arc was burned at the stake for donning a knight's armor and leading men into battle.

Demise of Subservience and the Active Ideal

Women had been required to cover their heads in public as a sign of submission and obedience to men since early Christian times. In the United States, hats, which some women had interpreted as symbols of middle-class respectability, were repudiated in the 1950s. As the wife of President John E Kennedy, Jacqueline Kennedy did popularize the pillbox hat, which sat on her wellgroomed hair like a crown. But by the end of the 1960s, no hat was in sight. (Journalists may describe the distinction as Jackie Kennedy versus Jackie Onassis.) By the late 1960s women also rejected other upper-class refinements, such as the attire consisting of a basic black dress, white gloves, and strand of cultured pearls. That attire was generally replaced with pants suits and slacks.

In 1982 actress Jane Fonda brought out her first aerobics videotape, helping to bring exercise to a whole new segment of the population, those who never venture out to an exercise class. Youthfulness and health were emphasized by women's magazines and the cosmetics industry, which encouraged more women to join exercise classes. The popularity of working out resulted in what reporters call "the fitness craze."

As aerobics and working out became popular, the dancer's black leotard and tights and the sweat suit were gradually replaced. In fabrics that stretch and styles that are comfortable, the unisex capri-length "wrestler" unitard is now worn over a cropped top. The unitard and similar two-piece sets are skintight. They hug the body and allow no place for bulges to hide. In addition to allowing for a greater range of motion, the attire encourages restraint in the consumption of food. The newest exercise attire, a thong-style brief or leotard with high-cut legs, permits a critical view of upper thigh muscles. This attire makes long, welltoned legs, a current fitness ideal, highly visible.

Throughout the many centuries, the Church's injunction to sex-specific attire has remained essentially unchanged. Like church fathers decreed long ago, the body continues to function as a blackboard upon which values and expectations for behavior are signified. Within the secular realm, styles of dress have at times differed from church prescription, dependent upon expectations for participation in the public sphere. As the male role became autonomous from that of the female, men's style of dress became visually independent from that of women. Images of masculinity and femininity evolved to support the expectation that men and women would function in separate spheres. Visual interdependence existed in the monarchic courts, where men were dependent on women to support their claim to the right to rule. Female attire developed around the same principles of power and authority as did male attire.

Economic and political conditions in the United States in the twentieth century gradually made it possible for women to reject visual signs of submission. Further, public education made it possible for American women to reject relegation to the domestic sphere. Women are now more than ever able to dress in attire that allows them greater ability to participate openly in decision-making roles. The women's movement for the past two decades has sought to modify the powerful influence of traditional male role models such as kings, warriors, and lovers, whose response to women has been that of tyrants, killers, and seducers. The movement has sought to legitimate feelings of tenderness and care, which had usually been stifled in the contemporary male gender role. And today, a new direction in male dress a masculine translation of female style is appearing.

In 1991 Italian and American designers seemed to respond to women's complaints and to their own experience. They addressed the man who is unashamed to acknowledge his vulnerability, as well as his virility, and to make light of gender distinctions. In a news story on male style, Ruth La Ferla reported that designers showed men's clothes in shapes and colors borrowed from a woman's wardrobe. Krizia embellished sweaters with nosegays, and Versace showed shirts, shawls, and vests in kaleidoscopic hues "as resplendent as a rajah's." Giorgio Armani altered the mood of the business suit by adding a shirt in a bright woodsman plaid. Keith Varty and Alan Cleaver of Byblos (a design company based in Italy) paired blazers with tapered ski pants. Similarly, Krizia, Ferre, Gucci, and others showed loosened jackets and track pants.

American designers Donna Karan, Calvin Klein, and Michael Kors have moved in another direction. They are attempting to introduce sexiness and flexibility into male dress. Donna Karan pants for men have no creases, eliminating the rigidity and stiffness of the image of authority. Klein is also introducing an extra measure of softness in men's wear. Michael Kors's collection includes separate pieces that can be combined as suits. "As in his women's wear collection, stretch fabric will play a part as will sexiness," reported Woody Hochswender. He quoted Kors as saying, "There is nothing wrong with dressing with a provocative edge," and, "Men want the same comfort level as women." According to Kors, the lycra and stretch fabrics used in women's fashions can give men a new level of comfort. At the same time, these fabrics provide a tighter fit, exposing shape and allowing pride in the physical male body.

Although the norm of gender-distinct attire continues, the injunction to modesty is being rejected. Expectations for women to renounce their intellectual capacities and for men to repudiate humane, emotional dimensions are slowly diminishing. More important, perhaps, the 1992 U.S. presidential election and the appointments made by then president-elect Bill Clinton suggest that the talents and strengths of both genders will be more equally respected in the future.

8

SEDUCTIVE DRESSINGS IN FASHION TECHNOLOGY

Introduction

Each culture develops its own definitions of attire that provokes sexual interest; those who wear such attire within that cultural milieu will be seen as inviting onlookers to engage them sexually. Alluding to the body beneath it, seductive clothing is part of sexual foreplay.

Seductive images are different from pornographic ones. Seductive images are designed to elicit interest in further communication and interaction, are "homemade," and can even be found in family gatherings and ordinary snapshots. Pornographic images, in contrast, address an already positioned audience interested in sexual acts. They are commodities constructed by professionals within distinct social and economic circumstances and are designed to furnish sexual pleasure.

Feminist scholarship suggests that in Western society the role of seductive tempter has been assigned almost exclusively to women. This designation stems from the early church theologians who placed Eve in this category. She not only succumbed to temptation and disobeyed God, but, even worse, she tempted Adam to do the same.

Although Adam and Eve were themselves condemned for disobeying God, it was through their sexual union that their Original Sin was transmitted to all humankind. From this Augustinian perspective, every sexual act could be viewed as a repetition of Original Sin. Because every human being must, of necessity, be conceived by such an act, we are all born in sin and subject to death. The resulting hostility to sex has become, in turn, justification for disdain of the body and antipathy to pleasure of any kind.

With knowledge of pagan sexual practices and biblical prohibitions, church fathers sought to prevent women from serving as a source of carnal temptation. They designated as seductive the use of color that inflamed lust, certain ornaments, and styles of dress that exposed the body or emphasized its curves. Women were not to wear such attire. The basic and most important category of seductive attire consisted of *alluring images designated by tile church.* These images are discussed in the next section of this chapter. The church fathers' claim that style of dress had the capacity to equip the wearer to think, feel, or act differently than otherwise is basic to the conception of alluring images.

The prohibition against color, ornament, and style placed women in a difficult position. Because they were dependent on men both socially and economically, they had to attract male attention. To attract the attention of a male, a woman needed to stand out. Over the centuries, Western European women developed modes of attire that remained within the bounds of modesty yet simultaneously enhanced their physical appeal. Such styles sometimes become popular and then disappear, only to be rediscovered later. These styles belong to a second category, *alluring images developed by women.*

In contemporary America deviant sexual preferences of some men have been legitimated by mainstream culture; they have become part of the vocabulary of seductive images. They form a third category, *alluring images initiated by men.* This category, too, will be discussed in detail later in this chapter. All three categories of images have become part of public memory and provide sources for today's designers.

Alluring Images Designated by the Church

Between A.D. 100 and 500, the church fathers defined the fundamental characteristics of seductive attire as ornamentation, varied colors of clothing, and styles of dress that exposed body parts. Clement of Alexandria (ca. A.D. 150-220) argued that to prevent male transgression, women should cover their bodies from head to toe. However, "their dresses should not be overly soft and clinging and should be hemmed below the ankles rather than above the knees. For that style of dress is grave, and protects her from being gazed at." "And," he added, "she will not fall who puts before her eyes modesty and her shawl; nor will she invite another to fall into sin by uncovering her face."

Clement required that women wear veils but forbade them to circumvent the purpose by wearing purple ones because colors attract attention and "inflame lusts." As Enoch, another of the church fathers, argued, "If God wanted dresses made of purple and scarlet wool, he would have created purple and scarlet sheep." In a diatribe against jewelry, Clement complained that certain ornaments used by women served as symbols of adultery. In a similar vein, Tertullian attributed to Enoch the observation that women learned about cosmetics from the fallen angels.

The objection to ornament and the injunction against adornment were clearly expressed by Cyprian in his work, *The Clothing of a Virgin*:

> *Let your countenance remain in you incorrupt, your neck unadorned let not rings be made in your ears, nor precious chains of bracelets and necklaces encircle your arms or your neck; let your feet be free from golden bands, your hair stained from no dye, your eyes worthy of beholding God.*

Similarly, in the first *Epistle to Timothy*, women are advised to "adorn themselves modestly and sensibly in seemly apparel not with braided hair or gold or pearls or costly attire but with good deeds, as befits women who profess religion."

The church's desire to dampen women's sexual allure by requiring that they keep their heads and bodies covered has had several unintended consequences. First, the woman's body has become like a chalkboard upon which she can write or erase sexual intentions. For example, after World War I, women wearing high heels and tight-fitting dresses with low necklines or sideslits that allowed some of the bosom or thigh to be discerned, as well as women letting their hair down when it was normally held up, were interpreted as announcing sexual desire.

The second obvious consequence is that because body parts that have been covered can be uncovered, all parts of the female body have been sexualized. A hemline shortened to expose the ankle or the removal of a glove to allow a glimpse of hand and wrist can arouse sexual interest. Likewise, a person who is partially clad usually provokes sexual interest. (In contrast, costume historian Lawrence Langner found that in cultures whose members do not usually wear clothing, it is the covered or clothed body that arouses sexual desire.) Thus, the church's insistence on covering the body had the paradoxical result of providing women with a means of contravening its original intention.

A third consequence is that proscribed attire became the category of dress identified as likely to arouse sexual desire; it was cataloged, recognized, and used deliberately for that purpose. This logical consequence was not necessarily unforeseen, since those who chose to wear such clothing provided a warning as well as an invitation: People knew which women to shun, and men knew which women to avoid or to seek out after dark. A law in England from 1352, for example, acknowledged that prostitutes needed special clothing to elicit sexual response. It stated: "No known whore should wear thenceforth, any hood except red or striped of divers colors, nor furs, but garments reversed or turned the wrong side outward upon pain to forfeit the same." The regulation thus recognized that both color and a style signify seductive intent.

In the nineteenth century, prostitutes' attire demonstrated the same characteristics as were stated in the 1352 law. It was made of cheap, flashy material (brightly colored and, as it were, turned wrong side out to suggest its closeness to the body) and "nothing besides in the way of undergarments. Bonnetiess, without shawls, they presented themselves 'in their figure' to male passersby." All of the early church fathers, of course, would have recognized from only their lack of head covering that such women represented the temptation of the Devil.

Alluring Images Developed by Women

The medieval whore in her gaudy headdress and the unbonneted nineteenthcentury prostitute readily attracted male attention: Each stood out in stark contrast to the norm. But attracting the attention of a desired male was also a goal of ordinary, "modest" women who sought access to wealth, power, and prestige. In a crowd of women covered from head to toe in dark-colored clothing, how was one to stand out? A woman's appearance had to be interesting and had to differentiate her from the others, and yet it had to avoid evoking disapproval or censure. To achieve this goal, her clothing had to remain within some definition of "respectable."

The women best known for achieving this goal were those who were "certified seductive" the royal courtesans. They were women who sought to attract the attention and interest of a monarch and succeeded. Their success in attracting a king and gaining legal recognition of their status legitimized their clothing style; consequently, they became what is today called trendsetters. Other women sought to copy their style. The courtesans were responsible for initiating and popularizing three distinct tactics (images) that were then adopted by more modest women: adapting elements of male dress, creating an image of harmony, and creating a glamorous look. These tactics, rediscovered in the twentieth century, continue to influence contemporary styles.

Adapting Elements of Male Dress

This tactic first appeared during a period of social and political change. The fourteenth century was a time of increasing prosperity in Europe. With the growth of commercial centers, such as Venice, Genoa, Barcelona, and Marseilles, and with the establishment of the great northern ports of Bruges and Antwerp, the feudal system began to disappear. Royal and princely courts were created in which political power was increasingly centralized. These courts were supported by a prosperous mercantile class and an ambitious bourgeoisie.

With the resulting growth in the number of powerful and wealthy families, members of the nobility felt it necessary to distinguish themselves from the rich merchants. Distinctions in clothing provided a readily available means by which the court nobility could assert its higher social rank, and copying the court styles became the means by which the rich bourgeoisie, in turn, could identify itself with the nobility and its privileges. Almost inevitably, the clothing worn by these groups displayed their wealth and power. As the new look of luxury in courtly attire spread across Europe, it became known as the International Gothic Style. For men, the wearing of jewelry embellished by precious gems, such as diamonds and pearls, became a mark of status.

In paintings from the fifteenth, sixteenth, and seventeenth centuries, women are sometimes depicted wearing elements of male dress. The credit for making such daring behavior acceptable usually goes to the first official courtesan in the French Court, Agnes Sorel. To set herself apart, she borrowed diamonds from the men in her family and had them mounted into a feminine-style necklace. By wearing the unexpected (diamonds had hitherto been worn exclusively by the male members of the royal family), she succeeded in catching the eye of the French king, Charles VII. As M. Baerwald and T. Mahoney noted, *the charm o the unexpected* is at work when women adopt elements of male dress.

Because Sorel succeeded in becoming the king's mistress, she quickly became a fashion leader. Other women copied her appearance. She popularized the high-domed forehead, a hairstyle that required that the forehead be immaculately plucked. It is the style she is wearing in the painting *Virgin and Child* by French painter Jean Fouquet. In this painting she was elevated by the painter to the highest status available to a woman placed "on a pedestal" as the Virgin Mary. Although the dress she wears in the painting is simple, its curved seams outline her figure smoothly, and one of her breasts is exposed. Round and seemingly full of milk, it is directed toward the baby on her lap. As befits the Queen of Heaven, a crown studded with gems and pearls sits firmly on her head.

Gloves, hats, and hoods were the other elements of male dress that women adopted in this period. In a painting called *Hunting with Falcons at the Court of Philip the Good*, all the guests are dressed in white as part of the theme of the festivities. The focal point in the painting is Duke Philip the Good, who is lounging elegantly against a banquet table in the center of a magnificent ensemble of courtiers. In different parts of the painting are clusters of guests, all in elegant costumes that seem more appropriate for display than hunting. In one cluster, among a group of couples participating in a stately dance, is a woman wearing scarlet gloves. Traditionally only cardinals wore scarlet gloves. But by the fifteenth century so many women had adopted this element of male dress that the cardinals refused to wear theirs. Despite their protest, the pope ordered them to continue wearing scarlet gloves. Masculine headdress, specifically the bourrelet (a round, padded roll placed over the hair), is worn by a few of the women in the painting, and women wearing this style of headdress appear quite frequently in other northern European paintings as well. Hoods worn by men were also adopted by women of the nobility. The trousseau of Agnes of Cleve included several hoods, at least two of which had bourrelets attached.

In a chronicle describing the customs and habits of the people of Venice, Cesare Vecellio reported that by 1590 the prostitutes had adopted elements of male dress as part of their seductive attire. Made of silk or other cloth, depending on the prostitutes' social class, their "vests were padded and fringed in the style of young men, particularly Frenchmen." Next to their bodies they wore a man's shirt "more or less delicate according to what they can spend." Instead of wearing a skirt, many wore men's breeches, which made them instantly recognizable.

In a double portrait of the Flemish painter Peter Paul Rubens and his wife Isabella Brandt, Isabella is wearing a man's hat. It rests precariously on one side of her head over a traditional female bonnet. It seems that by the seventeenth century women of the bourgeoisie had also discovered the charm of wearing elements of male dress.

The practice does not appear to figure into the art and fashion of the eighteenth or nineteenth century. But at the beginning of the twentieth century Gabrielle Chanel discovered its allure. Attending the races at Deauville one chilly day, so the story goes, she was cold. She borrowed a polo player's sweater, belted it, and pushed the sleeves up. Chanel was so entranced with the image that she soon produced similar sweaters for other women, and they sold immediately.

At the races she could be seen wearing a shetland sweater and pearls while other women wore silk and lace. Other elements of male dress that she introduced into female fashion were the leather belt, sailor pants, and the twin set, a combination of matching cardigan and pullover worn together. Chanel was also one of the first women to cut her hair short.

Elements of male dress worn by women call attention to the wearer because they are unexpected; since they are utterly contrary to the norm, they are "so absolutely daring." The novelty is disarming and sexually alluring. So found actress Marlene Dietrich, when in 1933 she made international headlines when she appeared offscreen in mannish attire. Warned by the Paris chief of Police that she would be asked to leave town if she continued to wear pants, she changed into a skirt, but she still wore a man's hat, collar, and tie. The tight-fitting jacket that she had worn came from a boy's clothing store. It emphasized her female curves. Perhaps male clothes make "femaleness" all the more obvious.

The oversized male shirt, or pajama top, the fedora hat, baseball and sailor's caps, the tie (worn loosely), and the male-style leather jacket were adopted by women in the 1970s. Giorgio Armani's use of haberdashery fabrics and Ralph Lauren's form-fitting tuxedo suit are 1980s examples. Designers had thus come to realize the seductive charm of the unexpected engendered by women who wear elements of male dress.

Creating an Image of Harmony

Creating an image of harmony was a tactic adopted by one of the best-known French courtesans, Jeanne-Antoinette Poisson, known as Madame de Pompadour. Two ideas seemed to animate her style. The first was that "the sensual and lighthearted" are "delightful"; the second was that "the elements of appearance should be fused to create a whole greater than the sum of its parts." These two principles were embodied in the clothing she wore when she set out to establish herself as Louis XV's mistress. The story goes that the king, long estranged from his Polish wife, Marie Leczinska, and brooding over the death of his most recent mistress, was restless and devoted much of his time to hunting in the Forest of Senart. Jeanne-Antoinette Poisson would follow the hunt in a brightly colored carriage. One day she would dress in light blue and ride in a rose-colored carriage; the next, she would wear a rose-colored dress and the carriage would be light blue. She followed a similar procedure in Paris, where she would arrive at the theater in full view of the king. She succeeded in catching his eye; then, under the cover of festivities and masked balls celebrating the marriage of the dauphin, she lured him to her bed. Shortly thereafter she was publicly acknowledged, and in 1745 the king awarded her the title Marquise de Pompadour. For nearly twenty years, until her death in 1764, she was considered de facto Queen of France.

In her time many court observers paid tribute to Madame de Pompadour's extraordinary beauty; however, despite their praise, her facial characteristics, as depicted in portraits and sculpture, were less than beautiful, scholars have insisted. They noted that the accuracy of the depiction is not in question. A number of artists (including Nattier, Boucher, Van Loo, Cochin, Droiuais, Lemoyne, and Pigalle) portrayed her at different times. Each depicted her with the same facial characteristics a round face with even features and a dazzling complexion, eyes not very large but most "brilliant, witty and sparkling."

Reports by court observers have suggested that it was her style of dress that attracted the king's attention and led, in turn, to the many tributes to her beauty. Following her belief, which was in keeping with the time, that the elements of appearance should be fused to create a whole greater than the sum of its parts and that the individual should be in harmony with nature, she chose fabrics of pale and delicate shades that complemented her dazzling pink and white complexion and her sparkling eyes. To provide a sense of playfulness, she wore her richly decorated, low-cut gowns adorned with many ribbons, flowers, ruffles, and lacy flounces. This profusion of exquisite tiny details, like those in the world of nature, was arranged to convey the impression of a unified whole. People who knew her almost never mentioned her beauty without also mentioning the "consumate elegance with which she dressed." Although the robe *à la française* (a dress of tight-fitting bodice, a low square décollete, and a ladder of bows down the front), which Madame de Pompadour adopted, had already come into fashion, her preference for it had an impact on other women. Throughout Europe, for the remainder of the eighteenth century, women's fashions were inspired by her clothing.

The desire for harmony in attire grew out of the rise of new ideas and disturbing questions about freedom, responsibility, and ethics in eighteenth-century France and England. Enlightenment thinkers argued that the development of science obviated the need for supernatural guidance. Instead, humans were urged to rely on the power of reason. These thinkers pointed out that the study of nature, unaided by divine guidance, had revealed it to be both knowable and regular and hence predictable. For many of them, the study of nature through the use of reason and logic replaced the study of the mysteries of God. In keeping with this change, writers began to emphasize that individuals were in and of themselves increasingly capable of good and that when they at last reached harmony with nature, they would be judged perfect. This desire for harmony also reflected a desire for political and social accord, the roots of which lay in classical Athens. When Athens was established as a democracy in the fifth century B.C., its citizens sought to limit dissonance among families and groups. Balance and order were viewed as essential for social life. In response to the value placed on harmony, artists of classical Greece strove to represent strength balanced with grace and gentleness in their statues of the gods. Symmetry and just proportions (in which the parts are subordinate to the whole) became the classical period's criteria of beauty.

Eighteenth-century philosophers who valued the harmony and regularity that they believed existed in nature readily adopted the classical Greek principles of beauty. In 1756 Edmund Burke suggested that beauty comprises a "smoothness" such that parts melt into one another. The definition of beauty by J. Barry in 1784, cited in the *Oxford English Dictionary*, similarly focuses on the unity that emerges when variety exists. The result, in art, is resolution a static, balanced artifact.

In the 1960s, with the "youth revolution" and the call for an "authentic self," women outside fashion centers were encouraged to reject fashion as "conspicuous consumption." women in small towns and suburban communities were listening to Suzanne Caygill, who toured the country lecturing on natural color harmonies. The principle underlying her talks was the Enlightenment idea that harmony with nature is basic to happiness. She lectured that the most effective way for a person to be in harmony with the environment is for him or her to dress and live in the appropriate color and style. In the natural world, she noted, the palette of each season consists of harmonious colors. Each individual's skin and eye coloring, hair, body contours, and personality can be complemented by a palette existing in nature. The effect engenders in both wearer and onlooker a feeling of being at peace – with oneself and with nature. Wearing these colors conveys a sense of unity and harmony." Caygill evolved and eventually codified for the public the principles that Madame de Pompadour had utilized so successfully. In *Color Me Beautiful*, Carol Jackson popularized Caygill's ideas about color and personal appearance.

Creating a Glamorous Look

A third tactic developed by women to make themselves stand out in the eyes of men can best be described as the creation of a "glamorous look." Glamour is particularly difficult to define. *Webster's* describes it as "mysteriously exciting and often illusory attractiveness that stirs the imagination and appeals to a taste for the unconventional, the unexpected, the colorful or the exotic." The term may also connote personal charm and poise, and may imply unusual physical and sexual attributes.

The nineteenth century witnessed a turning away from the profusion and richness of the Pompadour style. Decent, modest women were expected to wear structured dresses in dark, somber colors. Such colors and styles were in harmony with society's conception of the proper place and role for women. Women's styles in this period were not expected to create the impression of an individual as a harmonious whole. Rather, style served to express conformity with society's expectations for women. The dark-colored, enveloping garb appealed to middle-class women because it was practical, useful, and economical. During long, cold winters in small, drafty, sometimes smoky houses, the warmth of the relatively coarse, heavy fabric in such garments was useful. Equally important, most of the fabric was produced locally, as was the clothing itself, and production of the preferred dark-colored cloth did not require the use of costly dyes or dyeing processes. Hence, the garments were practical, useful, and inexpensive.

Wearing such garments, however, forced women to confront once again the problem of how to stand out among a group of women wearing the same "practical" clothing. To make matters worse, their voluminous, heavy-looking dresses, broad-brimmed bonnets, and enveloping capes in dark and gloomy colors stood in stark contrast to the white, light yellow, light green, and orange satins worn by the courtesans. The courtesans set out to look sensual. They decorated their clothing with dainty bows, ribbons, and frills. Trimmed with lace, their dresses emphasized their bosoms. Frivolity and lightheartedness characterized their appearance. Their attire glistened; it was soft and encouraged touch.

The courtesan was less than a mistress and more than a prostitute. As J. Richardson reported, "She is less than a mistress because she sells her love for material benefits; she is more than a prostitute because she chooses her lovers. The courtesan is a woman whose profession is love, and whose clients may be more or less distinguished." Often the women who became courtesans sought to escape the traditional constraints of poverty and marriage. Born between 1814 and 1830, they grew up in a time of economic and political change. The monarchy had fallen; the old aristocracy was discredited; and Napoleon's meteoric rise and fall served as a warning to any who might attempt to reach the heights of the pre-1789 nobility. Instead, industrialization, trade, and the burgeoning cities were the new sources of opportunity and wealth.

The courtesans sexualized sensuality. They reddened their cheeks and nails to stimulate passion and widened the pupils of their eyes with atropine, simulating sexual excitement. They were reputed to have raised interaction with men in general, and sexual intercourse in particular, to an art. They acquired the reputation that they were beautiful, talented, imaginative, and fun to be with. They were identified as "*les grandes horizontales*." Aided by being glamorized in the poetry, literature, and visual arts of the period, they became members of the fashionable set. They were international in origin, and they each had their own distinct features and style. They were described as "*grandes coquettes*"; they were flirty, gay, witty, and entertaining. As Richardson described:

All of Paris turned out to see the glorious sight of the courtesans in their handsome carriages and impeccable horses. Excluded from formal ceremonies by those who set the standards for respectability, this was most evident when they were not allowed to enter the grandstand at the Longchamps races. They had to park their carriages on the other side of the track. To offset this humiliation, the courtesans saw to it that their return from races would be like a triumphant procession. Reclining languidly against the plump cushions of their satin upholstered carriages, attended by footmen in elaborate and colorful uniforms and powdered wigs, they competed and often outshone the more respected wife. They drove from Longchamps to the Place de la Concorde, to the Bois de Boulogne and back again until nightfall imparting radiance as they and their carriages reflected the last rays of the sun.

Esteem accorded to a man from other men often depended on how well he had provided for his courtesan. For her services she would often receive financial support in the form of a well-appointed home, liveried servants, art objects, magnificent clothes and jewels.

To some women the courtesan's ability to attract a man, receive his gifts of support, and maintain his interest became proof of the desirability of the courtesan style. Many women, among them members of the court, tried to adopt a glamorous look.

In the United States, the radiance of satin, the zest of champagne, costly furs, and wealthy admirers characterized the image of chorus girls and movie stars. The media conveyed the message that any woman with beauty and talent could dance or sing her way to the top. They encouraged the notion that the United States was indeed a land of opportunity. Newspapers presented movie stars and chorus girls as modern Cinderellas, and the clerks and secretaries who swelled the ranks of women workers from 1900 to 1920 read with envy about their exciting lives, freedom, romance, and adventure. Female movie stars were presented as radiant and larger than life, and movies were capable of transporting viewers across all barriers of time, space, and class. Evoking the magic world of fantasy, the luminous quality of the stars' images modified the drab confinement of everyday life.

Women regarded movie stars as experts on appearance. Everything Gloria Swanson did was news. She became the epitome of elegance and feminine enchantment. When she bobbed her hair in the early 1920s, millions of women rushed to have their hair cut. Until then, throughout the centuries, women had kept their hair long and their heads covered. Short hair had been considered an affront, a violation of the norm of modesty. Suddenly it was seen as romantic, chic, and classy. The lacy, black negligee worn by Mae West in *Night After Night* was celebrated and copied by many women.

Two distinct seductive images were made popular by the show-business industry: that delineated as sexy by the church and that appraised glamorous by the media. The former consisted of sequins, color, plunging necklines, and dresses draped to swathe the body snugly. The latter was constructed with much less emphasis on female attributes; it merely alluded to the body underneath. Satin and makeup conveyed radiance and sensuality.

Alluring Images Initiated by Men: The Vulnerable Look

In the 1800s and 1900s sexual liaisons between older males and young females were satirized and usually discouraged. The term "dirty old man" reflects such sentiments. In a February 6, 1799, advertisement in *Diario de Madrid* for the *Caprichos*, a set of satirical prints by Francisco Goya, many of which mock older men who attempt to seduce young women, Goya described his art as deriding "vice and error." Goya was a keen observer of society and confronted directly the darkest and most basic human impulses, according to art historian Reva Wolf, who in 1991 curated an exhibit of Goya prints at Boston College.

In the art and literature of the 1950s, however, a liaison between the older, sophisticated mate and the young teenager was legitimized. The status of the young teenager as seducer was first seen in ballet, which had acquired a new importance in the post-World War II period. Designer Clair McCardle offered the "ballerina" look for everyday attire, making it popular. The style emphasized long limbs, flat-chestedness, ballet slippers, and hair swept back to reveal a long, delicate neck.

Embodying the essence of youthful innocence and the vulnerability of a new bloom, Audrey Hepburn, a former ballet student, was chosen by the writer Colette in 1951 to play the character of Gigi in the play by the same name on Broadway. Gigi is the story of an older, sophisticated male captivated by the innocent, childlike charm of a teenager. At the heart of all twelve romantic comedies in which Audrey Hepburn later starred is the same fantasy: a coy and playful relationship between a young teenager and a mature, sophisticated male. Her attire in each of the movies denied the attributes that traditionally anchor a woman in society: her breasts and hips. In the film Funny Face, for example, Hepburn is wearing a ballerina-style tunic, black turtleneck, and tights. Whether running with balloons in the rain, looking pensive in a railroad station, or floating down the steps in the Paris Opera, Audrey Hepburn gave to the films an aura of "enchanting innocence," as noted by reviewers. She was described as waiflike an image supported by her long arms, neck, and legs. Her popularity and success surprised her. She repeatedly insisted: "I have no illusions about my looks" and described herself as a "skinny broad." To her amazement she was chosen to represent a new seductive ideal. The *vulnerable look* was one that inspired the older adult male to view a woman as a child and perhaps as "Daddy's little girl," an immature being in need of care and instruction.

Cultural fascination with adolescent sexuality is reflected in the success of *Lolita*, a 1954 novel by Vladimir Nabokov that was initially banned, and in the "baby-doll" fashion that was popular by the mid-1960s. The baby-doll style featured little girls' attire. It consisted of a very short skirt, high waistline, puffed sleeves, jumper or apron effects, lots of lace and ruffles, and sometimes even bloomers. Legs were clad in lacy, pale stockings and feet in Mary Jane shoes. Geoffery Beene, Chester Weinberger, and Bill Blass designed attire in the babydoll look. The clothing was accessorized by elaborate makeup providing a doeeyed look, and by spiky eyelashes; the latter were sometimes painted on in a doll-like fashion. Cheeks were rosy and lips pale frosted, and hair was worn in ringlets around the face.

Without really knowing it, high school and college women offered a different version of the vulnerable look. Rebelling against fashion magazines because of their emphasis on gender differences, they rummaged in thrift stores and family closets for oversized men's shirts, sweaters, and coats. Their image was seductive for two reasons. First, it was familiar yet unfamiliar, because we are used to seeing women in women's clothing and men in men's clothing. Second, the teenager's body inside unstructured, oversized shirts, coats, or jackets seemed small and vulnerable, waifish. The softness of the look made her seem to be wearing her father's or big brother's hand-me-downs. She appeared lost and in need of male protection; some men would want to hold and comfort her.

Several cultural forces offered legitimacy to this image of vulnerability, giving it a place in the gallery of seductive images. Chosen by a panel of "analysts and sociologists" consulted by *Esquire*, it was included in the December 1968 issue of the magazine. The headline read: "Season's Greetings! $_4$ naughty dreams to last you till March." Lauren Hutton, a model and actress, used makeup and costume to represent four different seductive images, including the "baby-sitter." The teenager is portrayed in short shorts, bare feet, and an innocent-looking blouse partially unbuttoned. She is sitting at the edge of a kitchen stool holding a naked baby on her precariously stretched leg. Large parts of her body are exposed, and she looks directly at the viewer, unaware of danger. Since at least the eighteenth century a woman's extended pale leg, exposed to the thigh, and an undone bodice have alluded to sexual availability.

To summarize, the art and literature of the 1950s initiated a cultural dialogue that rejected old definitions and sexualized the "childlike" look. Adopted by teenagers, the vulnerable look represents the incorporation of a deviant male desire into the realm of public fantasy. This amalgam helped to widen the boundaries of the acceptable.

Implications

Seductive images designated or initiated by men differ from those developed by women, and they seem to have different effects on the the male-female interaction. Alluring images that emanate from men call attention to the body and define the male-female relationship more fully in terms of sex. Nourished by the view that sexuality is a biological drive pressing for release, or orgasm, the focus of the interaction is sexual satisfaction. Fulfillment entails mastery over the other, or the use of women as sexual objects.

Male-initiated seductive images can be seen as transporting men from "triumph to trauma." The male, in comparison to the female, enters a male-female interaction from a position of greater access to wealth, prestige, and power or triumph. Reaffirming such superiority, sexual intercourse may likely preclude female sensuality, warmth, and caring. Interaction with an "object" is likely to result in paultry long-term rewards. The rejection of an opportunity to take advantage of the nourishing qualities of women limits the experience, ultimately leaving men with a sense of unfullfilment and insufficient mastery over the situation. Such feelings may do violence to the male's sense of personhood, hence a "trauma."

Alluring images that women develop, in contrast, employ attire that encourages sensual pleasure. They can be described as enabling a woman to shift her lot from "trauma to triumph." The trauma stems from the recognition that she is shut out of significant social realms such as wealth and power. The clothing that women adopt allude to play and encourage eroticism, fun, and gentler sex. The courtesan's interactions with the king or other suiters enabled her to overcome her sense of humiliation over the condition of her birth. These women were given the opportunity to influence policy, to develop their talents and abilities, and to achieve economic independence. Their relationships with men made it possible for some of them to resolve the initial trauma and secure personal triumph.

❑❑❑

9

Clothing Symbol in Fashion Technology

Introduction

Tie-symbols are expressions of support, or association, with a particular idea, cause, predicament, or person. For instance, during the Gulf War in January and February 1991, people in the United States took to wearing clothing and accessories emblazoned with the American flag. Wearing the flag was associated with feelings of patriotism and showed support for the men and women in service. Flags could be seen on T-shirts, sweatshirts, swimsuits, beach towels, tote bags, and umbrellas.

A picture of the U.S. Olympic volleyball team printed on the front page of the *New York Times* in summer 1992 showed the teammates with their heads shaven. They shaved their heads as a gesture of solidarity with Bob Samuelson, a team member involved in a dispute with Olympic officials that caused a reversal of the U.S. victory over Japan. Their shaved heads matched his normal "non-do." For them, the shaved head was a tie-symbol; it expressed support for their teammate.

The most visible tie-symbol in 1992-1993 was the inverted red "V" ribbon worn to honor people who have died of acquired immunodeficiency syndrome (AIDS). Since 1991, when the ribbons were designed and worn by a fifteenmember group, Visual AIDS, thousands of the ribbons have been sold. They have become ubiquitous on award shows and on the streets. Their purpose is to display solidarity and sympathy for AIDS victims. A March 1993 report in the *New York Times* pointed out that the AIDS ribbon paved the way for other ribbons a pink one worn to show breast cancer awareness, and a purple one that calls attention to "the harsh realities of young people growing up in urban neighborhoods."

Tie-symbols are a means of self-association and self-expression, and their adoption is dependent on personal choice. Their term is short and they are ancillary to a person's attire. Concerns, fears, tensions, and hopes within a social aggregate may give rise to tie-symbols. Wearing one announces *sympathy with* a group, a political idea, or a public persona. The tie-symbol can stand for something or against something; it can be pro-social or antisocial. For the wearer, it may or may not have the meaning originally intended.

Advertisers have found that teenagers respond to hero images. These wishedfor identities are associated with overcoming obstacles. "Aspirational" has become a marketing buzzword. Aspirational ads are intended to make consumers aspire to, or emulate, the people endorsing the product. Recognizing the benefits of turning clothes into tie-symbols, Levi Strauss hired filmmaker Spike Lee to make the company's commercials. The 1991 ad campaign took viewers to such sites as East Rutherford, New Jersey, where Joe Hamm, a lighting technician, defied heights to prepare the stage for a Grateful Dead concert; New Braunfels, Texas, where spelunkers explored mysterious caves; and Las Vegas, Nevada, where people were making arrangements for a Mike Tyson fight. According to Levi's marketing director, Daniel M. Chew, the Levi spots were intended to make the target audience, the fourteen-to-twenty-four age-group, ask: "Gee, if these guys are doing all this, what could I be doing?" Lee's earlier campaign, "501 Button Fly Report," had been very successful. The ads provided the inspiration for a line of Levi's T-shirts carrying the slogan "Button your fly" and unauthorized versions saying "Unbutton my fly" Both slogans demand action.

Tie-symbols are important in the United States because they provide people with a means of finding out about their own values and goals. In more traditional societies a sense of identity and appropriate goals were handed to the individual by one's religion, family, and community. Such a path is often not easily available in more complex, contemporary societies. Tie-symbols make it possible for a person to play out different roles and try out different values; they also enable individuals to associate themselves with a desired persona, such as Madonna. Tie-symbols make it easier for individuals to find out about different paths and discover ones they might desire; hence, they are popular among the young and with those with less circumscribed lifestyles. Tie-symbols are used by individuals to help *define the self, maintain self-definition*, and *express political values and goals*.

Seeking Self-Definition

The term "reference group" was used by Herbert Hyman in 1942 when he described the phenomenon whereby individuals who do not belong to a particular group (the reference group) use that group's ideas, beliefs, and values to guide their behavior. The reference group provides the standard that is referred to in appropriating an appearance or behavior.

Grade school children are often concerned with *fitting in*, and they prefer wearing what other children in the school wear. They feel a need to dress "like the herd," Elizabeth Hurlock pointed out. They often reject homemade clothing in favor of store-bought clothes. They sometimes resist wearing what their parents want them to wear. Convinced that wearing clothes like those of their classmates will win them acceptance, they explain, "Kids don't want to play with you unless you wear the same clothing they do." Children in the lower grades see the attire chosen by the older students as the preferred style.

Since the 1940s the appearance of adolescents in American society has been remarkably similar to that of their peers and exceptionally different from both adults and younger children. Gaining the approval of their peers becomes paramount to youth during their junior and senior high school years, and their attire comes under close peer scrutiny. They realize that they have several choices and that the choices they make can lead to acceptance or rejection by their peers. Their concern with the questions "Who am I?" and "Who do I want to be?" may lead to periodic changes of style.

In the 1990s, spiked hair and pierced ears have been sources of parental anxiety. To gain information that might allay such feelings, Lawrence Kutner interviewed psychiatrists and developmental psychologists specializing in adolescence. The child development experts pointed out that "fashion statements" by adolescents are a part of the road to adulthood; hence, they are a normal phenomenon. Most people adopt the ideals and beliefs of their families when they become adults. The experts recommended that parents allow their children "to make choices and mistakes in this area. Wardrobes can be changed and hair will grow back."

Through the clothing decisions an individual makes, he or she gains greater awareness of a self that is distinct and separate from the family yet still anchored in society's basic ideas and beliefs. The act of wearing peer or self designated attire may make it easier to detach oneself from home and family, preparing the individual for the kind of adult independence required in American society.

Adolescent Peer Culture and Trendy Attire

"Schools are not supposed to be a fashion show, yet the halls of high school could pass for runways. For it is in these places of learning and the streets leading to them that many fashion trends are born," reported the *New York Times* in 1991. The story noted that the styles of clothing pervasive among rap artists, such as layered hooded sweatshirts, baseball caps, and cable chains with large medallions, have appeared in the collections of Karl Lagarfeld, Charlotte Neuville, and Isaac Mizrahi. Examining attire presently worn in high school may be of help in predicting future fashion.

Examining current styles in high schools in New York, Connecticut, and New Jersey, the reporters for the *New York Times* article found that bagginess was a major trend. Yet although some New York City teenagers insisted on widelegged, over-sized jeans that hang at the waist, sag in the back, and in some cases have two or three inches of cuff, others preferred tight-fitting, straightlegged jeans. In a high school in the Bronx, wearing leggings with long, loose sweaters was considered in style. In Westwood High School in New Jersey, button-down shirts in solid colors with baggy jeans were the representative attire. Students at Greenwich High School in Connecticut liked their jeans tight but torn; in Bridgeport, Connecticut, they liked the preppy look, corduroy and denim. The female students wore shorts and shirts with matching tights.

Bagginess also allows an individual to carry or transport implements of selfprotection, such as guns, clubs, or knives; tight-fitting styles do not. High school attire is thus sensitive to specific needs, such as the current concern with safety, and it depends on the cultural and socioeconomic background of the wearer. Students in violence-prone city high schools prefer boots and heavy Bass and Doc Marten's shoes with thick soles to sneakers.

A retrospective study of the clothing experience of students at the Fashion Institute of Technology during adolescence found that many of the students often heard their parents object that "kids go to school to learn, not for a fashion show." Their objections were to no avail, however. Wearing the trendy style enabled the adolescents to "feel at one" with their peers.

A strategy used by many adolescents is described in the following quote by one of the Fashion Institute students: "In the beginning of each year from junior to high school, I would look at what everyone else was wearing, then I would simply imitate. I insisted my mother take me shopping each year to remodel my wardrobe. Because if one was seen in last year's fashion, one would be the talk of the town, in a negative way." As another female respondent described the experience: "I can still remember my first pair of designer jeans Sassoon. Everyone had to have a pair, and everyone who was anyone did. We all looked like clones. But I felt I was a part of a group. It is incredible what a pair of Sassoon jeans could do for one's image. They gave me a sense of security, of being accepted." And another said:

My best friend had a pair of Nike sneakers, which I wanted very much but they were too expensive. Forty dollars was too much at the time. Any kid in school wearing a pair of Nike's was considered "in." I felt "out" because I didn't own a pair. When I finally got the courage to ask Mom to buy me a pair she said "no" and yelled at me for trying to be flashy. I begged and nagged her every day until she couldn't take it anymore. I'll never forget the day she took me to Herman's Sporting Goods Store to purchase my sneakers. I was so happy you couldn't wipe the smile off my face. But then in junior high Skippy was the "in" sneaker. All my girlfriends wore them. They were under ten dollars so I bought a few pair. This made my mom real angry, since just the year before she bought me the Nikes, which I stopped wearing. I told her nobody at school wears them anymore, so I couldn't wear them and look stupid. As usual she could not understand why I had to follow what all the other kids wore. I guess parents don't understand peer pressure and the need for kids to feel wanted by a certain group of friends.

That mothers are often cost-conscious and teenagers style-conscious is exemplified in the following story:

> *My mother took me and my sister school clothes shopping, which always turned into a nightmare. I wanted the latest fashion and my mother wanted clothes that would last. Buying them a little big so I could wear them the next year also. We often had screaming matches in the stores. Eventually my father had to take me, which was great because he let me get what I wanted and would spend more.*

Some teenagers whose parents cannot or will not buy them the "right" clothes steal, mug, and even murder to get such clothes. Most, however, go to work. A young man whose family had immigrated from Taiwan when he was eight years old described his experience in this manner:

In junior high school I became brand conscious. I started working on the weekend delivering Chinese food and earning $200 to $250. This was disposable income. Everything I bought was "brand-labeled." Nike and Puma sneakers, Calvin Klein and Sassoon and Sergio Valente jeans. Members Only jackets. I almost had everything I wanted. During my high school days Japanese fashion became "in" [1982-1983]. The clothing [*sic*] were layered and loose fitting. They were not cheap. A jacket was $350 to $450 and sweaters $100 to $150. They were not boring and made me feel great. Now I was an American. I belonged.

The desire for peer approval has often incorporated a concern with weight. "The height of the disco period was in my ninth grade," reported a female student. The movies *Thank God It's Friday* and *Saturday Night Fever* were very popular. As she described it:

> *The common dress for girls my age were Danskin bodysuit worn with designer jeans. We competed with one another to lose weight. I was very successful at losing ten pounds and decided to keep on dieting. My anorexia craze ended once I reached a hundred pounds. My menstrual period stopped for six months and was extremely painful when it resumed. I learned my lesson the hard way.*

Impact of a Public Personal

At Brooklyn Technical High School, across the street from Spike's Place, Spike Lee's retail shop, many students wear baseball caps with the letter "X," a promotional item for the director's movie on Malcolm X. Some students at Brooklyn Tech and other schools say they wear the hats, Malcolm X buttons, and other accessories because they support the slain leader's more aggressive approach to black civil rights.

Becoming popular among men in the summer of 1992 was the bandanna handkerchief tied on the head in an urban-gypsy style. It was folded into a triangle, pulled back over the skull, and knotted in back, as Woody Hochswender reported in the *New York Times*. He noted that John McEnroe wore a pink paisley bandanna for the U.S. Open and "was savagely chic." Photographer Bruce Weber was well known for the practice and not just for hacking around in the garden: "He went hanky-on-top to Anna Wintour's [the editor of *Vogue*] little soiree at the Paramount Hotel last week." Weber gave legitimacy to the look by wearing it to Anna Wintour's party.

For teens of the 1980s the movie Flashdance, and MTV were important sources of style. Referring to Flashdance, one said, "I remember going home and cutting up all my sweatshirts." Another noted, "My mom thought I was crazy cutting up perfectly good shirts and turning them into rags." And another related, "The movie had a big impact on us kids who watched it. Even guys wore cut shirts and sweatshirts that bared their shoulders and belly buttons." A ripped sweatshirt became the desired style.

With the start of MTV in 1981, music and fashion began to go hand in hand for the younger teenage group. Madonna's style had a significant impact. Prior to 1983 and Madonna's impact, the oversized man-tailored shirt and tight jeans were the most visible trend for this age-group. Only a few other trends were seen, such as the short dresses, usually in black, of teens in the Punk movement in the East Village in New York. Madonna's videos Borderline, Lucky Star, and Like a Virgin showed her first "look": a short black dress, big cross earrings, silver and rubber bracelets, black crosses and many silver chains worn around the neck, and a bare midriff. The short tube skirt, tank tops, cropped leggings, and fingerless gloves that Madonna wore became "required attire" among the younger teenage set. Fashion forecasters predicted these elements would be the rage for girls up to sixteen. Hundreds of young girls showed up at Macy's in New York for a "Desperately Madonna Contest," a look-alike contest held after the movie Desperately Seeking Susan. As one respondent described it: "I loved the way Madonna dressed and I dress like her: lace outfits, spandex leggings, tight miniskirts, and tons of rubber bracelets."

Anticipatory Socialization

Starting high school marks a critical turning point in the lives of most youth in the United States. It often entails a dislocation from the past and feelings of loss. The sense of belonging and established feelings of familiarity are upset. High school students must step out of the life conditions they had earlier experienced, step away from their playmates and friendships, and adjust to new classmates, classrooms, and schedules. Moreover, they must establish an identity. Reference group attire that is associated with a particular type of music often helps to solve the problem of connectedness. A T-shirt with a political message, brightly colored and spiked hair, and metal bracelets and chains are also examples of tie-symbols that announce affinity with a particular set of ideas and beliefs. They enable the student to establish a recognizable identity, which facilitates social participation and interaction.

Music and dress offer growing adolescents a means of self-definition. One of the basic motivations of high school students for seeking a job seems to be to acquire the means to buy the clothes and music they want. Through them teenagers learn to recognize particular values and specific orientations to social life, encouraging self-definition. These representations (clothes and music) may also act to link the young to the adult world, a form of anticipatory socialization. As presented in a recent exhibition, five different reference groups appear to have emerged in American high schools: preppies, greasers, jocks, freaks, and nerds. Each is identified by a well-defined style seen in the foods eaten, level of expected higher education, occupational goals, leisure activity, and, of course, appearance.

Maintaining College Groups

The Yale School of Drama is "filled with suffering artists dressed in black," reported Alex Witchel in a 1991 article in the *New York Times Magazine*. Entering college freshmen adopt a particular type of sneaker, jacket, or color in vogue in a particular school. It reaffirms and maintains their new association.

A 1982 study by Margaret Rucker and her colleagues at the University of California, Davis, provided information on how the problem of self-definition is worked out in college. The researchers found that students in different majors tended to wear different styles: A long ethnic dress identified female students majoring in art; a suit (blouse, skirt, and jacket) characterized textile and clothing students; jeans and plaid shirts were the choice of engineering and psychology majors; overalls were worn by those studying animal science. Students adopt the appropriate styles to show they are connected to a particular social aggregate. They thus announce that they have a particular identity and a social base within the larger university population. Here, reference group attire acts to *deindividuate*. It helps to create a social entity within a context of ongoing interaction.

Homosexual Subculture

Until the 1980s most gay men felt pressured to remain invisible to the world outside the gay community. Many did, however, come up with subtle ways to let each other know who they were, as

Michelangelo Signorile reported in *Outweek*. Often they adopted what is now called the Old Clone look. They wore jeans, lumber shirts, jackets, and heavy boots and sported a moustache and sunglasses. Instantly recognizable by other gay men, the look would not offend at work, for most nongay colleagues would miss its significance. It gave the wearer the feeling that he was in one sense openly gay, even if most straights did not realize it. The masculine clone look also helped to prevent violence from "queer bashers."

As a means of denouncing the strategy of hiding, some gay men adopted another style. These men believed they were free-spirited rebels, and they chose innovative attire "with heavy sexual innuendo": close-cropped hair, small drop earring, "Read My Lips" T-shirt, leather motorcycle jacket, silver whistle, leather wristband, wide black leather belt, tight-fitting, cut-off gray Levi's 501 jeans, white sweat socks, and black Doc Marten's boots.

These factions, the "invisible," the "clone," and the "rebel," provide gay men today with distinct modes of dress, allowing for a greater sense of affiliation. The author of the Outweek article, a gay man himself, observed that the choice of style offers a means of belonging.

Tattoos

Robert B. Edgerton and Harvey E Dingman found that of the 2,282 residents in a residential school for the mentally retarded (ages twelve to twenty) 90 percent had acquired tattoos shortly after their arrival, and most of the tattoos were selfinflicted. The tattoos fell into four different categories: 30 percent were associated with powerful gangs outside the institution; 40 percent referred to a love object, such as "mother" or the name of a boyfriend or girlfriend; 10 percent proclaimed the individual's personal attributes as a fighter or a lover, for example; and the last 20 percent consisted of circles, squares, parallel lines, question marks, and other symbols that had no conventional meaning and therefore could not be understood by others. The tattoos in the latter group presumably communicated something about the self to the self in a private system of meaning. Here, in a new and unfamiliar environment that they were not allowed to leave, the residents connected themselves symbolically to an outside source of support, one that was.most meaningful to them. The tattoos helped them cope with a sense of institutional isolation.

The style of a tattoo may be a form of symbolic affiliation also for those outside the institutional setting, as Clinton R. Saunders reported in his study of commercial tattoo settings. He noted that proprietors pride themselves on having a large selection of designs, although only 10 percent of these are chosen by clients with any degree of regularity. According to Saunders, tattooists emphasize that they are involved in a "business" activity in which "the customer is always right." They stress that they are involved in popular culture production rather than creator-oriented fine art.

The wearing of tattoo tie-symbols can also help an individual overcome a sense of alienation, as noted by Goffman in his discussion of the meaning of tattoos for sailors. Sailors with tattoos are often expressing their "life experience solidarity," Goffman pointed out. The tattoo marks the individual as a sailor and, thus, distinct from the "land society" By adopting the tattoo the sailor acquires a social base, a group of peers. The tattoo enables the sailor to protect himself from feelings of alienation and isolation. He shows that he is not alone, that his behavior is not idiosyncratic or deviant, that he operates within the safety zone of a group of peers.

Imitating a President's Wife

Copying the personal preferences of the president's wife, that is, the color and style of her clothing, has often been a means of creating a sense of connectedness to the established social order and the mythic "First Family." When U.S. President Theodore Roosevelt was in office, his daughter Alice was looked upon as "Princess Alice." Light blue was her favorite color, and it soon cropped up in clothing throughout the country under the name "Alice Blue." A popular song of the time, *"My Sweet Little Alice Blue Gown,"* reinforced the style that she wore.

The predominant color of Florence Harding's wardrobe when she came to the White House in spring 1921 was a darker shade of blue. It became the newly desired color. When Grace Coolidge displayed a preference for red, there were few women around the country who did not possess a red garment of some sort. Jackie Kennedy's fondness for bouffant hair and her adoption of the pillbox hat spread throughout the country. Nancy Reagan's passion for red led to the acceptance of bright-colored clothing among the general population. It also caused White House correspondents to start donning red dresses or red ties as a way of catching Ronald Reagan's eye at news conferences. The color took on a regal significance when Reagan staged formal news conferences at the end of a long, red-carpeted hall. Once the vivid emblem of the Russian Revolution, red became "Reagan red," a new and very different tie-symbol from that used during the Russian Revolution.

Expressing Political Values and Goals

Groups and aggregates desiring, protesting, or rejecting a political agenda may signify their sentiments in their dress. In the United States such expressions vary. They may involve (1) identifying the side one is on, (2) taking a stand and dressing the part, and, sometimes, (3) hiding one's identity.

The most familiar, popular, and least tumultuous example of political attire is the slogan T-shirt, which came into being in the 1960s. Many artists were involved in such projects, the best known being British designer Katharine Hamnett. She received so many requests for her T-shirts that she had to stop making them in 1987.

In 1991 T-shirts were used as a means of environmental education and a form of fund-raising for environmental causes. James Brooks reported in the *New York Times* that T-shirts were being sold to adults to raise funds for research on how to protect sea turtles and were being given free to schoolchildren as a means of educating them about the endangered species.

Benetton, an Italian-based company that produces and distributes colorful sportswear for men, women, and children, has been portraying itself as antiracist. The company's trademark, "The United Colors of Benetton," depicts people of all ages and different races holding hands and being visibly happy about it. Since its initial advertising campaign in 1983, the company has used the themes of racial equality and civil rights to appeal to the consumer rather than pictures of actual garments. Its ads, the company claims, are intended as a hymn to global understanding, racial and multicultural harmony. They often carry more than one message. To promote AIDS awareness, for example, condoms, in pastel colors and out of their wrappers, were placed horizontally next to one another on a white background. In one sense, the multicolor emphasis suggested global unity; at the same time the ad championed social responsibility.

Revolutionary Tie-Symbols

Rejecting the Vietnam War and the draft, hippies adopted an appearance and clothing that reflected their "revolution" against rationality, self-restraint, and goal-directed behavior, the values underlying institutional discourse. In contrast to the conformity of the gray flannel suit and the impeccable, modest mien required by the establishment, they looked disheveled and unkempt. They wore their hair long, and jeans and work shirts became their "uniform." Young men often wore Indian headbands, amulets, shell necklaces, beads, and embroidered vests instead of shirts. See-through outfits flaunted sexuality.

The hippies of the 1960s demanded the right to full self-expression. In a study of hippie communities, D. L. Wieder and D. H. Zimmerman found that immediacy, spontaneity, and hedonism were favored over sobriety and industry. Property was rejected by the hippies because it identified privilege, and they had no qualms about receiving welfare or panhandling.

As a cohort, a group of people born during the same time period, this generational unit was critically aware of inequality and the mindless pursuit of affluence. Rejecting traditional concepts of career, education, and morality, they produced a culture in opposition to technocracy. They searched for alternatives to the prevalent traditions of lifestyle and occupationally linked identity. Their disaffiliation took different forms. For some it was militant and political; for others it was mystical and religious.

Other groups, long before the hippies, also wore revolutionary tie-symbols. The Protestant reformers, who rejected the morality of the official church and searched for a new connectedness to God, are an example. They refused to accept the church's contention that to commune with God elaborate ritual was necessary. They regarded as false the need for sumptuous vestments. The name "Puritan" was first used in 1566 because this group of reformers sought to "purify" the church in England. Puritans campaigned against clerical attire, religious statues, stained-glass windows, and sacred music, which were seen as impediments to spirituality. The Puritans felt that spirituality emanated only from a direct relationship with God. Self-direction and conscience, not simple submission to those in authority, became the new determinants of behavior. Adopting dark and plain clothing made of wool or cotton was in keeping with the Puritans' ideal of religious simplicity and directness.

In eighteenth-century Paris, the name "sansculottes" was used for the attire worn by urban workers at the time of the French Revolution. Instead of wearing the fitted breeches (culottes) worn by the aristocracy, the workers wore long trousers striped in red and blue. In addition, they wore white shirts open at the neck, short, loose jackets, wooden shoes, and the red Phrygian cap, a symbol of revolution. The antiaristocratic attire indicated their desire for complete social equality.

Reactionary Tie-Symbols

Members of the Ku Klux Klan, the notorious white supremacist group, hide behind a white pointed hood, mask, and gown. Their attire is more precisely a costume; it is worn only at group gatherings. On such occasions it acts more as a tiesign than a symbol, since it is required attire and has only one meaning. The original Klan appeared after the Civil War and sought a return to the racial caste system. White people in the South, particularly middle-class whites, were impoverished as a result of the war. Many were deprived of the right to vote because of their participation in the war against the Union. The Ku Klux Klan, with its strange rituals and ghostly costumes, provided a means for frightening the local black population into a servile demeanor. The activity of the Klan continued until it had accomplished its racist goals of empowering white people and reducing the black vote. By 1877 the original Klan had been officially disbanded.

The twentieth-century Klan was formed in 1915 by William Joseph Simmons at Stone Mountain, near Atlanta, Georgia. Klan activities were now directed against Roman Catholics, Jews, and the foreign-born as well as blacks. This Klan claimed to protect the racial "purity" and moral values of the native-born, white, AngloSaxon Americans and claimed a higher morality and dedication to religious fundamentalism. Because the Klan was not strictly regional in its appeal, its influ- ence spread to other parts of the country such as Colorado, Indiana, New Jersey, Oklahoma, and Oregon. Its tactics for inculcating fear and intimidation included whipping, tarring and feathering, branding, mutilating and lynching. The Klan reached the height of its power in the early 1920s when it probably had between four and six million members. As a political force the Klan was effective, and it prompted the election of many pro-Klan officials on the local level. In 1924, after the Klan helped split the Democratic presidential convention, its influence began to wane.

The Klan was again revived in Georgia after World War II. In addition, other white supremacist organizations arose in the South as the movement for increased civil rights for blacks spread, particularly after the Supreme Court decision on school desegregation in 1954 and the Civil Rights Act of 1964. Many bombings and murders were attributed to the Klan.

Similar angry feelings fuel the hatred that Skinheads feel toward AfricanAmericans and other minorities. Beatings, stabbings, and killings in the defense of "white power" have occurred in cities as diverse as Portland, Oregon; Denver, Colorado; and New York City. Skinhead attire is their everyday dress; unlike the Klan, their attire is not limited to special occasions. It also incorporates more variety than the Klan costume. Their heads are almost completely shaved and they wear caricatured working-class attire: old-fashioned shirts, suspenders with shrunken trousers, and heavy, oversized shoes or military jackboots.

□□□

10

Luxury and Restraint in Fashion Technology

Introduction

Simple, elegant and restrained, American designer Marc Jacobs' work epitomizes the 1990s minimalist aesthetic. His spring 1998 collection comprised a series of easy separates, little soft grey cardigans, flirty pleated skirts, contrasting fuschia macs and sporty clamdiggers. There was a slight hint at 1950s style in the cut, but not so much that the modern feel of the collection became swamped with nostalgia; there were enough references to trend-based shapes and colours that the potential consumer could feel comfortably fashion-conscious, but there was nothing too extreme, too difficult to wear. As such it seemed perfect for contemporary women's lives: streamlined, stripped of clutter, functional yet beautiful.

Importantly it also drew upon the undoubted allure of luxury fabrics. The cut of the clothes may have been restrained but the luxury of the materials, soft cashmeres, and fine wools meant that the wearer was able to indulge in the tactile pleasure of expensive fabrics next to the skin. Since the late 1990s we have liked to believe in the simplicity of the minimalist lifestyle, with its pleasing connotations of controlled rationality, which creates a tranquil space in the chaos of urban living, but we also crave the comforting embrace of luxury. While the idea of capsule wardrobes, made up of infinitely interchangeable key separates, may be enticing, there is also a desire to retain a sense of distinction, particularly from the mass-market copy. The look may appear democratically accessible, but the cost of such minimal styles is prohibitive. While high street fashion may have become increasingly quick at replicating the latest catwalk looks, quality has, however, remained harder to emulate. And as was pointed out in the *Observer Magazine* in July 1998,

> *'[Fashion] has decreed a massive swing away from easy, throwaway fashion to divisive, elitist, luxury.' In this chapter I want therefore to unpick both the precedents of 1990s minimalist fashion, as well as questioning its deceptively simple style. It may appear to be an innocently easy way to dress, but as ever in fashion there is a web of contradictory meanings attached to its streamlined exterior.*

Tyler Brule, the editor of *Wallpaper* magazine, wrote in an article entitled 'It's smart to be simple' in the *Independent on Sunday* in 1996 of the growing trend towards 'downsizing', 'voluntary simplicity', 'beyond basics'. He felt the roots of this shift were on the West Coast of America, where it had become increasingly fashionable to discard unnecessary elements of your life, casting off excess in both possessions and lifestyle, and, influenced by both the economic impact of the recession, and the moral imperative to avoid extravagant display, lead a simpler existence. The term 'minimalism' was understandably appealing. He cited both the Chic Simple collection of books, and a Seattle newsletter *Simple Living,* as examples of this apparent emphasis on scaling down of both wardrobe and home. So powerful has this move been that even designers like Dolce e Gabbana, who are not usually known for their love of restraint, used advertising in their Autumn/Winter 1998/99 menswear campaign that evoked a simple, rustic lifestyle. A male model clad in a pale polo neck sweater and contrasting dark trousers and jacket stared out at the viewer from a blank, white interior; on the other side of the double page spread was a still life adding detail to this scene. On a rough wooden table a collection of simple bowls and eating utensils, a loaf of bread, fresh fish and olives were displayed. They spoke of a rural Italian lifestyle, a simple, honest and healthy existence, unhampered by the pressures of the city, the constant drive of commercialism. Minimalism had become a lifestyle that could be sold on this very contradiction: it seemed to offer an escape from constant consuming, from the confusion and violence of contemporary society and yet, ironically, as Tyler Brûlé pointed out, this frequently involved buying more.

Another element in the shift by many fashion designers towards this restrained style, is the rejection of overt display that had been seen as characterizing the 1980s. The glittering excess of designers like Gianni Versace was felt by some to be too vulgar, too brash for the intelligent consumer. His eveningwear was cut to slip around the body, revealing the figure to the eager eye of the tabloid press. Its extravagance attracted celebrities, keen to be turned into curvaceous femme fatales. However those who sought the apparent cool rationality of simple clothes rejected designs that flaunted this image of women as spectacles of sexually charged flesh and glamour. Simpler dress seemed to offer women freedom from culturally defined notions of the body that focused attention constantly on the ability to fulfil current physical ideals.

It was not just the obviousness of sexual provocation that led to minimalism becoming an alternative to the Versace aesthetic. Designers wanted to move away from ostentation and the perceived bad taste of the gilt logo, which was seen as too blatant a symbol of wealth and excess. This represented a turning away from the ethos of conspicuous consumption as the motivating force when buying fashion. For the designers I will be concentrating on, a much subtler, but no less powerful form of status assertion was brought to play. This could perhaps be called inconspicuous consumption: wearing clothes whose very simplicity betrays their expense and cultural value, when quiet, restrained luxury is still revered as the ultimate symbol of both wealth and intelligence. This contradictory consuming is apparently untainted by slurs of vanity, and brashness, since its style seems so clearly to be about restraint and abstinence.

Douglas Coupland's satirical definition of the significance of Armani's appeal mocks the contained sophistication of the designer's unstructured, modern tailoring, but it betrayed the potential, covert meanings of this style, 'Armanism: After Giorgio Armani: an obsession with mimicking the seamless and (more importantly) controlled ethos of Italian couture. Like *Japanese Minimalism,* Armanism reflects a profound inner need for control.'

While Armani appeared to snub the decadent extravagance that is such a feature of high fashion, its focus on detail, on Armani's desire to demonstrate an intellectual distancing from trend-led fashion's frivolous ephemerality, his work constructed an alternative set of expensive obsessions. This was noted in the *Sunday Times Magazine* in 1990: 'Armani can measure his success as a series of subtractions'.

An advertisement from his campaign of 1994 epitomized the unstructured tailoring that is Armani's signature. Both male and female models were clad in muted fluid linen, their posture conveying a feeling of relaxed confidence; even the collars of the women's suits were smoothed away, reducing the jackets to their most essential form. Nothing was allowed to distract from this reduced silhouette the models' hair was swept back tidily from the faces, their sunglasses added to the air of rational anonymity of their figures. Their natural surroundings reinforced ideals of simple, authentic design, echoed in the organic unforced lines of their clothes. This aloofness offered a protective sense of security to the wearer, who was well dressed but never calling out for attention, never a spectacle of display. Armani's clothes were at once anonymous in their simplicity yet recognizably expensive when inspected up close, their fabric and cut betraying their elite status. Armani's need to strip designs to their most basic form expressed not only an admirably modernist aesthetic, but also his desire to police definitions of 'good' taste. Indulgence in clothing is allowed only within the realms of those knowledgeable enough to appreciate the subtlety of a well-cut jacket, the sensuality of luxurious, yet deceptively plain, fabrics. Financial and personal indulgence is as much a part of consuming the sleek trouser suits made by Armani, as it is in the purchase of a sparkling Versace outfit, but the former wear the mask of puritan abstinence, of rational, functional design and the longevity of the 'classic'. Such clothes are, Rosalind Coward commented, 'designed to make a statement about what they feel like. They are designed to connote a sophisticated sensuality, that enjoys touching itself all the time.'

Designers like Jil Sander whose signature style is pared down, minimalist design is seen as producing clothing for women with careers, women too busy, and too powerful to wish to dress in the decorative or the spectacular. Abstinence from such traditionally feminine pursuits is perceived as a sign of this power, perhaps because it has for so long been seen as a masculine trait. This essentially is what designers like Armani, Jean Muir and Nicole Farhi have sought to do: to give women a sense of ease and confidence in their clothing, a rational anonymity that belies the quality and expense of their garments. This modesty and understatement provides a 'neverending dialectic of status claims and demurrals,' at once ascetically simple, yet decadently expensive.

Minimalist fashion is concerned with more than its surface simplicity, which is really an inscrutable mask presented to the world as a feint, belying the undercurrents of sensuality hidden in the soft fabrics which shift against the skin. This mask also disguises the wearer's aspirational desires, their search not just for tactile experiences, but also their wish for legitimate status, valid unquestionable identity, which is traditionally associated with 'old money', stability increasingly hard to find in the fluid job market of the late twentieth century. As Bob Colacello noted in an article on Sander in *Vanity Fair* in 1996, 'As with [Ralph] Lauren behind all the restrained good taste is a romantic yearning for something more, not less.' In Jil Sander's view the worst thing is to be judged déclassé, to expose any trace of lowly status, any slip into bad taste.

This ideal has a series of noble precedents that illuminate the attitudes that have built up around this manner of dressing. The dandies of the early nineteenth century allowed for no indulgence in decorative detail or unnecessary elements in a design. Beau Brummell, who personified the minimal style of the first dandies in London, viewed dressing as a ritual of washing and preparing the body and then clothing it in the most exquisitely restrained examples of each garment: austerely cut dark cloth coat, perfect pale pantaloons, plain waistcoat and shirt and simple accessories, yellow leather gloves, hessian boots and a neat hat. The only area left for any sartorial expression was the white cravat, which was to be dexterously tied in the most modishly elaborate manner.

The dandy was obsessed with self-adornment, even though the end result was so simple in its appearance that it was viewed with deep suspicion by the popular press at the time. This can be seen in a French caricature of the 1820s, when dandyism crossed the channel to Paris. The caption 'Egotism personified' reinforces the cartoon's satirical view of the dandy as a selfabsorbed narcissist. The dandyish young man seated at the centre of the image seems so concerned with collecting the chairs in the room together to support his elaborately graceful pose that he has rudely allowed the women to stand. He appears oblivious to the fact that his spurs have ripped one unfortunate woman's gown and that his walking cane is poking another in the eye. This lack of attention to anything other than his own appearance was an affront to the nineteenth-century ideal of active manhood, prompting the historian and writer Thomas Carlyle to ask 'And now for all this perennial Martyrdom, and Poesy, and even Prophecy, what is it that the Dandy asks in return? Solely, we may say, that you would recognize his existence; would admit him to be a living object; or failing this, a visual object, or thing that will reflect rays of light.'

It is ironic therefore that such sobriety was to become a defining feature of much nineteenth-century menswear, coming to be seen as the mark of the respectable bourgeois male. Heaven forbid though that men should seem too preoccupied with achieving this sober ideal, masculine attire was to appear effortless, demonstrating the gentleman's ease with his status. Brummell's close attention to detail and fanatical allegiance to the puritanically austere was a lesson in control and restraint that Coco Chanel later transferred to the female body. Fashion designers' desire for a simple style that would sweep away the multi-layered excess of the early years of the twentieth century was epitomized in Chanel's work. Her designs were at the cutting edge of couture fashion, mocking bourgeois sensibilities that still clung to the more obvious wealth of rich fabrics and complex designs. Utilitarian fabrics like jersey were given high fashion status by virtue of the image and ideals conveyed by their designer. Chanel worked within the rarefied atmosphere of couture, but she attracted avant-garde and daring customers at the start of her career. Potential wearers had to be willing to risk the misunderstanding of onlookers, unversed in the coding of inverse status symbols. There is a history of artists and intellectuals adopting simple, utilitarian clothing as a symbol of their contempt for fashion's constantly shifting whims and a sign of their loftier concerns. However, the bourgeois fashion consumer needed to be sure of the unassailable nature of her status to embrace such simplicity of style. Chanel provided women with clothing that was appropriate to their new, more active lifestyles, and which viewed femininity as confident and streamlined, rather than as a decorative confection. She encouraged women to dress as plainly as their maids, but this did not mean that they should necessarily be mistaken for such lowly creatures. Chanel's sleekly minimal designs fused the tenets of dandyism: close attention to detail, high quality, basic forms, with an irreverent attitude, simple black dresses and separates were piled with the previously declasse glitter of fake jewelry.

Another earlier form of pared-down design is exemplified in the work of American designer Claire McCardell who rose to prominence in the 1940s. In her work we see minimal fashion as an expression of laid-back functionalism rather than any adherence to introspection. Her clothing is about allowing the body to move and work, to take part in an active and healthy life. The simple shapes and utilitarian fabrics she favoured came to epitomize American style, based as they were upon a belief in democratic ready-to-wear, not the elitist couture of the Old World. As one commentator remarked, 'She thought the couture mode too structured, too formal and wanted to create accessible, easy clothes for busy women in a fast world.'

McCardell dressed the proto-career woman of the 1940s and 1950s, freeing her from the New Look and giving her instead an easy-to-care-for wardrobe of sports-inspired separates. In a Louise Dahl Wolfe photograph of a McCardell bathing costume of 1948, the soft grey tones enhance the feeling of harmony between body and fabric. The model wears a clingy knitted jersey costume which forms around her figure, its patterned weave echoed in the gentle ripples of the sand she lies on.

A McCardell empire line dress of 1946 shows her commitment to clothing that allowed for a variety of body sizes, the definitions of its line provided only by drawstrings at the bust and neckline, rather than by cut. Its simple silhouette also exemplifies the timeless quality of this type of dressing: its 1940s heritage is given away more by the evening gloves and costume jewelry that it has been accessorized with, than by its style. McCardell sought to include certain key pieces in each of her collections, decrying the usual fashion imperative for seasonal trends. She wanted to make clothing easier, providing women with six-piece travel wardrobes, popover dresses that just slipped cleanly over the head, durable denim and gingham outfits that could be worn year after year. For her such basic forms expressed the vitality of the wearer, and the vitality of modernity. In the 1954 entry of Current Biography, McCardell's approach was described thus: 'The designer's idea is that clothes should fit the individual and the occasion, and should be comfortable as well as handsome. The color and line should flow with the body.'

Even her more obviously glamorous eveningwear draws its allure from the use of a few striking elements. In an example from the Metropolitan Museum in New York's collection, rose-red pleated silk, and the wrapover form of a kimono, add sophistication and allure to a simple column dress, rather than any elaborate decorative devices that might distract from its essential silhouette.

Anne Hollander sums up this easy style and potential problems relating to simplicity of form by saying, 'American modernization allowed women's clothing to participate equally with men's in the new impersonal character of American modern design itself. When a designer's original idea can so easily be adapted to mass production and can become familiar to many people in many different contexts, it quickly loses the look of an individual invention.'

The democratic nature of simple designs can make it hard for consumers to distinguish between brands, or indeed to discern the need to pay more for minimalist clothing. Townley, the firm McCardell worked for, lost money on one of her most dramatically pared down designs, the 'monastic' dress, a basic a-line style, cut on the bias to swing down from the shoulders and flatter the figure. Customers could see no difference between her version and the cheaper copies that soon filled the stores, and chose economy over the cachet of owning one of the originals. For later American designers this need to distinguish the brand became paramount. In the 1950s Robert L. Steiner and Joseph Weiss revised Thorstein Veblen's theory of conspicuous consumption to demonstrate the elite's need to constantly create new status symbols to maintain their position as tastemakers, in an increasingly prosperous America, where more and more could afford the obvious splendours of luxury. Steiner and Weiss wrote, 'As a result of the long practice of conspicuous consumption, ornate objects have become associated in the common mind with vast wealth. Therefore, if the old elite is to demonstrate a disinterest in money, it must deplore ornateness and adore simplicity.' This so-called 'counter-snobbery' ensured that the old elite maintained the moral high ground, able to assert their superior style, through their apparent contempt for such base instincts as the accumulation and display of vast wealth. However, as the authors pointed out, 'underneath the shy, retiring, unassuming ways and masquerading as quiet, good taste, shines forth a distinctive exhibitionism quite as flagrant as the pomp and circumstance of former years'.

This contradiction was encapsulated in the 1970s by Roy Halston's designs. Halston's work was the favourite of fashion insiders, who enjoyed the contrast of minimalist clothing worn in the context of the decadent extremes of New York's Studio 54 nightclub. He added sensuality to McCardell's utilitarian aesthetic by using fluid luxurious fabrics to enliven his trademark twinsets and wraparound skirts. In a double page spread from a 1975 edition of American *Vogue,* Halston's easy daywear is displayed in the clean lines of a mulberry car coat and olive suedette trouser suit. His eveningwear was more daring, for example in a purple dress which is slit to the waist, seemingly held together only by the broad yellow belt, the restrained feel of the silhouettes undercut by provocatively revealed flesh. His work stood out as coolly sophisticated, at a time when most designers were dabbling in hazy images of romantic nostalgia.

However by the end of the 1980s simple clothing, had come to be associated with a conservative need to ensure the validity of the status claim rather than as a preoccupation of the fashion cognoscenti. While McCardell, like Chanel, had been regarded as avant-garde, labels like Donna Karan and Calvin Klein were viewed as taking a 'safe' approach to design, providing the essential wardrobe for those who wished to be viewed as serious and career-minded. American designers' more casual diffusion lines were also signifiers of a functionalism and conformity that sidestepped the flamboyance of much of the era's fashions. Even in the 1990s the New York collections are famous for making the more outlandish trends from European catwalks palatable to the consumer, rather than for their innovative ideas. A Calvin Klein outfit of spring/summer 1997 demonstrates this commercial talent. The influence of Helmut Lang's layering is discernable but here it has been translated into shiny stretch fabrics rendering the ensemble sportier in feel than the Austrian designer's edgier style.

While Klein has sought notoriety for his label via controversial advertising campaigns, Donna Karan has emphasized her empathy with the female consumer. Also drawing on the McCardell look, she has, like her forerunner, been seen to personify the easy elegance of her style. Using a limited palette of mainly blacks, greys and soft putty colours and simple shapes she has created an empire of clothing and home ranges. In a 1993 coatdress, she paid homage to McCardell in the basic wrapover style and the 'important belt' McCardell advised adding to plain dresses to enliven them for social events.

Karan's eveningwear is equally laid back a supple dress of 1993 comprised a column of greige fabric, illuminated by the subtle glow of a pale gold collar. However, there is a need to create an aura of exclusivity and glamour around such simple clothes, since they lack the instant status cachet of more elaborate designer fashions, enticing consumers with the visual images attached to the designer's name. Both by association with glamorous star names, (Demi Moore and Bruce Willis for Donna Karan, Jodie Foster and countless other Oscar candidates for Armani), and using lifestyle-enhancing marketing campaigns, the prestige of such labels was raised. The crucial links between editorial, social and advertising pages that this publicity created forged a link in the consumers' minds between image and reality, elevating the status of simplicity. Halston, himself a purveyor of reworked classics, remarked at the height of his fame that, 'You're only as good as the people you dress.' This is a dictum that has helped many of the designers discussed to raise their turnover. Mass market brands like Gap's utilitarian basics fulfilled a need to 'downsize', to strip away unnecessary objects that cluttered up already complex and confusing lives, in a manner that was cheap and accessible. However designer goods provided the rational cachet of the stripped-down lifestyle, with the cocooning feeling of exclusivity.

In 1995 Lisa Armstrong wrote in *Vogue*, 'Eighties snobbery may have been simplistic, but it was democratic, easily grasped by everyone. This new version, by contrast, has taken to its heart a completely different system of status symbols that, far from being recognized from the other end of Bond Street, couldn't be identified from next door.'

For many designers and wearers of minimalist clothing though there is a series of subconscious meanings hidden beneath the surface. It is clear that simplicity of form can be a more deliberate search for new definitions in dress. In Rei Kawakubo's work for Comme des Garçons, the relationship between body and fabric, and the spatial planes they create in combination are intrinsic parts of her design approach. In an outfit from her Spring/Summer 1994 collection layers of black linen cloak the body. The silhouette was reduced to a simple column, but within this there was a play of dark and light, transparent and opaque as the folds of tunic and skirt met and crossed over. For Kawakubo designing is always about questioning and testing the boundaries of fashion; in this case the asceticism of the resulting garments is a means of forcing the viewer to concentrate on the forms and textures of the clothing. The Western couture tradition of extravagance and overt luxury as the key signifiers of wealth and status are challenged by this erasure of decoration and the contemplation instead of simple, clean shapes. As Harold Koda has demonstrated she draws upon Japanese philosophy of sabi 'poverty/simplicity/aloneness', and wabi 'transience/decay and rusticity' to produce 'an aesthetic of external denial and internal refinement'.

In Yohji Yamamoto's work a similar philosophy of design is in operation. As with Kawakubo, colour is often negated, leaving only shades of blackness, or garments are drenched in a wash of colour in a full-length dress of 1998 warm golden yellow, that adds richness to the felt fabric. In contrast to Sander and Armani who tend to favour expensive fabrics to add dimension to their designs, for these Japanese designers the poverty of the material speaks of the reflective nature of their work, and potentially of the wearer who looks inwards too, the austere shell of her garments a symbol of inner thought and tranquility. The simple forms provide the space for introspection and higher thought, once again, as with the European designers discussed, minimalism is held to be a sign of intelligence.

Hussein Chalayan's work is another example of this belief in asceticism, in the denial of flamboyance and distracting decorative elements, as a tenet of an alternative form of beauty. The forms of a grey, caped, sleeved jacket photographed for *Frank* magazine in September 1998 had an organic feel, heightened by the illuminated fronds of the leaves in the background of the image. The curving line of the sleeves drew the eye inwards towards the deep black of the skirt, revealed beneath the rounded hem of the jacket. In this example a minimalist aesthetic was used to give a sense of purity to the forms, of unity and wholeness, and an invitation to seek meaning, rather than a mask to conceal the codes hidden under the simple designs.

By the 1990s there was a growing anxiety, exacerbated by the economic recession, abcut fashions that flaunted their expense too flagrantly. Consumers' feelings of exhaustion with obvious labels compounded this after the huge rise in awareness surrounding designer fashion, which had become so closely tied into the entertainment business and gossip columns in the previous decade. People at all levels of society were more familiar with prestige fashion brands than ever before. Designers at the cutting edge of fashion's elite like Helmut Lang were able to assert minimalist style as the obverse of 'vulgar', obvious designs that by the 1990s seemed so unfashionable. His subtle style is shown in an outfit from 1993 where narrow-cut leather trousers and single-breasted jacket were teamed with a synthetic printed tee-shirt. While excessive designs continued to make headlines for Versace and Mugler, it was Lang's cool, urban silhouettes that married basic shapes with edgy colour combinations and advanced technological fabrics, which were both the crucial look for fashion insiders, and the key influence on other designers, eager to find a new vision of the modern.

Lang helped to reinvigorate the fashion for simplicity. By using cheap, industrial fabrics, and discreetly complex construction methods, he added an urban sophistication to his designs, a feeling that the consumer had to have greater fashion knowledge to appreciate the complexity of such seemingly basic items. His clothes suggested cultivated taste, and, as Bourdieu noted, in the case of consuming to demonstrate knowledge, rather than just wealth, 'What is at stake is indeed "personality", i.e. the quality of the person which is affirmed in the capacity to appropriate an object of quality. The objects endowed with the greatest distinctive power are those which most clearly attest the quality of the appropriation, and therefore the quality of the owner.'

Prada was the other label which helped to bring minimalist style to the forefront of 1990s fashion consciousness. The designers' need to construct an identity which spoke of both cultural and fashion capital was acute at a time of anxiety and insecurity, both the etiolated, androgynous chic of Lang's work, and the ironic subtlety of Prada's inverted status symbols, enabled consumption that was gratifyingly fashionable, yet eluded the taint of obviousness. A red coat from Prada's Autumn/Winter 1998/99 collection showed her attention to detail in horizontal slits that broke up the smooth surface of the coat, adding a dissonance to its simple form.

However, as the decade wore on, the understatement of minimalist style became increasingly influenced by, on the one hand the revival of luxury and detailing that came via couture's newcomers, and on the other the desire to possess less easily pirated objects, that relied on the supreme luxury of expensive fabrics. Narcisco Rodriguez created midnight blue or oyster cashmere separates that glimmered with the iridescent shine of constellations of self-coloured sequins; and Gucci played with the minimalist aesthetic, fusing it with a sense of decadence shown in an advertisement of 1996. The two models pose languidly in a fashionably simple interior, the stark lines of which are softened by the natural light shining onto the stone walls. They are clad in Halston-style columns of white, betraying the 1970s nostalgia of the Gucci look. The woman's tubular dress is broken only by a neat circular gap in the fabric at her hip, revealing the white strap of her underwear and an oval gold buckle that sits against her tanned skin. The image conveys an underlying sexuality that belies the simplicity of the style.

This sensuality became more explicit in Gucci's 1998 collection that revelled in the contrast between the simple lines of the minimalist and a love of excess. The tailored structure of one catwalk model's midnight blue coat and pencil skirt were defused not just by the flesh revealed beneath her semi-transparent top, and visible bikini pant strap, but also by the blinding glitter of the rhinestones that lined the coat. As the model walked down the runway the ensuing light show teased the seriousness of minimalist design, injecting a glittering brashness into its normally sober contours.

This love of luxury has meant that late-1990s minimalism has been less and less about the denial of tactile pleasures in dress. Even the starkly utilitarian ethos of workwear was reinvented. The appeal of Ralph Lauren's white cashmere cargo pants of autumn/winter 1998/99 was based at least in part upon their very impracticality, the delicious irony of this military basic being transformed into a decadent status symbol.

Sportswear was given the same treatment, its status as the ultimate functional form of dress once again hijacked by high fashion, and translated into slouchy sensuality in Marc Jacobs's cornflower blue hooded tops of 1998/ 99. Once again cashmere was used to add the distinguishing mark of luxury, of expense. The ambiguity of such simple garments and their omnipresence at all levels of the fashion industry was a motivating force in this shift towards quality fabrics rather than the cheaper more durable materials of earlier designers discussed, like Chanel and McCardell. As has been noted, minimalist fashion is never as simple as it seems and it constantly shifts between the seemingly opposing values of luxury and restraint, reflecting in its balance between these elements of decadence and abstinence the fears and desires of contemporary culture.

So how might the meaning of the style be assessed? The various attitudes that are reflected in minimalist designs discussed the controlled, confident elitism of Armani and Sander, the avant garde modernity of Chanel and McCardell, the intellectual introspection of the Japanese designers, the edgy urban cool of Prada and Lang, and finally the decadence sparked within the recent trend in pared-down-dressing presents an interesting complex of meanings. What do all these strands imply about the contemporary minimalist? Minimalism may strip down garments to their basic form, provide an escape from clutter and confusion, but is the resulting ambiguity of pervasive simplicity fulfilling in itself?

In Calvin Klein's advertisement campaign of autumn/winter 1998/99, the mood was not languid and confident as in the earlier Gucci campaign. The models appeared tense, the outside world of grass and trees seemed distant and cut off from them, as they sat in a claustrophobically Spartan interior. Amy Spindler of the New York Times described these Steven Meisel images in terms of alienation, saying, 'they are images depicting the height of isolation, figures in close proximity but their eyes never meeting'. For her minimalist designs had become a distancing device, the blankness of the clothes' surface hiding the wearer's identity from prying eyes. The pervasiveness of these basic garments turned them into conformist anonymity rather than allowing the space for introspection. Indeed for her there was anxiety rather than tranquillity in the scene. She went on, 'What if nothing was happening, and we finally had time to sit and think, but our minds were as minimalistic as the room, as blank as our faces, and as empty as our eyes?'

So is the escape into minimalism of the last years of the twentieth century a mask for our anxiety? Perhaps, but this style also provides a space that can generate new ideas, new definitions, that are harder to create in more defining fashions. Marc Jacobs's designs for Louis Vuitton of autumn/winter 1998/99 demonstrated the easy-to-wear forms that minimalism generates, and the gentle lines they create around the body, flowing softly around the figure, rather than restricting or idealizing it. These clothes also marked a shift in attitude towards prestige brands, and at the end of the decade a number of more progressive designers were recruited by luxury brands to revive their profiles, most notably, Martin Margiela at Hermes. His first collection for them in 1998, consisted of deceptively simple reversible shortsleeved sweaters, worn with soft suede gauntlet gloves, and gentle long skirts. Rather than the challenging designs that he is known for, the look created was simple and luxurious. But, as Sarah Mower wrote, 'What more mordant a put-down of current Paris runway sensationalism than a statement of wearable classics for older women?'

And this is the key to a more positive reading of such designs. Their simple forms and subtle colours do not try to dictate a particular ideal of beauty, either in terms of body shape or age. As Donna Karan's advertisement campaign for autumn/winter 1998/99 showed in its images of a statuesque fifty-something woman clad in a thickly knitted sweater and slim black skirt, these clothes allow a space, a break from seasonal fashion. Inherent in the cut of the clothes is a reverence for longevity, for the notion of timeless classics, which are wearable by any woman, not just the modelesque. And in an era obsessed by the perfection of the body, the chasing of idealized youth, this may still be considered liberatingly avant-garde.

11

Indian Fashion Designers

Fashion design is the art dedicated to the creation of wearing apparel and lifestyle. Please see also Fashion for a more complete definition.

The first person who could really be considered as a Fashion designer was Charles Frederick Worth (1826-1895.). Before he set up his maison couture (fashion house) in Paris, clothing design and creation was handled by largely anonymous seamstresses.

When he started his business, his customers could attach a name and a face to his designs once they learned that they were from the House of Worth, thus starting the tradition of having the designer of a large company is not only the creative head but the symbol of the brand as well. After Worth, Paul Poiret started with a concept which is nowadays considered as general fashion design/ marketing and Haute Couture, and is also credited with starting the trend of removing the corset from female fashion. Although fashion itself has a long history which leads back to the early civilisations, the people who designed and produced garments before the late 19th/ early 20th century were seen as anonymous artisans, not well-known public figures.

Following in Worth's and Poiret's footsteps were: Patou, Vionnet, Fortuny, Lanvin, Chanel, Schiaparelli, Balenciaga, and

Dior. By the 1960's, Haute couture was not the only trend dictator anymore. Under influence of Fashion Icons (like for example Marlyn Monroe, Audrey Hepburn and Jackie Kennedy or the models like Twiggy, Youth culture and the independent women's movements, it became acceptable for fashion to ascend from the people rather than be handed down by large couture houses.

Fashion brands not only just produced garments anymore but also started to create their own image or started designing for certain target groups and/or sub cultures. Vivienne Westwood for example "created" the image which is now generally considered as Punk. The Trend dictation of the Old Couture Houses was over.

Modern Fashion Design and Designers

Modern fashion design is roughly divided into two categories, Haute-Couture, and Ready-to-Wear.A designers Haute-Couture collection is meant exclusively for private customers and is custom sized, cut and sewn. To qualify as an official "haute couture" house, a designer or company must belong to the Syndical Chamber for Haute Couture, a Paris-based body of designers governed by the French Department of Industry that includes American, Italian, Japanese, and other designers as well. A Haute Couture house must show collections twice yearly with at least 35 separate outfits in each show. It is often shown on the catwalk and in private salons. Ready-to-wear collections are not custom made. They are standard sized which makes them more suitable for larger productions. Ready to wear collections can also be divided into Designers/createur collections and Confection collections. Designer / creator collections have a high quality, a superb finish and a unique cut and design. These collections are the most trendsetting compared to Haut Couture and Confection. Designer / createurs ready to wear collections contain often Concept items which represent a certain philosophy or theory. These items are not so much created for sales but just to make a statement. The designers ready to wear collection is also presented on the international catwalks. Confection collections are the once we see most commonly in our shops. These collections are designed by Stylists. The brands that produce these collections aim only for a mass public and are in general not searching for new grammar for the language or a new point of view on/of fashion.

Although a lot of the modern fashion designers are still working in a somewhat "traditional" way- making clothes that are very fancy and expensive but still look like "normal" clothing, there have been designers who break these "rules" over the years, some from the mid-nineties onward, some, like Japanese designers Yojhi Yamomoto, Comme des Garcons, and Junya Watanabe from the early eighties to the present, and some now-deceased designers such as Elsa Schiaparelli, who worked in the thirties, forties, and fifties. Fine examples of modern-day "rule breakers" are Martin Margiela and Warmenhoven & Venderbos. These designers approach clothing, Fashion and lifestyle from new angles and explore also the boundaries of Fashion itself in order to create "new" concepts and views for Fashion design. Their collections are not only restricted to garments (ready to wear as well as couture) and other Fashion related products, but also contain work in other media. The works of this breed of designers can also be placed in a certain Art movement.

Most fashion designers attend an Academie of fine arts. Fashion design courses are considered as applied arts just like graphic design and interior design. Often the types Stylist and Designer are mixed up. A stylist inspires his/her designs on existing things, trends and Designers collections. A Designer starts from scratch; he/she develops a unique concept and translates this into garment collections, other Life style related products or a statement in various other types of media. Some Designers approach their work just as a fine arts painter or sculptor.

Inspiration for fashion designers comes from a wide range of things and cannot be pinpointed exactly. However, just like all artists, they tend to keep an eye on things going on world-wide to inspire themselves towards making their future clothes lines. Most fashion designers are well trained pattern makers and modeleurs. A typical design team is made up out one or more: Designer(s), pattern maker(s) /modeleur(s), sample maker(s), buyer(s) and salesman (men). For presentations and catwalk shows the help of hair dressers, make-up artists, photographers modeling agencies, the model and other support companies/professions is called upon. As Fashion became more and more a large business, Designers started also with licensing products. (For example: Perfume, bags and all sorts of products)

Abu Jani and Sandeep Khosla

'The boys', as the twosome of Abu Jani and Sandeep Khosla are known in the fashion circuit, can be considered among first names in that made it big, by way of success, attention, fame and hype. It is a creative alliance that exudes attitude and talent.

They were one of the first to display their creations at Harrods. Ever since, the Abu Jani and Sandeep Khosla show is a much awaited, though not so frequent event.

Though they lack in professional training, they push ethnic fashion to the limits, almost to the dictates of their fancies. No wonder they claim that they do not make garments, they make heirlooms.

Aki Narula

A recipient of the Damania Fashion Designer Award, Aki Narula has been in the fashion business for four years. Available at India's premier design salons - Ensemble (Delhi, Mumbai), Ogaan (Delhi, Calcutta), Melange (Mumbai), Ffolio (Bangalore), Cinnamon (Bangalore), Sosas (Goa), Kali (Calcutta) - Narula's designs are understated, the accent on drape and texture.

Kimonoesque wraps where the dictate in zen; unisex accentuating leisure, Narula designs for both men and women, Indian and Western wear. Having worked as a stylist for various fashion shoots and ad campaigns, Narula has also designed costumes for theatre and a national award winning Bengali film. In recent months, Narula has also taken to designing lifestyle linen, candlestands and screens.

Arshiya Fakih

Araiya was conceived of and launched by sister duo Aaliya and Arshiya Fakih. They come from a family, which has contributed extensively to the garment industry. After graduating from Sydenham College of Commerce and Economics, each sister took to her own path in honing their creativity.

Arshiya attended Sir J.J. School of Fine Arts, NIFT, Mumbai and the Fashion Institute of Technology (FIT) in New York. She interned with Ralph Lauren, and Onyx Noir and worked full time with Neil Beiff. Aaliya completed her diploma at the NIFT-Mumbai and then went on to FIT, New York. Aaliya went on to work for California Concepts - an export house in New York.

Araiya was formally launched on 6 November 1998 at Hotel Marine Plaza in Mumbai. The overwhelming response to Araiya's brand of fashion led to several other showings of its collections. Within two months of its launch, the city had recognized the founder designers of Araiya - Aaliya and Arshiya, among the top 20 newsmakers of the year 1998-1999.

With the commencement of its operations in India, the sisters extended their presence to the export market. Araiya periodically exports its creations to Saudi Arabia, Fiji Islands, South Africa, London and New York.

Araiya is known for its hip and trendy western and Indianwear, which is an effulgent combination of eveningwear and casuals for the active women and men of tomorrow. The designs are cast mostly in fabrics such as Polyester and Cottons blended with Spandex and other knits such as Jersey and Stretch Chiffon.

Araiya is entering a strategic tie-up with Eskay Knits (India) Limited. They are going to undertake an extensive brand building and brand awareness exercise that will cover the entire country. To begin with they plan to open one more retail outlet in Mumbai at Linking Road along with an attached ' Araiya Café ', which will be the first of it's kind in India. Over the next year Araiya will have retail outlets in Delhi, followed by Bangalore, Goa, and Madras. By the end of three years Araiya will have 10 stores across all metros and mini-metros in the country. In addition to these outlets in Mumbai, they also intend to start outlets in Dubai and franchises in Los Angeles and New York.

Anuradha Vakil

Anuradha sees herself more as a revivalist of textile crafts than as a 'fashion designer', simply because the base of her designs are always traditional Indian textiles and in her own small ways she contributes towards their preservation.

Her label Noor came in to being four years ago, out of her passion for handlooms and now retails from Ogaan in New Delhi and Kolkata, Melange in Mumbai, Ffolio in Bangalore, Madras and Cochin and her own shop Noor in Ahmedabad.

She works mainly with hand woven natural fibre fabrics and travels extensively in her search for the unusual and beautiful. She works with master weavers and crafts people in most textile centres, which range from Kalamkari hand painters in Kalahasthi, Andhra Pradesh to Bandhani karigars in Mundra. Her designs are timeless and are very simply cut, as the focus is always on the textile, the weave, the print, the craft.

Anuradha designs for a woman who has a finely tuned sense of aesthetics, someone who is as committed and passionate about things created by hand. Predictably, she has a clientele from the fields of arts, theatre and design. Being an ardent lover of Indian classical music and kathak, she doesn't really mind her clothes being labelled 'arty'. She prefers that her clothes are worn by a selective few.

Every season, new collections are put together which are usually based on a particular textile craft. Each of these comes after months of intense travels and experiments and with sheer ingenuity of her craftsmen.

Lately, the emphasis in her work has been on using vegetable dyes in most craft traditions. With the world waking up to the environment issues, these are so much more relevant today.

Anamika Khanna

She started her career on a promising note by winning the 'Damania Fashion Awards' and now retails at Carma (New Delhi), Ogaan (New Delhi & Kolkata), Ensemble (Mumbai & New Delhi), Espee (Kolkata), Ffolio (Bangalore and Chennai), and other prominent stores.

Anita Dongre

Anita was thrust towards the world of fashion immediately after schooling. Although initially in University she worked towards a Commerce degree, she simultaneously enrolled into the prestigious Indian Fashion Design School S.N.D.T. and completed the course with flying colours in 1983. Wanting to give back to her Alma Mater, she began teaching at S.N.D.T. and continued to do so for 2 years.

Anita's urge for putting her design skills into practise got her into establishing her Ethnic Indian wear studio and she began retailing under the label Masque. Subsequently, she began supplying her designs to renowned stores such as Sheetal in India, Damini in London and a host of stores in cities like Vancouver, Singapore, and Dubai. She continues to supply her Indian Ethnic Designs in these markets.

Anita then made a gradual transition and launched her western women's wear label AND in mid-1999. Market sensitivity and a keen understanding of the growing Indian woman's need for comfortable, stylish, branded and affordable clothing was the primary factor in the positioning of the AND label. While AND retails in Mumbai from India's premier mall, Crossroads and another store located at Linking Road and at New Delhi from South Extn. I, plans for turning AND into a national brand are on the anvil and she is focused on this objective.

A couture design label has always been one of Anita's dreams. Having been involved for over 15 years with the fashion world, she felt it apt to launch her couture label ANITA DONGRE. The ANITA DONGRE label is a fitting combination of the exemplary world of Indian creative crafts, clean cuts and simplistic value. With Anita's positive understanding of an international look, the ANITA DONGRE label was appropriately launched at an international forum - IGEDO in August 2000.

Her garments made waves in Dusseldorf and also hit the front pages of Germany's National newspapers and to date Anita has been the only Indian Designer chosen to showcase her garments at the Finale of the IGEDO Spring Summer Fashion Show.

Anita began retailing her couture collections from the Taj Khazana stores at New Delhi, Kolkata and Chennai and has recently opened her ANITA DONGRE couture and prêt store in Mumbai's upmarket OM Chambers, Kemps Corner.

Anjana Bhargav

In the evolving Indian fashion landscape, Anjana Bhargav has carved a niche, for herself. She is best categorized as a woman who designs for individuals with 'substance', She insists on designing "real clothes" for "real women".

Initially on an extremely small level, Anjana started designing for her friends. Armed with a formal degree in Textile Designing and Pattern cutting combined with an inherent sense of aesthetics, Anjana was encouraged by the overwhelming response she got. She established Studio A, a design studio in New Delhi. She launched her first collection at a fashion show in 1994 with Bina Ramani, one of India's leading designers and pioneer of the Indian Fashion Industry. This was soon followed by a solo fashion show 'An Indian Summer', which was held at the prestigious UNESCO Hall in Paris. Since then, Anjana has had several showings in Sharjah, London, Kathmandu and New York along with showings of her collections in New Delhi.

Anjana was recommended by the Ministry of External Affairs to represent 'Women Entrepreneurs' at the OECD Conference held in Paris in the year 2000, where over 300 women entrepreneurs across the globe shared their experiences.

The Anjana Bhargav label reflects silhouettes where each collection has an inspiration, with accessorized garments as her hallmark. Her collections present an exclusive range of embroideries on romantic fabrics, thus recreating the splendour of an ancient era. Her designs resurrect patterns and skills of ancient arts into the rhythm of modern life, keeping the accent always on comfort, wearability and affordability. The penchant is always on minimalistic styles that extend easy wearability and understated elegance. Not merely celebrities, but individuals who are achievers like Arundhati Roy, Shahnaz Hussain, Dr. Kiran Bedi, Shubha Mudgal, Romy Dev, Feroz Gujral and Femina Miss India Asia Pacific first runner up Divya Chauhan, are some of her clientele.

Anjana has been actively designing for the Usha International group of companies. Usha International has the largest network of Usha sewing schools across the country. She has been commissioned to upgrade and develop the curriculum for the Usha International Fashion Institute.

Anjana's creativity is not restricted to fashion alone, but extends to interior designing as well. She has to her credit projects as diverse as private homes and farmhouses to commercial establishments including the revamping of the New Delhi Stock Exchange. Here again her designs reflect her creative yet practical approach.

Anjana's recent venture is Perfect 10, the complete personality institute, a first-of-its-kind, not only in the capital but also in the region. Perfect 10 is about grooming, appearances, conduct and a sense of style. Anjana's fifteen years of passionate involvement with lifestyle designing imparts a distinct and discerning touch to the Perfect 10 institute. Her shows also reflect her quest for individuality. In October 2000 she unveiled her Fall/Winter 2000 Collection paying tribute to mothers and daughters. Some of New Delhi's most distinguished mothers and daughters showcased her collections. In April 2000 along with the ambassadors of several countries, she organized a show where Latin American girls modelled her outfits for 'Udayan' a trust for orphaned and abandoned children.

Anshu Arora Sen

After finishing her course in Fashion Designing from NIFT in 1997, with an award winning collection, Anshu went on and launched her label 'A Small Shop' in December 1998.

Anshu's clothes are vibrant, using a palette of colours, simple yet interesting shapes, and traditional hand crafted detailing reworked in the contemporary context. The styling is largely casual and easy to wear. The look is not about an age group but more a certain mind set, and is targeted towards those who willing to have some fun with clothes!

Aparna Jagdhari

Aparna's resume boasts of a variety of creative and artistic endeavours, but her focus has always been on fashion. After graduating from NIFT, Delhi she worked on product, computer aided design, textile-weaving projects and designed costumes for several plays.

Realising that fashion was her true calling she established her store Freefalling in 1999. She describes her silhouettes as basically western but with an Indo-western look. The colours, fabrics and embroidery details are Indian in their interpretation. Colour is the very essence of expression, and the main focus in her clothes is colour blocking. Bold colours are juxtaposed in a graphic style. Her clothes allow the freedom of self-expression in that they can be worn as separates or combined in various ways. The look can be very bold, or more subdued.

Her ideal collection would be the prefect amalgamation of diverse techniques in textile surface techniques, which are prevalent in India with the modern methods, which are being explored around the world.

Freefalling clothes are supplied to Ensemble and Melange in Mumbai, Ogaan in New Delhi, Ffolio in Bangalore, and Taj Khazana.

Arjun Khanna

Ajun's Khanna's return to India in 1989 evoked a major change in his approach to fashion. Graduating from the American College of fashion in London, Art has always been his first love - the only subject he excelled in since childhood. What followed were a course at the Blackheath College of Art in London and a photographic course from Pillia's school of photography.

He started off with what he felt to be a challenge -'Men's wear '. His first collection was aimed at a limited audience - men's western wear featuring the Oxford look followed by the Dick Tracy line of 30s and 40s. "It was a period when I designed for my own satisfaction and my clothes were wild and at that time unwearable."

Starting with a mens line at Ensemble' Arjun has spread his collection to Vama in Mumbai and Santoshti in Delhi. It shows so clearly his eye for detail. He has designed for Padamsee's production 'Begam Sumroo' and styled for the winners of the 'Graviera contest.

Garments with clean styling and cut, embroidery used judiciously and a good finish make an Arjun ensemble. Experiments with trends have always interested him. His silhouettes vary without prior warning. The garments appeal is not restricted to its outer appearance only. The lining of the garment plays a major role so do the seams hems fusing and the internal mechanisms.

Ashima & Leena Singh

Ashima and Leena Singh have always had a unique, distinctive style and an original, traditional appeal in their collections. An established and well-reputed label today, their designs speak of tremendous and superb craftsmanship. They specialize in Bridal and hand embroidery. They also love playing with colours and are famed for their special colour effects and a variety of fabric developments.

Their design philosophy strives to bring out the best in each woman through designs that are both traditional and contemporary. Their product range of Indian and Indo-Western Wear include a large variety and assortment of fabrics, drapes, silhouettes, embroideries and colours to choose from. Catering to all the conventional as well as the bold, with emphasis on quality and attention to detail is their hallmark. For their Bridal wear they create exquisite and delicately handcraft masterpieces. They aim to create classic and timeless clothing that can be passed on through generations.

With their combined strengths their business growth has been phenomenal. They were one of the few who combined the designer concept with the commercial aspect as a marketing strategy. They were the first designer designers to join hands with retailers and have teamed up with Jewellery Designer Paayal Seth to set up India's Premier Retail Outlet - KAAYA - The store for Women at South Extension, New Delhi. They have recently had a series of successful exhibitions as the U.S. and U.K. They also have the honour of being the official designers of Miss India 1999 'Gul Panag'.

Ashish Soni

Ashish graduated with a bachelor's degree in Design & Clothing Technology from India's most respected Institute, the National Institute of Fashion Technology, New Delhi in 1991. Having made it to a batch of 25 students from the 7000 applicants that year was not all. He further proved his mettle both as a designer as well as an entrepreneur by successfully establishing & positioning his label, standing for nothing short of painstakingly high quality & design. Soon after, Ashish launched his own label "Ashish Soni".

Ashish's imagination, creativity and ability to create designs for men and women rapidly gave his label a reputation of quality and style. Ashish's creativity is rooted in a fiercely Indian family background, enlarged by western influences through an education largely abroad. His multiple exposures developed a clear and sharp aesthetic, which earned him a prominent place in the world of Indian haute couture.

Since the launch of his label, he has held eight very successful solo fashion shows. He has also showcased his Spring/Summer collection exclusively at the Carlton Towers, London in June 1998 in collaboration with 'BVLGARI'. Another calendared event is the unveiling of his Summer Collection every year at the World Trade Centre, Dubai for "Fasateen", the biggest retail outlet of High Fashion clothing in the Middle East. Ashish has also participated in the Festival of India 1996 in Thailand, Hong Kong and Singapore and in AEPC Road Show held in New York, Paris, London. His creations are retailed at leading outlets throughout the country including own studio "Ikos".

The quality of his shows coupled with his creations has won him much deserved acclaim. Needless to mention the clientele that Ashish boasts of today is a veritable of who's who of public figures, media personalities, and leading entrepreneurs. His creations are retailed throughout the country starting from his own studio "Ikos" and Carma in New Delhi, Ensemble, Vama and Pyramids in Mumbai, Ffolio in Bangalore and Madras, Ogaan in Kolkata. Overseas, Ashish's creations can be found at "Fasateen" in Dubai.

In August 1999 Ashish launched his ready-to-wear label "as by Ashish Soni". At the beginning of this year Ashish presented a Costume collection as part of the Millennium Celebrations at Khajuraho - the only designer to be selected by the Government of India.

Ashish's Signature lines are characterised by extreme simplicity, immaculate cuts and a perfect finish. His intuitive and original sense of style, his panache and his originality combine with an impeccable garment construction ability to make stunningly simple yet dramatic garments. Ashish is married to Misha Grewal, former national squash champion.

Azeem Khan

Mumbai designer Azeem Khan counts Hillary Clinton and Naomi Cambell among his elite clientele. His designs are top-of-the-line. The area of Colaba at the Cathedral doted tip of Mumbai resembles both a fishing village, a Navy installment from Rudyard Kipling days and a burgeoning mix of fashion boutiques and art galleries. Those who live there like to think of the neighborhood as COHO-Colaba and Cuffe - Parade - similar to New York's trendy but funky Soho area.

Fashion designer Azeem Khan is one of the innovators of Mumbai's Coho, with his cool and snazzy boutique next to the Colaba Post Office, and with his background of a being a real New York City Soho inhabitant, living and working downtown.

"Our family S.U.Zariwala has had its operations here for three generations. My grandmother started it off by selling embroidered hankies door to door," laughs the charming 30 years-old designer, sitting upstairs in the office of his boutique. "My grandfather Shansheed Khan bought a paan-beedi shop in this very same place and I have kept the same wooden and brass enhanced door."

While S.U.Shansheed Khan changed his name to the generic embroidery and sequin Zariwala title, it sparked the neighborhood Zariwala art, which thrives in nearby shops and studios. Azeem's father's work is known in the Indian film industry with his famous sequined sarees draping Nargis Dutt to every other heroine in the movies.

"Our company S.U.Zariwala is currently India's number one in exports to Italy, France and New York and every year, business increases by 25 per cent," says Azeem. "Most of the companies in the west don't want to deal with Indians, maybe because they are so laid back and can't always deliver. My three brothers carefully supervise all the work, one living in America, the other in Europe and one is involved in the manufacturing unit."

Despite his illustrious family lineage, Azeem Khan was not always going to be a designer. He originally studied medicine and architecture, and said his father did not pressure him to get in the family line but allowed him to "Find myself".

Azeem "found" himself going to New York City in 1989 and studying at F.I.T. He received the "Design of the year" award there in 1992 and got a scholarship to study at the prestigious Parsons School of Design.

"I am basically not happy in one place, and I like to jump from place to place," said Azeem. "Parsons is a private school. The competition made me focus on what I'm good at. I got on the Dean's list and then Geoffrey Beene offered me a job as an Assistant Designer."

Azeem became totally 'down town" from going to school down town and living the New York Soho life, as he worked for this well known designer. He said that after two years working for Beene, he considered staying back and getting U.S citizenship but Mumbai beckoned. His father's store represented yet another place for his restless creative spirit to flow.

The designer's Miamoto sports coupe is parked in front, the Kohli fisherwomen appear to float past this stone and brass store, blending into the environment. In fact, the boutique is so much in sync with COHO, that it is the only non-art gallery participating in the monthly "COHO Art Night", where everyone is invited to go gallery hopping. Azeem Khan's store is a stop on the art journey.

"I like to work hard and I party hard also at night," laughs Azeem, whose good nature is apparent through an exuberant "Split personality of work and play" Azeem's international designing skills were earlier demonstrated on super model Naomi Campbell when he designed an elaborate Indian bustier for her saree when she did a fashion shoot in Dubai. He also designed the clothes for Italian jewelry designer Marina Bulgari's launch at the Taj Hotel in October.

"Bulgari contacted me to be a partner and I was restricted to five sets," said Azeem. "I did the show for fun and deigned clothing that wouldn't be astonishing, to compliment the jewelry. I was really surprised to later receive many calls and requests to buy those clothes."

Azeem Khan's first show in India, the Diwali '98 Collection, was held on October 10 in his boutique. It was in his words, "Very casual, like Soho, where you don't sit on a chair - so different."

He elaborates, "I started with ten outfits and in a burst of creativity, designed 26 outfits for the two models, Jaswinder Sachdev and Pooja Mishra," said Azeem. "I like doing things like that, subtle and beautiful because it's just not a matter of buying clothes."

It was a special "downtown" style, lounging on the stone slabs, sipping foreign champagne and wines-to have what Azeem prefers, "A happy buzz". His second show held at The Taj, was in general opinion, "The show of the millenium".

"I wanted my show to be an experience and full of drama, with the models draping the clothing differently, like wrapping the materials around their head," said Azeem.

"Sarees are very sexy but don't show anything. I teach my client how to wrap the saree. You must wear my clothes with an attitude, and appreciate the bizarre. Sometimes at a party, if I see a woman wearing one of my designs, she might apologize that she has not worn it with the same flair that I intended. My training with Geoffrey Beene taught me to mix all the styles to one to make one statement."

The collection was a dazzling array of the glittering and intricate Zariwala work and painted designs that are clearly unique. The price range of Rs. 15000 to Rs. 40000 appeared not too over the top.

Although Azeem has been asked to teach at NIFT, he has declined the academic route. But he does offer some advice for new designers. "My advice to young designers is to never copy. Always be original. Everyone has a certain style and you must bring that out."

That is the look - confident, different and full of style that Azeem Khan has now bridged from downtown New York - to downtown Mumbai.

Deepika Govind

Deepika believes that style is simplicity. Her clothes have a defined cut, and portray a very contemporary look. She is especially focused on the final touches, as she believes that a tacky finish ruins the entire look. Versatility is her strength. But dealing with individuals according to body types and personalities, creating wardrobes and trousseau in accordance to a person's lifestyle has always been her forte, besides ready-to-wear of course. A playful sense of humour belies an incisive mind and a reputation built on an instinctive knowledge of what a woman wants to wear - and how to deliver it.

She retails at her own store Divinite and has other retail outlets and individual buyers across the country. She retails under four labels. Label 1 is Abstinence: A purist line. Fabrics being the starting point of purity, she uses special hand woven fabrics and works together with the weavers to create fabrics according to her vision. She also uses tailoring and craft techniques in silks and cottons alone. Her clothes are simple, clean cut, and with a lot of detail. Label 2 is D2G (D-square-G): This is her Ready-to-wear line. Her pret collection has the cutting edge of modernity, and is known for its wearability. Label 3 Aura: This is her ornamental, more ostentatious line. Unique eveningwear and garments ideal for a trousseau. Her attention for detail is painstaking and she uses the most exquisite embroidery. Label 4 Dee: A line of accessories, which she is currently working on. Versatility truly seems to be her strength, as she has also branched into menswear. Not being satisfied with the designing aspect alone, she has styled several shoots and ad campaigns for prominent magazines and she has been a fashion columnist with the Times of India, Bangalore.

Hemant Trivedi

Hemant Trevedi - Fashion Stylist, choreographer, design professor and undoubtedly, one of India's foremost and most important fashion designers. He graduated from the Australian Technical Institute of Fashion Design and furtherd training at the Fashion Institute of Technology, New York.

International labels have pursued him and yet he returned to India in early 1980 as one of the first professionally qualified fashion designers, because "This is a land that I call my own. I was born exposed to colour of every hue, in a country rich in culture and diverse in its people. How could I ever live elsewhere when India, as an inspiration has it all! Ultimately, my aim is to make a contribution in quality growth towards the Indian Fashion Industry and not live in an insular or directionless world".

Today, Hemant is Fashion Director at Sheetal, India's leading fashion store. He has also been associated as design professor at S.N.D.T University at Mumbai, India for the past 20 years.

Trivedi has presented some of the most breath taking fashion presentations both in India and overseas, including countries such as U.K., U.S.A., China, Egypt, Mauritius, Sri Lanka, U.A.E., and the Far East.

His most impressive artistic direction has been seen at the Femina Miss India pageants for which he is in charge of choreography and grooming of the pageant delegates.

He has launched the careers of hundreds of fledging models and turned many into virtual super-stars.

He is a man who has created the winning wardrobes for several former Beauty Queens and particularly for Miss World 1995 Aishwarya Rai and Miss World 1998 Diana Hayden, who besides countless others, remains his most favourite client and the present Miss World 2000 Priyanka Chopra

Trevedi's contribution to the Indian fashion scene cannot be denied. Being one of the first professionally qualified designers in India, he has a feel for the industry and its growth.

While he does not seek the limelight, it is equally difficult to ignore him. Many a fashion critic has said that Hemant has the uncanny ability to predict a "look" well ahead of time. His creations have often become trendsetters and he has a faithful clientele to prove it.

Jattin Kochhar

Jattin Kochhar believes that it is his ability to amalgamate his soulful Indian heritage with true urban influence that has been the foundation of his design ideology. Having no formal education in fashion design has never deterred him in his career. Simplicity with absolutely clean and defined lines has been the hallmark of his creations. He enjoys designing simple, practical lines both for men and women. Keeping in mind the urban lifestyle of his clients, he lays major emphasis on a basic design, which can be worn both casually as well as formally by just changing the accessories. Strappy, slinky eveningwear for women and trendy semiformal attire for men is an essential part of any of his collections.

Having been in the business for the last 10 years he feels he has matured as a person and also as an artist. "Keeping in tune with the millennium spirit I have worked on a fusion line, which reflects my Indianess in truly universal designs, by using a wide variety of ultra modern fabrics embellished with Swarovski crystals for which I have an absolute fascination", says Jattin.

JJ Valaya

Known for his knack of combining clothes, and his unique experimentation, JJ Valaya is regarded as one of the fashion czars in the industry. Like his clothes, his list of achievements is incredible. His career has had a large number of firsts, reiterating his role as a trendsetter in the industry.

He was the First Indian Student to win the prestigious Prix d'Incitaion in Paris, and was the first designer to hold a solo show in India. He continued to do this annually. He was also the first Indian designer to show along with prominent International Designer Todd Oldham. In 1992 he launched his Couture label-JJ Valaya, and introduced this label in upmarket stores in India and abroad. JJ Valaya 'LIFE', India's largest single designer store opened in New Delhi in 1994. With this store he branched into Furnishing, Tapestries, Accessories and Art.

In 1998 he launched his Prêt label, Studio Valaya, both in New Delhi and Mumbai and went online with www.studiovalaya.com. He also opened his JJ Valaya Couture Store in Mumbai at Crossroads in 1999. He also was the first designer to hold four solo shows in the same season.

Kiran Uttam Ghosh

Her training with prominent British designer Jasper Conran in London, gives her clothes an international feel. She skilfully incorporates the traditional Indian, and the international. Her clothes are understated, with shaped silhouettes and characteristic drapes. She refuses to be typecast into the Eastern and Western brackets, and instead designs for individual women. She focuses on reality and simplicity in her designs.

Her label Kimono is one of India's highest selling designer labels and her clothes currently retail from Ffolio in Bangalore and Chennai, Ogaan in New Delhi and Kolkata, Melange, Ensemble and Crossroads in Mumbai, Elahe in Hyderabad, Elan in Ahmedabad, Espee and Zenon in Kolkata and RCKC in London, Origins in Hyderabad and Vama in Mumbai.

Krishna Mehta

Krishna Mehta's tryst with designing began in February 1982. Accomplishing the fashion-designing masters in 1987 from Sophia Polytechnic, Mumbai, Bachelor of Commerce degree from Sydenham College of Commerce & Economics, Mumbai in 1981 and an extensive training in weaving at the Weavers Service Centre, Mumbai, Krishna joined the family business of garment exports in 1982. Working her way up from a Co-ordinator to merchandiser to fabric incharge and then to designer in a span of nine years.

In 1991 Krishna took the fledgling Indian fashion industry by storm with her menswear. Her perfectly cut and impeccable finished lines soon established her as a respected name in men's fashion. The first menswear designer soon came up with an Indo-west line and fusion lines for women in 1994, which were also indeed the first of their kind to be seen in the country.

Krishna Mehta opened her flagship store " Krishna Mehta" in Mumbai in January 1996, specialising in Indian, Indo- West and Western Couture garment lines for men and women. This was followed by the opening of a "Krishna Mehta'" franchisee store in Ahmedabad.

Krishna Mehta is a label synonymous with classic designs of understated elegance. Relaxed yet bold, in keeping with the pace of contemporary life. Today, Krishna Mehta could easily be called the priestess of classicism who has continued perfecting her designs and styles, realising the acute awareness about Indian Fashion on international levels. Be it her prêt or couture lines, those who know her style can spot a " Krishna Mehta" creation from miles away anywhere in the world.

Lalit & Sunita Jalan

Lalit's passion for creating is rooted in his childhood obsession with clothes, and 'dressing up'. His innate sense of style has brought him a long way since those childhood games and he is now regarded as one of the most successful designers for male couture.

His meteoric rise to success was far from easy. Lalit had to overcome several obstacles to achieve his dreams. He has always been a risk-taker, breaking out from the family profession to become a couturier at a time when designing was hardly considered a legitimate profession. Destiny brought him together with Sunita, who became his wife and business partner. Their marriage led to the inception of 'Lalit Jalan' an ethnic label for the high profile man of the '90s.

Their flair for design led to and shaped into Hunar, the Design studio, the first ever store for ethnic men's wear in Kolkata. Their entry into the competitive fashion industry marked a resurgence of Indian Ethnicity and the demand for ethnic male wear. Initially they were met with apprehension and scepticism by Kolkata's fashionistas. But together they won over critics with their unique experimentation with age-old tradition. They celebrated their success with the establishment of Hunan Forte. The curtain raiser to the national scenario followed with their first act in Mumbai's reputed studio Glitterati. Nationally acclaimed shows, immense media coverage and positive feedback led to Lalit and Sunita being featured in the annual Femina Book of Fashion exclusively for male trousseau.

Their collections are hallmarked with subtle, sombre tones of creams, peach, browns, mauves, and greens all creating a very mellow effect. The clothes are known for their intricate embroidery and the symbiosis of concepts and silhouettes on fabrics. The skilful combination of classic silhouettes gives their clothes a contemporary mould. The effort is painstaking; the fabric is scrutinized for every weave, texture drapability and ease of maintenance. Constant supervision at every evolving stage of production and experimentation gives a seal of quality to Lalit's creations. Every ensemble speaks of personal interpretation. Their work is subdued yet blatantly honest. Lalit Jalan's HUNAR escapes definition because of its abstract essence of uniqueness.

Their dream of creating globally acknowledged clothes became a reality when famous Japanese designer KENZO visited India, and asked Lalit to design his personal ethnic wardrobe.

In their own, quiet way, Lalit and Sunita have successfully spread their work to HUNAR at Kolkata, Ensemble in Mumbai & New Delhi, Ffolio in Bangalore & Chennai, and Portfolio in Cochin.

Lina Tipnis

Lina Tipnis belongs to that band of designers that has steadily climbed the ladder of success with hard work and a disciplined business sense. Lina began her career by designing in 1987 for her retail outlet at the Oberoi, Mumbai. She is candid about her lack of professional training when she says," I have had no formal training in designing. I am fortunate to have an inborn desire to create garments"

After having retailed for 5 years, the next logical step was wholesaling. In 1992, her label sold Indian semi formal and fusion co-ordinates to select stores in India and abroad. In 1997, she launched her label Linarika that is now sold in over 30 stores in India as well as the U.K., Southeast Africa and the Middle East. While the Indian semi-formals are marketed through these outlets, the fusion lines with a very international flavour are aimed at the European markets. Today, the label has a loyal customer base amongst its target audience profile.

In 1997, Lina was invited to showcase her collection at one of the world's largest and most prestigious garment fair- CPD (Collection Premieren Dusseldorf) hosted by the IGEDO Company. Her collection received an overwhelming response.

Ever since then, Lina has been successfully exporting her fusion lines to stores in Europe. The fusion lines which are available across Europe are simultaneously sold in India through stores like Melange in Mumbai, Ffolio in Bangalore and Chennai, Ensemble and Kaaya in New Delhi and Elahe in Hyderabad. While her much in demand ethnic prêt lines are sold at Piramyd, KBN, Kala Niketan, Roop Kala, Eternia in Mumbai besides stores in Ahmedabad, Hyderabad, Bangalore, New Delhi, Chennai and Pune.

With the philosophy of 'less is more', her garments are essentially minimalistic ensembles that are modern and simple. Emphasis has always been on engineering and wearability. Working on natural fibres has been Lina's forte. The reason for her success is her capability of having her finger on the pulse of consumer's needs and her ability to compromise with the ever-fluctuating trends of the highly volatile fashion industry. Lina has stabilised in the fashion business by moving into both genres of styling. That is her formula for success besides her marketing and promotional skills.

Lina Tipnis has been exploring fusion couture for some seasons now, and has arrived at a look, which combines classic elegance with a soft sensuality. She has also used fashion for a cause. Post the Kargil war; she initiated a program with Mélange wherein she roped in other designers to sell garments at 50% discount off the regular price. All the proceeds were given to the Kargil fund.

Lina is also a consultant to the Raymond group for setting up of their designer stores selling Prêt. Over the years, Lina has noticed that customers have no loyalty for stores but there is a gradual evidence of designer loyalty building up. Hence, prices have to be constant across stores. Also, she is very keen to work in collaboration with other designers to nurture the fashion business and give it industry status. "The market is very large and there's room for everyone. Designers must first work towards increasing fashion consciousness collectively and then create brand loyalties.

Manish Malhotra

At the age of 25, Manish Malhotra forayed into Bollywood by designing for Juhi Chawla in Swarg. Today, at 34, his name is synonymous with style in Hindi films. He revolutionized the fashion scene in Bollywood by envisioning a 'look' for the character. His tenure as a costume-designer has seen him clothe most of the leading actresses in the film industry from Sridevi, Urmila Matondkar, Karishma Kapoor, Kajol, Raveena Tandon, Manisha Koirala,

Madhuri Dixit, Twinkle Khanna, Shilpa Shetty, Kareena Kapoor, to Aishwarya Rai, Rani Mukherjee and Preity Zinta. Although he doesn't design regularly for male actors, he has attired Shah Rukh Khan and Aamir Khan on several occasions. Manish Malhotra's list of films includes several blockbusters since Rangeela, where he metamorphosised Urmila Matondkar and turned her into a raging sex symbol. He repeated the magic with Karishma Kapoor and changed her image through Raja Hindustani. From Dilwale Dulhaniya Le Jayenge, Khamoshi, Hero No.1, Judaai, Kuch Kuch Hota Hai, Dil To Pagal Hai, Hum Saath Saath Hai to Kaho Na Pyar Hai, Mast, Phir Bhi Dil Hai Hindustani, Satya, Dhadkan and Mohabbatein, he has been associated with nearly all of the decade's most successful films.

His work has been greatly appreciated and he has received several awards. He was awarded the first and only Filmfare Award for Costume Design for Urmila Matondkar's look in Rangeela, the Showtime Opinion Poll Award for Raja Hindustani, the Siemen's Viewer's Choice Award for Dil To Pagal Hai, the Lux-Zee Cine Award and the Bollywood Award in New York for his work in Kuch Kuch Hota Hai. He has also been graced with Indira Priyadarshini Memorial Award for his contribution to the fashion industry, felicitated by National Institute of Fashion Technology, New Delhi and the Indo American Society for his contribution to fashion designing, and was also named the most Stylish Designer Of the Year at the Elle Style Awards in 1999.

Manish Malhotra decided to branch into mainstream designing in 1998 with his high-profile couture store Reverie - Manish Malhotra. The store received a tremendous response and his clientele featured socialites Tanya Godrej, Tina Ambani, Haseena Jethmalani, Rhea Pillai, Avanti Birla as well as important members of the NRI community. He has done several wedding trousseaus for reputed families. His popularity soared during this period when he was exclusively asked to design clothes for Michael Jackson for his appearance during the Bollywood Awards held in New York. The performer was so please that he requested Manish to design outfits for his show in Munich and to design clothes for his children.

Malhotra's first fashion show in November 1999 was eagerly awaited and the talented designer did not disappoint. His clothes were received with great appreciation and almost 70 percent of the clothes were sold out within three weeks. Malhotra created a coup of sorts by having Urmila Matondkar model the showstopper, an act followed by several designers for their shows later. A part of his collection was the embroidered denim wear that became a rage all over the city. International model, Naomi Campbell picked up a pair on her visit to the city.

Manish has managed to achieve that delicate balance between designing for film, as well as haute couture. Now with Sheetal Design Studio, Manish wants to conquer further horizons in the fashion industry. His plans include a pret a porter line for women along with his couture label and also a couture & pret line for men.

Manoviraj Khosla

Manoviraj Khosla launched the 'Manoviraj Khosla' label in 1990. Starting with menswear, he moved to womenswear under the same label. Then in 1995 he tied up with the UB Group to launch his second label - the ' Kingfisher Line'

Moving from men's wear to women's wear to the sporty, casual ready-to-wear Kingfisher line gives Khosla the variety he seeks.

Variety is a hallmark of Khosla's work - he designs both Indian and Western styles, and experiments with cut and fabrics. The Indian clothes have greater emphasis on style and cut rather than embroidery. Fabrics such as lycra and synthetic knits are used for Indian women's wear, which gives the clothes a more International feel. Indian men's wear - kurtas, sherwanis or bandhgala, are all done with minimal embroidery work.

Western wear for both men and women are in variety of fabrics and styles, catering to teens and older connoisseurs...in keeping with Khosla's own sense of style.

Meera and Muzaffar Ali

Through a decade of detailing and upgrading craft of Lucknow and Kotwara, Meera & Muzaffar Ali have brought centuries' old tradition back to life. Both Chikan and Zardozi today have become contemporary and the label of KOTWARA is internationally associated with the philosophy of clothes that integrates aesthetics and humanity, peace and harmony. The wearer of Kotwara, experiences an inner tranquillity as a contrast to a highly consumerist outlook. Living Sufism has been able to establish a hitherto unknown genre of clothing created amidst nature and music with love and sensitivity.

Their endeavour has been to look at style in the broadest sense of the concept and create products with a universal appeal and relevance. By using the sense of fine detailing, which has evolved in India over the centuries, the range extends from innovations in Indian and western forms using simple craft techniques of chikan, zardozi, tukdi and appliqué with hand detailing to create dramatic effects. The label of Kotwara has thus acquired a style of its own which is both avant-garde and traditional and evokes an image which is an interesting blend of detailing and innovation, modernity and old world charm. From the traditional Lehnga they have a wide range of western forms from long coats to shorter jackets, dresses, skirts and trousers. They are gently quilted, subtly embroidered and delicately hand finished.

Clothes for Meera and Muzaffar Ali are the epitome of inner grace, and for that matter they don't have to be expensive. They are the essence of nostalgia, the fragrance of the present, and the dream of the future. When Muzaffar sketches clothes he designs in a trance, made of moments of the past and present, and projects them as valuables that people would cherish. To him these clothes are sacred as they enclose the temple of the human form. Muzaffar Ali, filmmaker, painter and designer, draws deep inspiration from Sufi poetry and music. He stepped into designing through his films and his deep involvement with his village made craft an ongoing relationship and a means of providing employment for the rural craftspeople of Kotwara. Each day in Kotwara they dream to look ahead, create new feelings, innovate new details. Not only with the craft but the life of the craftswomen and her children, their education, outlook and livelihood.

Since 1990, Meera & Muzaffar Ali have held several fashion shows in Delhi, Mumbai, Kolkata, Bangalore, Madras, Singapore, Kuwait, London and New York.

Mona and Pali

Mona and Pali, the formidable sister duo from Bengal, who have placed Kolkata on the national map share a home and a passion for designing.

After graduating Mona Lamba chose teaching as her profession whilst Pali Sachdev, who has a legal background underwent intensive training in a reputed fashion institute in Singapore. Soon enough they gave in to an inner desire, a natural aesthetic urge and opted out of their respective professions to pursue a dream with total dedication and determination. They were amongst the first few designers to hit the catwalk more than a decade ago.

They started from home in 1985 at the behest of their friends, who had persuaded them to design their clothes, which they executed competently and successfully.

In 1987, they flagged off their boutique 'Monapali' in Kolkata making their dream a reality. After that, there was no looking back as they moved on to become stalwarts of the Indian Fashion industry retailing through their outlets in New Delhi (Hauz Khas Village), Ahmedabad and other prominent stores all over India.

Their clothes range from casuals to heavy formals. Their clothes are an eclectic mix of design elements most of which are inspirations from the ethnic cultural roots of India. What makes the designs distinctly Monapali is an unconventional mix of mediums. Be it in textures, textiles, print or embroidery. They were the ones who revived Kantha, Folk (Madhubani, Warli, Patta Chitrai) tribal motifs and the Alpana from the realms of oblivion and elevated it to the status of haute couture culture. They combined block print with spray/smudge print and hand paint, and cut through layers of fabric to create a distinct pattern.

They have used multifarious embellishment technique and worked in ceramic cord, terracotta, mouli, ropes, wooden and shellac buttons, and gauge. It was in 1996, they created the first collection in Shibori the Japanese stitch dye technique capturing the element of ethereal earthiness on slim lined Indian ensembles and saris. For them each collection is a challenge, and they work with whatever has triggered, intrigued and excited their creativity.

They have held several shows throughout the country and abroad. Along with other designers their shows are a yearly event in Folio (Bangalore) and Glitterati (Mumbai). Time and again they have been invited by the Govt. of India and NIFT to participate in various events all over the country. They represented India in China in the 'Festival of India' in 1994 and the Bridal summit- Asia Pacific in 1999, in New Delhi. They have held as many solo shows in Mumbai, New Delhi, Kolkata and Ahmedabad.

Quiet, reticent and self-effacing, they are considered by fashion pundits as the 'Silent Contributors' to the revival of simplicity on the catwalk. Rohit Khosla, the father of the Indian Fashion Industry, had applauded their work and remarked that they were one of the most innovative and original designers of all times.

Monisha Bajaj

It was to discover the great Indian Pandora box of design that this young designer returned to her illustrious roots. A graduate from the Fashion Institute of Design and Merchandise, Los Angeles, she chartered a new course for her design .One that infused folklore of the past in a totally contemporary palette.

Today, just five years down the line Monisha Bajaj is India's leading light in couture. A fashion designer who is focused in her design style Monisha is a synonym of under-played chic. One of the most versatile member of the couture industry in India; she has many a firsts to her credits. Including the decision to emerge from the confines of the Indian boundaries and find a place for her design internationally. After showcasing her collection at the Dubai Fashion Week in Summer 2001, she is now all set to take her Fall Collection 2001 to New York for a solo showing at a high profile charity event.

For Monisha fashion is all about belonging to an aesthetic idiom. Borrowing inspirations from elements that go with her innate style and creative disposition. Essentially a classicist she brings in the thrill of experimentalism too into her design. Fine detailing with heritage fabrics, the use of embroidery for textural enhancement and the crafty use of silhouettes that are functional yet feminine; Monisha creates fashion with a strong flavour. Her textile story is lure. Her colour statement is varied with the binding force of Bajaj's colour palette being the art of mixing bold with soft and neutral with colour. Weaves are a strong statement .So is the interplay of fit with form, integral to the Indian drape tradition. Monisha's design sense is innovative yet moulds well to classical forms.

It was in 1996 that Monisha Bajaj launched her own label after a successful career abroad working in the Contemporary Design Department of the store Fashion Destination. Since then Monisha has showcased her collections in shows all over India and abroad .She presented her first solo in Fall-winter '97 at Park Royal, New Delhi. Taking the label further, Monisha in '98, opened her solo store in Defence Colony titled Monisha Bajaj. Avidly reviewed and retailing from most of the reputed design stores of India, Monisha Bajaj for summer 99 had a ramp show at Imperial hotel .The same winter the designer created 'Millennium Magic at Manesar', Heritage Village with a eclectic collection that had folk, traditional and contemporary elements blending well together.

In the summer 2000 Monisha joined hands with the high profile NGO Savera to show-case her Spring-Summer line at a charity do in the gracious lawns of the British Ambassador's residence .In the first ever Lakme India Fashion Week, Monisha Bajaj presented her collection of prêt a porter in a solo show that combined wearable chic with some fine touches. This year as well Monisha will present her prêt and diffusion lines for the Winter of 2001 at the 2nd Lakme India Fashion Week to be held in Mumbai this August. Last year Monisha Bajaj took her collection to New York, Los Angeles and other ports abroad. The label met with critical acclaim at every destination. The 'Monisha Bajaj' label is classic yet contemporary: Suited both for the contemporary Indian and western markets.

Monisha Jaising

Under the label Azzura, Monisha Jaising is responsible for pre-empting Prêt as she made inroads into the international arena way before the inception of Lakme India Fashion Week. Monisha Jaising graduated from the American college for applied arts in London in the year 1989 with a bachelor's degree in fashion design [duration of study--4 years]. She has been working as q designer cum manufacturer of ladies garments since December 1989.

She was one of the first designers to show with Ensemble, as early as the 80s. This is one designer who has shown consistency and skill in her styling. Known as the princess of 'bohemian luxe' she contours a clean and body conscious silhouette for women, with an evidence of a fusion of both Western and Eastern elements. During that time this was quite the side step from the routine popular 'fashion' yet ironically this proved to be her calling card.

Monisha got noticed due to her wonderful prints, the softness and sculpt of her professional cutting and her price consciousness. To date she continues to keep that formula and balancing the fit with functionality. Though Monisha is a well-respected name in the Indian designer segments very few people are aware that this lady retails at the more popular designer wear stores in the world such as Voyage, in London; Ensemble in Mumbai and New Delhi and now @esthetics in Dubai.

Niki Mahajan

Niki Mahajan, a designer with panache has devoted the last 15 years in promoting the talent reserves of the Indian subcontinent working with the immensely talented artisans from Bihar, Gujarat, Rajasthan, Assam and other remote corners. The endeavour is to retain an umbilical connection with the huge talent resource of the country mysterious interiors. Working with tribals, Niki has created a fabric called "Reeds" which is made by splitting grass and treating it with natural elements. A recipient of the Yuv Ratan award for excellence in promoting the production of unique fabrics by the Ministry of Textiles, she has had the opportunity to learn about the crafts at the grass root level. Currently she retails from Bangalore, Madras, Cochin at Folio, Oorja at Hyderabad, Kali at Kolkata, Casa at Pune, L'affaire, Heritage and her own studio at Vasant Vihar, Priya Cinema Complex, New Delhi and the Designer Studio, Mumbai. Specialising in trousseau, occasion wear and Prêt lines, with an emphasis on clean-cut silhouettes and intricate hand work.

Payal Jain

Studio Payal Jain took root in 1993 after her return to India as a graduate summa cum laude from the Fashion Institute of Design and Merchandising, San Francisco, U.S.A. Awarded the President's Honour Roll at the Institute, Payal gained valuable experience working with some prestigious European fashion houses during the course. During her stay in the U.S., Payal also worked at Fritzi California and San Francisco Clothings Bank. Subsequently Payal worked with leading couturiers Jacqueline de Brey and Ulrich Engler in Europe.

Since its inception Studio Payal Jain has come a long way. It is recognised today as a leading salon de couture in India. And the Payal Jain oeuvre is to be found at exclusive boutiques in India, Greece and England.

A singular feature of Studio Payal Jain is the seamless integration of design and production processes with the revival of traditional crafts being an important leitmotif. Most fabrics used in Payal Jain ensembles are unique and have been hand-woven in the Studio's weaving unit. Working with diverse fabrics like silk, cotton, wool and linen, she endeavours to experiment and to create something different.

Printing is done manually with natural vegetable dyes at the Studio's print atelier. Combining age-old Indian techniques with a modern approach, master printers at the atelier produce striking, unorthodox prints. Different each season, these eclectic prints are a hallmark of the Studio. Another strength of the Studio is hand embroidery where traditional motifs and techniques are continuously re-interpreted to suit contemporary fashion trends. The forte of Studio Payal Jain is women's wear including eco-friendly accessories like jewellery, scarves, shoes and hats.

The modern, fashion conscious woman has three lines to choose from, each with exclusive designs and garments that are one of a kind. La ligne heureuse is an exciting and adventurous line of constructed daywear consisting vibrant and chic silhouettes for women of all ages. La ligne mur is a simplistic line with an emphasis on design and fit. The range consists of sophisticated, career and evening suits for women executives. La ligne elegance has formal evening ensemble, graceful and elegant with rich fabrics flowing into extravagant silhouettes.

Apart from the three Prêt-a-porter collections a year, the Studio also does Haute Couture for discerning clients. With the individual being the focus of every design, these garments complement the personality of the person they are designed for. Highly aware of its social responsibilities, the Studio utilizes its creative abilities towards various social causes, from raising of funds for worthy charities, working for co-operatives, to bringing about social awareness. In fact, every fashion show done by the Studio is for a voluntary organization, a small contribution to help their efforts in making our world a better place to live in. Working together as a large family, it is the Studio's tireless workers who have made it all possible. A result of their resolute trust and commitment.

In the near future, the Studio plans to move into lifestyle design consultancy. Becoming a single source for a complete wardrobe, fabrics, home furnishings, travel accessories and furniture.

Poonam Bhagat

'Taika' in Finnish means Magic. And that is exactly the image that Poonam Bhagat's clothes create. Romantic, mystical, and at the same time powerful, her clothes have a dreamlike essence.

Her design philosophy is understated chic. And this is reflected in both cut and use of fabrics. She refuses to use synthetics, focusing on natural pure fabrics. Cottons, voiles, chanderis, crepes, tussars and khadi silks are her favourites. Her silhouettes are mostly Indian, but fusion wear forms an important part of her collection. Her clothes are greatly appreciated by critics and consumers. She retails at Taika, Ogaan, Signature, Maarwaris, Gyans, Maestros and Kaaya in New Delhi. Zenon and Kali in Kolkata, Melange in Mumbai, Ffolio in Bangalore and Aparao Galleries in Madras.

Priyadarshini Rao

After graduating from Design school at SNDT University, Mumbai she began her career as a designer for womenswear at Shoppers Stop. In early 1996, she quit her job and launched her signature label at Ffolio in Bangalore. Her label started getting noticed, and she began retailing at Melange and Ensemble in Mumbai and New Delhi.

She launched her Men's wear range in the year 1999 at a preview at Melange, which was noticed and sold out. This encouraged me to create a new menswear line for each successive season, and today I have begun enjoying designing for men, far more than creating the women's wear ranges.

Comfort is an essential aspect of her clothing. Her clothes are clean cut, with an appreciation of the fabric and finish being used. She believes that the texture of the fabric is an important, and enhances the aesthetic appeal of the garment. She refuses to embellish her work with heavy work or embroidery as she feels it would detract from the clothes. She has experimented with silhouettes, and loves the language of the bias. Clothes must enhance the personality of the wearer, and vice versa, and her collections are based on this dictum.

Puja Nayyar

Puja Nayyar studied fashion at the National Institute of Fashion Technology, New Delhi. Puja had her debut showing in the fall of 1997 and since has shown her collection in Khazana, Taj Mahal hotel, NASSCOM Conference at Oberoi Hotel (Mumbai). She has also created conceptual ensembles for the 'ARJO WIGGINS' paper show at the India Habitat Centre. In Nov.'99 Puja's collection was shown at Sao Paulo, Brazil for the 'India Fashion Show' amongst many more showings.

Puja's forte lies in the creation of a clean and minimal image. A perfectionist for details and finish, she pays scrupulous attention to her handcrafted ensembles and she develops exclusive fabrics by the use of specially treated yarns and painstakingly intricate textures by varied surface treatments.

Puja believes that clothing for today's women needs to be fashionable, individualistic, intelligent, stylish must have an attitude and value for money. Her ensembles are textured, beautifully embroidered in innovative embroidery techniques or simply minimalist both in woven and knits. In addition, she creates scarves, stoles, bags, caps, lifestyle products like made-ups and screens. Her foray into menswear has been the emergence of specially created fabrics for jackets, shirts and textured ties.

Puja sells from prestigious fashion stores in New Delhi, Mumbai and Bangalore and works out of her studio in New Delhi.

Ranna Gill

In the vibrant world of contemporary fashion few designers have consistently stood out of the crowd for their creativity, talent and attention to the aesthetic detail. Ranna Gill is one such rarity.

Having completed her associate degree in Fashion from the countries premier fashion institute NIFT in 1991, Ranna went on to complete her graduation from the Fashion Institute of Technology, New York in 1994. While studying at F.I.T., Ranna spent the formative years of her career in fashion interning with Donna Karan, and later joined one of the world's most prestigious fashion houses Polo Ralph Lauren (Women's wear division) at their world head quarters in New York.

Upon her return to India Ranna launched her self-styled label Ranna in 1996. The spring opening of her boutique "Ameera" and the Spring Summer 2000 show (the latest in a series of many successful showings) marks her 5th year in Indian fashion. She has had a number of fashion shows abroad, and in India as well. For this designer every season is an experience. Every collection is a journey into the inner self where she discovers yet another aesthetic realm to draw her creativity from. A realm that is new, dew fresh and off the predictable track.

Rina Dhaka

As a child Rina Dhaka was always a dreamer, and not it is that very quality that is an asset to her work. A visual person, for her images are more important that words.

After college, Rina did a training project with Intercraft, and with designer Evan Grandhal. She also set up a 'Salwar Kameez' boutique for one of her acquaintances. Around this time 'Mutiny' and 'Ensemble' were just coming up as fashion houses and she made a line of designs for them. Her clothes were well received, and she entered the fashion fray. Rina Dhaka has been a part and parcel of the Indian fashion scene for the past fifteen years. Early in her career, one of her designs for the Miss India events caught the eye of Rohit Khosla, the only fashion designer back then known for his innovativeness. She was encouraged by his appreciation and has striven to keep up the spirit of innovation. She is best known for her theme collections - sheer trousers, crochet, stretch jersey, woollens and spider web motifs. Her forte remains western wear and she prides on the fact that her pieces can be worn as separates. . "I personally feel fashion for women is about giving options. It is about severity and seduction," says Dhaka on the charge that clothes reveal too much.

Designing, for her, is basically a lot of fun. She loves to give shape to her inner feelings, and she believes in being true to her creativity. She has also opened a studio in Hauz Khas Village for Lycra.

Success is what counts and Rina Dhaka seems to have it all! Appreciation for her work has extended Indian shores and international fashion magazines 'Vogue' and 'Elle' have featured her work. Her recent show in Singapore, which was attended by their President, was an astounding success. She says, "My strength lies in designing knits. I love doing it for Western wear. Now I've also started doing Indian garments in knit and other fabrics. Indian wear basics support my western wear creations; a purely western line is otherwise, difficult to sustain."

Indeed, with Indian women beginning to work in the outside world and becoming more independent, there's a market for both western and Indian clothing, party wear and office attire. As Dhaka points out, "We need both clothing. I'm not going to go to an Indian occasion wearing my pants; I'm not an angrezi mem. We have beautiful Indian clothing, antique Indian shawls and old sarees and now we have us, Indian designers, who will try hopefully to keep the culture intact and make a strong fashion statement."

Rina Dhaka emphasizes silhouettes and is willing to take risks. In one collection she mixed fur and boots with her Indian outfits and always gives five or six looks in each collection.

She says she is impatient with the shapeless jackets and lenghas, which are worn at all weddings. "I'm bringing back a lot of the fitted clothes, the churidhars which were done earlier, in the sixties.

Nothing comes back exactly the same; it's just a reference point. I'm bringing it into my Indian clothing too. You know, the jilmil sitare look, like Mumtaz had. Bollywood can be very glamorous, it was so trendy then. Now of course it's so confused."

Ritu Beri

Ritu graduated from Delhi University in 1987 and during the hiatus that followed she was driven to find something occupy herself with. Given the sad lack of choice in Delhi at that time, she began designing outfits for herself. This led inevitably to creating clothes for her friends-and suddenly she was in business!

She enrolled in the national Institute of Fashion Technology in 1988. This institute is affiliated to F.I.T, New York and had just opened its doors in Delhi. She was amongst the first batch of 25 students chosen from a large number of applicants country-wide studio 'Lavanya' in December 1990. She achieved instant success with this collection even in the fashion Meccas of London's Regent St., where a couple of her creations were a sell-out in 'Liberty! Further collections followed. SANSKRITI 1995: 'Sanskriti ' was a path-breaking way of tracing her roots.Her creations were the result of India's scintillating cultural heritage in retrospect she divided her collection into 4 sequence..

Ritu Beri makes her mark at this century's greatest peace time event. The Indian contingent will be walking out in style at the opening ceremony at Atlanta. India's ace designer, Ritu Beri has joined in the Olympic fever, by creating a special collection for the contingent to be worn at the opening ceremony.

According to Ritu Beri," Designing clothes for the Indian contingent is a great honour and a big challenge.

Ritu Beri launched 'Caring means sharing' for People for Animals- a project to fund animal-care centers. She introduced her new and unique line of animal styled products range called, 'Caring means sharing. This collection comprises of T-shirts, caps, stuffed toys, jugs, notepads, posters, postcards, pens and keychains. The funds raised through sales of this product line for "People for 'Animals' will be instrumental in the creation of additional animal-care centers throughout India.

For Ritu 'Caring means sharing' is a dream. Ritu Beri says- "Today, the world is still my oyster-and I appear to have succeeded in prizing it open just a little bit."

Ritu Kumar

In the late 1960s India was going through profound changes; plastics had replaced mud, brass and silver; factory produced papers and woods took the place of sophisticated handicrafts and nylons displaced an ancient heritage of cotton and silk. It was not only a battle between tradition and modernity; it was also a confrontation of lifestyles and values.

During this time, a small group who had benefited from unique opportunities of study and travel began to see the depth of the craft and design heritage of their own country. They discovered that India was a reservoir of delicate skills. In an attempt to merge their international experiences together with the skills of their people, they became aware that contemporary designers must revitalize their own roots and identity. This was essential to take Indian creativity out into the world in such a way that benefited both craftsmen and the modern consumer.

This scattered group, including Ritu Kumar was to become the country's leading designers of the buildings, garments, fabrics and accessories. Ritu began with hand block printers and two tablets in a small village near Kolkata, and in the last 28 years, Ritu's team of dedicated designers have progressed to produce some of the country's most exquisite garments and accessories in cotton, silk and leather. These ranges embrace both traditional textile crafts and the lineage of Indian design.

Ritu has pioneered the term 'fashion' in the Indian context, and more importantly has demonstrated that hand made products can be as profitable and even more glamorous than those made by the machine.

Ritu Kumar's forte is traditional Indian clothes, that draw heavily on the textile and embroidery heritage of India and remains classics of their kind. But she evolved another style for European buyer. Her Indo-West fusion wear has all the trappings of block prints, embroidery and craft inputs on a western style.

Ritu's global achievements include the wardrobes comprising of the winning three Miss India's, for their participation in the International beauty pageants (Miss Universe, Miss World & Miss Asia Pacific respectively). At least six of these, to mention a few: Manpreet Brar, Ruchi Malhotra, Rani Jeyraj and recently Lara Dutta, have won the award for the Most Outstanding Evening Gown in International pageants.

Ritu has opened many outlets all over India. International style icons such as Late Princess Diana, and Jemima Khan wear her outfits, putting her designs and India's talent on the world map. Ritu has also launched her book ' Costumes and Textiles of Royal India' published by Christie's, London.

Rocky S.

As a college student he studied commerce, however he always had an inclination towards a more creative & artistic field. After formal training to the J.D. Institute of Fashion Designing, after which he got a job as a designer at departmental store, ROOPAM. After gaining the experience and the technical expertise, he decided to enter the film industry.

Akshay Kumar was the first artist he designed for. He was Rocky's launch pad in BOLLYWOOD. Soon I started getting several inquiries to design costumes for actresses. To keep up with his orders he set up a small-scale manufacturing unit. Keeping all interests in mind he took up a few artists & interacted with the likes of Raveena Tondon, Shilpa Shetty, Rekha, Manisha Koirala, and Sridevi. Now he designs for Hrithik, Amisha & Aftab. These artists are often looked upon as role models & people have the desire to look & dress like them. Media being a very effective form of communication, particularly films, definitely has a strong influence in the world of fashion.

After establishing himself in the industry he decided to branch out into the commercial aspect of the trade. He opened a store retailing exclusive ladies & men designer wear, located at Juhu named ROCKY-S. This Brand label selling prêt was greatly appreciated.

The drive to gain international fame & success took him to Dusseldorf- Germany where he participated in the IGEDO fair in

1996 September. Now he plans on venturing into the international market and globally be recognized as a trendsetter.

Rohit Bal

Fame rests lightly but with certainty on Rohit Bal, whom Time magazine in its recent Special Report on India profiled as 'India's Master of fabric and fantasy.' The regard he commands among the top echelons of Indian fashion is endorsed by a discerning, high profile clientele, that includes some of India's biggest names in the media, film, fashion and corporate world.

His affair with the media has been long-standing and passionate. Never, it seems, has one man been the focus of the attentions of so many. Reams of adulatory print continue to roll off the presses as he unveils one collection after another, each one more fantastic than the last.

Intensely concerned with design as an art form, he draws upon history, fantasy and folklore to create his masterpieces, which retail for up to 15,000 USD. These are gone before you know it, snapped up by the discerning and needless to say, the wealthy. So completely does he seem to have understood the psyche of the target consumer, that fashion pundits credit him with setting the trend for every season. His address to the fashion scene is intelligent and studied, yet imaginative and inspired.

Graduating from New Delhi's St. Stephen's College with a first class (Hons.) degree in History, the compulsive designer worked for a few years with his brother's export company. In 1990 he created his first line, traditional designer wear for men and the rest, indeed, is history.

The 34-year-old designer's sense of aesthetics is finely honed, and each of his creations is handcrafted to perfection, with meticulous attention to detail. He has access to the best the industry has to offer in terms of materials and workmanship. From villages where local craftsmen weave dreams with magic fingers, to factories, workshops and outlets where retailers jostle for survival, to the opulent grandeur of glitzy boutiques and malls at the best addresses in the big cities of high fashion, Rohit Bal can lead one to the doors of discovery, and he holds the key.

Rohit Gandhi and Rahul Khanna

ROHIT GANDHI- After graduating and working with a New York based fashion house for five years, he launched H2O a brand of mens' shirts and ties for the domestic market. After the success of H2O, he teamed up with designer Rahul Khanna and launched 'CUE'.

RAHUL KHANNA-After completing a course in Apparel Merchandising at NIFT, he worked as a freelance designer and stylist for various leading export and fashion houses in New Delhi and Mumbai, in 1998 joined designer Rohit Gandhi and launched 'CUE'.

Their collections are based on Straight Line clothing, retaining the very basic elements of style & quality, and keeping in mind the increasing demand for western wear in India, which has been ignored in the past.

They keep their silhouettes sharp and defined with an emphasis on fabrics, cuts and a lot of detailing rather than on embellishments. The look this year is understated chic.

The look this season for men is very comfortable. The suits are unstructured with concealed plackets and stylised collars. The fabrics used are very body friendly and wrinkle free. The fabrics have been chosen very carefully keeping body comfort...and the rapidly changing Indian seasons in mind, which means a lot of High Twisted Yarns, Blended linen Crepes, Light weight stretch performance fabrics and Ash Sprayed Knits.

The colour palette is neutral with subtle dashes of pastel colours such as aqua, orange, lilac and mint green. Polka dots play an important role in the collection. At Cue, they celebrate style and this is reflected in their clothes.

Shahab Durazi

The designer in Durazi is satisfied with the way his career has shaped in a decade in spite of being a one-man show who has laid strict restrictions on his creativity and career.

"I don't do ad campaigns, clothes for beauty queens or uniforms or display my garments at various fashion shows.I play the design game my way and I have got where I wanted to strictly by sticking to my straight and narrow road. I do everything myself including cutting every garment in my collection. I do not have assistants because I don't want to dilute my work. I want to guard my trade secrets close to my heart and yet I have managed to do everything I aspired for."

The designer who put Indian women into tailored jackets took a decade to make them a part of their wardrobe. Shahab Durazi has successfully carved a niche for himself when he returned from the Fashion Institute of Technology, New York in 1989 hoping to create a new look for the Indian women.

From the broad heavy shoulders and narrow waist to give the Indian female torso a more slimming look Shahab Durazi who till 1993 made only businesswear, moved into formal evening garments in that year with his butterfly look using for the first time embroidery.

In 1995 he softened his collection silhouette even further moving into chiffon and organza and using embroidery to add textures to his fabrics rather than for ornamentation. By 1997 his black, white and grey look for autumn-winter had the typical Shahab Durazi touch remaining more classic rather than flamboyant.

For Durazi the year 2000 will mean an ultra chic and simple yet modern and very urbane image that will suit the lifestyles of the new millennium. My garments will be outstanding having the advantage of that sleek cutting edge." From daywear and formalwear for men and women I have also designed all the accessories for my collections."

Durazi has also turned into a more tolerant designer. There was a time when he designed for the svelte and slim woman fitting into 6-12 sizes. Today he has added on sizes 14 and 16.In the future Durazi would like to widen his base not only in sizes but also in collections. Maybe it is because Shahab Durazi has done it all his way and not succumbed to popular demands that has made him a designer label women and men long to possess.

Shantanu & Nikhil

Shantanu & Nikhil, is a label with an eye on the global young and trendy Indian garments market. The company is in business of manufacturing high quality Indian ethnic garments both for the Indian and the overseas market. Shantanu, did his MBA from the University of Toledo, Ohio, USA and Nikhil, is a product of FIDM (Fashion Institute of Fashion & Merchandise) Los Angeles. They decided to pool in their entrepreneurial & designing skills in a business that was not new to the family. This led to the birth of Shantanu & Nikhil as a brand label in 1998.

Shantanu always felt that the Indian fashion industry had all the necessary ingredients: creativity, a vast variety of fabrics, and a treasure of kashidkari to prosper in a huge industry but what it lacks is professionalism, The degree in business administration has helped Shantanu understand the market, its needs and the various intricacies involved in effectively marketing their product. In short, Shantanu's business skills have lent a professional touch to Finesse International, the company started by Mrs. Nicky Mehera, their mother, in 1986.

Since his early school days, Nikhil was always the more creative one. He joined Fashion Institute Of Design & Merchandising in Los Angeles, California for an advanced fashion design program. He has been awarded with some of the most prestigious awards and scholarships. Nikhil was invited to design a collection for a prestigious store "Georgio Beverly Hills" in Los Angeles and was featured in L.A.Times to be the only Indian designer to have had a show in Universal Studio, Hollywood.

Saluting the new age of power dressing at work and elegant chic socially, in a short span of three years, Shantanu & Nikhil have a series of signature stores to their credit besides having a strong presence at a variety of designer stores internationally.

Sangeeta Chopra

Sangeeta Chopra stepped into the world of fashion at an early age of 16 years, more than 2 decades ago. She choreographed and directed her first fashion show & since then had directed more than 900 shows, both in India & across the globe.

Her foray into the field of design began 15 years back. She studied fashion design at the prestigious Fashion Institute of Technology In New York for 2 years.

Since her return she has combined both careers successfully. Currently she operates out of a studio in South Mumbai by appointment only. She had designed the Miss Universe wardrobes for various Miss India's including Sushmita Sen, Madhu Sapre & Namrata Shirodkar. Several music videos and several advertising campaigns- both press & film - have seen her designs. Her collections have also seen extensively on the runway all over India & abroad for many years.

Though presently her outfits are only available from her studio, she is looking towards the LIFW to put a foot in the retail market. She is looking forward to the interaction with buyers from all over India & sees the efforts of both FDCI & IMG as a step in the right direction to take Indian fashion to great heights.

Savio Jon

Goa-based designer and stylist Saviojon recalls cutting the bottom of grocery carry bags, placing them on hangers, pretending them to be tops and organising garage sales with friends at age six.

They were unbearably wearable and didn't sell a single one. Two decades later he is better known to do the same. His love-hate relationship with clothes began at an early age, and learnt to cut and sew watching his mother do so at age eleven. With support from cartoonist friend Alexyz, Saviojon put together and exhibition of clothes cut and made entirely by him. While still at high school, he was also asked to design stage costumes by rock star Remo Fernandes.

Not so fascinated by the regular academic path, he applied at the NIFT, New Delhi, to formally learn the craft. His dreams were shattered when he was disapproved due to his work profile. Determined a career in fashion, Saviojon took hands-on approach and apprenticed with asymmetricalist Wendell Rodricks while freelancing intended for various export houses. His career took off in 1993 when he won at the first Shopper's Stop Designer of the Year Award, while giving him a regular retail space at their outlets. He felt an absolute high when Diana Hayden wore his creation at the Cannes film festival the year she won the Miss World title. In 1999, the Taj Exotica, Goa commissioned him to design their entire uniform. Ever since, there is no looking back. Though he has no formal training, Saviojon believes that learning is a forever process. Being an absolute control freak he still cuts every piece from his collection and likes to blend street with avant-garde making the clothes unbearably wearable. Better known for his wild fashion sensibility he believes in quality not quantity and his focus is on craftsmanship and detail. His designs reveal that clothes aren't just about appearance but as he says, "Changing the way you feel." Effectively he has been able to bridge the art/fashion world divide without sacrificing wearability.

He admires Gaultier for his humour, Yves Saint Laurent for his laid back glamour, Chalayan for his intellectualism, Helmut Lang for his minimalism & Galliano for his madness. Although he has a rebellious sensibility, don't expect the usual line. He has evolved from clumsy couture, distressing, indie punk to the current selvedge chic. His involvement with fashion has been from the start ard is very high street than high fashion.

At a time when fashion is brushing up on the glamour front, Saviojon has made it his mission to tamper with anti-fashion and funk. Although fashion temples such as Melange, Ogaan, Ensemble and Sosa's are snapping up his collections, commerce hasn't dampened his passion for art. His permanent focus is to have fun.

Tarun Tahiliani

Tarun Tahiliani's clothing epitomizes style, craftsmanship, quality and refinement.

Tarun started his professional career in management, with a degree from the Wharton School of Business. In 1987 he conceived of starting a world-class fashion store in Mumbai that would house up-market designer clothing. Tarun and his wife Sailaja chose a handful of talented young, undiscovered designers, which led to the birth of Ensemble, and along with it a revolution that would change the face of the fashion industry. Tarun's own design career also had its inception in the birth of Ensemble. Although he had the flair he honed his technical knowledge in design by qualifying for an associate degree from the Fashion Institute of Technology in New York. Style, craftsmanship, quality and refinement are the defining symbols of Tarun's garments. His collections attempt to rejuvenate ideas towards a renewal for contemporary Indian life. A wide spectrum of silhouettes and styles complement his trademark drapes and subtlety. Today, Tarun, the master of drape, is one of the most sought after and successful fashion designers in the country whose clients cover a domestic and international arena.

Recently, Ensemble inaugurated a boutique in New Delhi. Tarun Tahiliani's first ' store within a store' at Ambawata, Mehrauli has an attached couture salon where bridal and occasion wear will be designed and fitted in consultation with clients. Menswear and home-furnishings are also retailed from this outlet. Ever since the tremendous success of his first solo show "The Rubaiyat" in September ' 1994 at the Dorchester in London, he has continued to present exclusive, well attended and highly publicized shows in major cities all over the world.

Vandana Roy

The glitterati in their endeavour to look great and feel good place their faith in the hands of a few designers and a price tag with endless nulls. Our mailbox had a lot of enquires from women wanting the same feel of the garment but at an affordable tag. Another dimentions to it was the fact that this segment wanted wears that were subtle as a casual wear yet trendy when party borne. A survey through the shopping havens across the terrians of our country led us in search of the affordable yet elegant salwar kameez that would do any women proud. The gaints in retail trade like Modern Silk House in Lucknow, Sona's Favourite Shop in Bangalore, Pralochna in Coimbatore, Sri Krishna in Chennai, Nikhar in Jaipur, Seasons in Mumbai and Asopalav in Ahmedabad were a few destinations that compelled us to believe that ingenious ideas have been plotted in making this dressing a branded product. We narrowed the search and discovered a single brand that has been visionary and a cult figure in dressing....Sentiments.

How did the Sentiments brand of Salwar Kameez's touch similar sentiments of an invigorating mix of culture and people across the country, makes you wonder what made it click. Was it the fashion genius creating wearable attires or was it a marketing revolution?

Probably it was both. A few unanswered questions made us search the history of Sentiments and we discovered a woman.

"Please let me be low profile," she screams from behind her desk in her design studio, wearing an elegant salwar kameez which we presumed was nothing but Sentiment. The name behind the desk was Vandana Roy, the designer and the businesswoman of Sentiments. So in this age of recession how has she managed to make a success? "Give your client value for money and she remains with you," replies Vandana Roy. However clinched it may sound but then that is the reality in this recession infiltrated season. Salwar Kameez is a necessity in today's wardrobe but at the same time within a given budget the woman wants to feel indulgent and luxurious. "The focus is on the intelligent woman who has more than just taste and is not looking for cheap imitations of big designers," thinking 17s to the mature 30s and rightfully so as we gather.

"You cannot, I repeat, cannot compromise in the quality of your garment even if you want to cut corners in the pricing." comments Vandana. The fabrics are exquisite and there is an exceptional attention to detail in the making every garment even if it is mass-produced. "Even if we are mass producing, we at Sentiments ensure that not more than two to three pieces of a single design in one colour reaches the retail outlet in one city," beams the lady, proud to maintain exclusively in spite of being a production house. "It is this mass production that makes it physically and financially visible for me to travel to jaipur just for Bandhanis, to Coimbatore for handloom cottons, get my jute linens from Bhagalpur, Jamevars from Banaras and get Bagru printing work done from Sanganer in Rajasthan," says Vandana, explaining the intricacies of producing more garments than one at a time. The quantities in question make it possible for the brand to directly deal with the craftsmen, weavers and artisans all around India and extract quality work from them. A tight reign on the prices by eliminating middle men is passed on directly to the women who adore the garment for its fit and style. So how does she design keeping in mind the different choices of a consumer in coaching to the one in Calcutta? "The choices may be different but the bottom line is the same, every women wants to feel beautiful."

The arduous journey of creating acceptable designs begins with fabrics and colours. "The fabrics ought to have a character and the colours a charishma," the designer proclaims. Their tie up with all the leading fabric manufacturers in India and suppliers abroad ensures that the same fabric is not dumped in the market for a stipulated time. This gives them enough lead time to introduce garments in the fabric that no one has touched before. Vandana Roy did her two -year course in Dress Making and Fashion Co-ordination from the SNDT institite in Mumbai. Besides this, the designer has a fabulous hand for art and painting, which she uses to create soulful dressings for Sentiments.

She laments the fact that in spite of such talented people coming out of fashion institutes, not one of them looks towards mass production as a medium of creating dressings. "Every one wants to be a top of the line and media hyped designer," comments this successful manufacturer of Salwar Kameezes. She believes that if there are more players and competition in this industry, it would eventually be prospering the consumer and anything less than perfect would be a passe. So are there any other players fishing in the same grounds of Sentiments? There are a few more players in the branded segment but are far from being a recognizable symbol like Sentiments. There are nearly two hundred shops all over India convincingly retailing the Sentiments brand. "These retail outlets are personally selected by us and we ensure that there are no more than one or two outlets in a city." says Vandana while discussing her marketing strategy. Sentiments do not intend to increase the number of retail outlets any further because they do not want to oversell and wish to retain their characteristics aura in each city, is what we gather.

Where there is an original, can the fakes be far behind in a country that has shoab of pirates. Retail outlets that could not get the coveted Sentiments brand indulge in blatant piracy, creating 'Just-like-Sentiments' designs. But a consumer so used to the insignia of Sentiments at the nape of the garment, refuses to be fettered by the fakes, but then can there be greater accolades than having the losers ape your design to make a living. "The fakes still cannot compete with our brand because the moment they try to change the fabric and compromise on the quality of the garment which is a give away,"suggests Vandana. Sentiments create 30 to 40 designs every month and before the copiers get a whiff of it, the designs are changed in the coming month. These not only ensure a variety, but also translate into repeat purchases from feminine genders, especially when there is so much to choose from. Sentiments has been creating these sophisticated silhouettes that meld style with the couture look to give a timeless and contemporary look within a range of Rs.1200 to Rs.3000. Whether you float with a pretty embroidery pattern or pack a punch with lycra, you are always ready for a look which is all woman. Be it the traditional Bandhani print or the abstract batik print, the fashion is becoming in nay garment that flaunts the Sentiment label. It has been a decade of existence for this brand of clothing which breaks away from predictability. "Good things in life need not come for a scandalous price," a smile ensures from Vandana Roy who still prefers to let her work speak more than her image. Commercializing a brand and yet satisfying all discerning clients is no mean feat. Sentiments has managed to do just that. Women will continue to succumb to the brand. Sentiments through Vandana Roy will continue to energize the gentry with their collections. The future is endless. The Sentiments are endless.

Vijay & Shobna Arora

Art is boundless. It sifts through the sands of time conjuring an aesthetic equilibrium around which life reverberates. It is the very being of existence influencing every nuance of living, and fashion is but, one aspect, of that.

'ANANT' the label promoted by designers Shobhna & Vijay Arora is synonymous with 'perennial' in Sanskrit and in sync with their philosophy, to style ensembles that are evergreen, aesthetic, and timeless.

Embroidery and embellishments are the forte of the Anant label. The silhouettes are clean, streamlined and the focus is intricate hand embroidery that makes style statements. The look is always sophisticated, either understated or strong creating an impact.

Vijay Arora did his MBA from Cornell University, USA. He never made a concerted effort to become a designer. His first collection was in 1993, which was a range of men's kurtas and churidas. By

1994 end the transition was made as women loved the men's kurtas and wanted them to be made feminine.

So far, they have designed 70-80 collections together. Anant by Shobhna & Vijay Arora is about understated elegance that a connoisseur would understand: Simple, yet effective, aesthetically correct, wearable contemporary & traditional ensembles for men and women.

□□□

12

Notable Fashion Designers of World

Introduction

Designers are people with a desire to create. They combine practical knowledge with artistic ability to turn abstract ideas into formal designs for the merchandise we buy, the clothes we wear, the Web sites we use, the publications we read, and the living and office space we inhabit. Designers usually specialize in a particular area of design, such as automobiles, industrial or medical equipment, home appliances, clothing and textiles, floral arrangements, publications, Web sites, logos, signage, movie or TV credits, interiors of homes or office buildings, merchandise displays, or movie, television, and theater sets.

The first step in developing a new design or altering an existing one is to determine the needs of the client, the ultimate function for which the design is intended, and its appeal to customers or users. When creating a design, designers often begin by researching the desired design characteristics, such as size, shape, weight, color, materials used, cost, ease of use, fit, and safety.

Designers then prepare sketches or diagrams by hand or with the aid of a computer-to illustrate the vision for the design. After consulting with the client, a creative director, or a product development team, designers create detailed designs, using drawings, a structural model, computer simulations, or a full-scale prototype. Many designers use computer-aided design (CAD) tools to create and better visualize the final product. Computer models allow ease and flexibility in exploring a greater number of design alternatives, thus reducing design costs and cutting the time it takes to deliver a product to market. Industrial designers use computer-aided industrial design (CAID) tools to create designs and machine-readable instructions that communicate with automated production tools.

Designers sometimes supervise assistants who carry out their creations. Designers who run their own businesses also may devote a considerable amount of time to developing new business contacts, examining equipment and space needs, and performing administrative tasks, such as reviewing catalogues and ordering samples. The need for up-to-date computer and communications equipment is an ongoing consideration for many designers, especially those in industrial and graphic design.

Fashion designers design clothing and accessories. Some high-fashion designers are self-employed and design for individual clients. Other high-fashion designers cater to specialty stores or high-fashion department stores. These designers create original garments, as well as clothing that follows established fashion trends. Most fashion designers, however, work for apparel manufacturers, creating designs of men's, women's, and children's fashions for the mass market.

Fashion designers who work for clothing manufacturers or wholesalers design clothing and accessories in many sizes and colors in order to meet the demands of the general market. A smaller number of fashion designers create custom designs for individual customers, specialty boutiques, or their own stores. These high fashion designers are usually self-employed and charge high prices for their designs.

A successful fashion designer must be good at predicting the future. Since it takes between eighteen and twenty-four months for an article of clothing to go from rough sketch to final production, the designer must understand buying trends as they are developing. Therefore, research on fashion trends is an important first step in the design process. Some designers do this research themselves, while others base their designs on research conducted by others, such as industry trade groups. Fashion designers go to trade shows or visit textile manufacturers to select fabrics for their designs.

Once they have picked their fabrics and sketched their designs, fashion designers make prototypes of the clothing using inexpensive materials. These prototypes are tested on fashion models to see if any adjustments are needed. Some designs may be thrown out entirely and the line of clothing narrowed to fewer pieces. Once the designs are finalized, samples of the item are made using the actual materials. These samples are taken to fashion shows or marketed directly to retailers.

In recent years, computers have changed the way many fashion designers do their work. Most designers still make their initial sketches by hand, but more and more are using computer-aided design (CAD) software to create designs that can be easily viewed from different angles in different colors on different virtual models. CAD also makes it easier to make adjustments to the original designs.

The scope of a fashion designer's work varies according to where he or she is employed. Fashion designers who work for large design companies usually take the lead in creating designs and choosing colors and fabrics, but they may then supervise others who transform the designs into finished products. Fashion designers in these firms may also be responsible for working with manufacturers and textile suppliers. Fashion designers who are new to the trade, or who work for smaller companies, must often do their own sewing and patternmaking. This chapter is covering World notable fashion designers.

Carlota Alfaro

Carlota Alfaro (born June 4, 1933) is a fashion designer from Puerto Rico. She is perhaps the best known Puerto Rican fashion designer.

Alfaro showed a passion for design ever since she was a child, often designing clothes for family and friends.

Alfaro reached international fame in Latin America, Europe and the United States during the 1960s, decade in which she also created the Instituto Carlota Alfaro, aimed towards passing on her knowledge to young fashion design students. Alfaro's specialty was haute couture.

Alfaro has received many international awards, and her collections have been sold at a variety of famous stores including Fifth Avenue and Zacks.

Pegah Anvarian

Pegah Anvarian is a Los Angeles-based fashion designer. She is designer of the Pegah Anvarian Collection.

Anvarian grew up in Richardson, Texas (a suburb of Dallas), the daughter of a photographer father and educator mother, who taught her how to sew at the age of six. Her family encouraged creativity in the home, prompting Anvarian to design her own clothes from age eight. In 1996 she moved to New York City and began assisting as a costume designer and stylist. Anvarian relocated to Los Angeles in 1999, and continued styling, doing extensive editorial, celebrity, and advertising work. Anvarian currently resides in Hollywood, California, with her fiance, photographer Andrew MacPherson.

The Pegah Anvarian Collection began in 2002 with her first sets of orders coming from Henri Bendel in New York City and Madison in Los Angeles. The Pegah Anvarian Collection is currently distributed internationally, and is available at Henri Bendel in New York City; Madison in Los Angeles; Gregory's in Dallas, Texas; and Talulah G's in Las Vegas, Nevada. The Collection is produced in Los Angeles twice yearly.

Dana Buchman

Dana Buchman is an upscale women's fashion brand, and its founder, Dana Buchman, an American fashion designer and creative designer of the same name. It is owned by the Liz Claiborne fashion company.

History

Dana Buchman was born and raised in Memphis, TN. Always a top student, Buchman graduated from Brown University. She was a President's Fellow at the prestigious Rhode Island School of Design and earned an Advance Degree in Fashion at London's St. Martin's School of Art. After graduating, Dana Buchman became a creative head for Ellen Tracy.

In 1982, Dana Buchman was personally approached by influential American designer and executive Liz Claiborne and joined the corporation with a design job in knitwear. After five years with Liz Claiborne, Buchman started her eponymous bridge collection under the Liz Claiborne corporation. By the mid-nineties, Buchman's brand became one of the leaders catering to the bridge segment of the population and by the late-nineties saw annual profits skyrocket over $250 million.

Dana Buchman has been a member of the Council of Fashion Designers America since 1991. She married her husband Tom Farber, a New York State judge, in 1985. They have two daughters Charlotte and Annie Rose. In 2006, Buchman co-authored "A Special Education: One Family's Journey Through the Maze of Learning Disabilities." Written with her daughter Charlotte, the book reveals Charlotte's struggle with her learning disabilities, as well as Buchman's own path to self-discovery. Buchman donated the profitSs from the book to the National Center for Learning Disabilities.

Jay-Z

Shawn Corey Carter (born December 4, 1969), better known as Jay-Z, is an American rapper and current president and CEO of Def Jam and Roc-A-Fella Records. In addition, he co-owns The 40/40 Club, and is co-owner of the New Jersey Nets NBA team. He is one of the most financially successful American hip-hop artists.

Known for his flow and blending of street and popular rap, Jay-Z has become one of the best-selling rappers in the hip hop industry. He is admired for his ability to compose lyrics without the use of pen and paper (his critically acclaimed album The Blueprint was written in only two days). He also returned from retirement in late 2006 with the album Kingdom Come which sold 680,000 copies in its first week, Jay-Z's highest-selling album in a one-week period.

Along with Damon "Dame" Dash and Kareem "Biggs" Burke, Jay-Z was one of the founders of Roc-A-Fella Records, a hip-hop record label. Jay-Z is the second richest Hip-Hop Entertainer (behind Sean "Puffy" Combs, a.k.a. Diddy), having a net-worth estimate of $340 million.

Charles David

Charles David is an American designer of luxury leather goods and shoes. The family owned company began U.S. distribution of European shoes in 1987. Its first retail store opened on Melrose Avenue in Los Angeles, CA in 1988. In 2005, it had 25 retail stores across the U.S in Arizona, California, Florida, Illinois, Massachusetts, New Jersey, New York, Pennsylvania, and Texas. It also sells handbags and shoes in department and specialty stores nationwide, such as Nordstrom, Macy's and Bloomingdale's.

In Spring, 2004, Charles David launched their junior lines, Charles by Charles David, and Exchange by Charles David. Charles by Charles David features the latest trends in affordable prices. Exchange by Charles David is a younger, funkier line from the popular signature line. Charles David shoes have been worn by stars such as Debra Messing, Eva Longoria, Jessica Simpson, and Halle Berry.

Eric Gaskins

Eric Gaskins (born 1958) is a New York based fashion designer known for his craftsmanship and technique.

Gaskins was born in Germany and grew up in Groton, MA. He attended Lawrence Academy and graduated from Kenyon College with a degree in Fine Arts. He moved to Paris where he was trained by Hubert Givenchy. After his return to the United States he designed for Koos Van den Akker, Bob Evans, and Scott Barrie. In 1987, he launched his own label in New York, where he currently lives. His design philosophy is "to create clothes that are essential, without artifice or contrivance".

Gaskins releases his couture collections four times annually under his own line. It is modern day and evening wear. He mainly focuses on dresses, suits, and gowns.

His designs have been featured on the covers of Cosmopolitan, Spy, Bazaar, Glamour, Vanity Fair, and Palm Beach Illustrated. Other significant editorial coverage included such magazines and television programs as: Self, New Woman, Elle, Essence and Entertainment Tonight. Among his celebrity clients are Salma Hayek, Melanie Griffith, Vanessa Williams, Mariah Carey, Geena Davis, Maria Shriver, Jada Pinkett, Jennifer Lopez, Allison Janney, Kim Cattrall, Kathy Bates, Marcia Gay Harden and Goldie Hawn.

Heatherette

Heatherette is a fashion company and design house run by Traver Rains and Richie Rich. It is located in New York City. It owes its roots to the designers' culture life as the "Club Kids".

In late 1999, Rains and Rich began collaborating on t-shirts and leather goods as a hobby on their living room floor. Rich showed up at a party in one of his own customized leather tops and caught the attention of Sushi, the creative director and buyer at the downtown store Patricia Field who ordered twenty of them on the spot. Heatherette has been seen on Gwen Stefani, Pamela Anderson, Mya, Kelis, Pink, Paris Hilton, Aubrey O' Day and other celebs.

Heatherette made a splash in the fashion industry very early on, receiving editorial credits in such magazines as Vanity Fair, W, Surface, Paper, YM, InStyle, ID, Flaunt, Italian Vogue, and Rolling Stone.

Heatherette is featured in New York Fashion Week.

Trivia

- Heatherette was featured on the third cycle of America's Next Top Model, as the designer for a fashion show the contestants were in. Particularly happy was contestant Norelle Van Herk, whose favorite designers are Richie Rich and Traver Rains.
- Heatherette was also featured on MTV's TV show Made , My Super Sweet Sixteen (They design Teyana's dress), and the movie My Super Ex-Girlfriend.
- An especially wild Heatherette fashion show, which featured Anna Nicole Smith and Boy George, is chronicled in the 2006 nonfiction book, Confessions from the Velvet Ropes by Glenn Belverio.

- Lydia Hearst, the daughter of famous Symbionese Liberation Army kidnap victim and John Waters' film actress Patricia Hearst, has modeled in several Heatherette runway shows. For the Fall 2007 collection she and the Heatherette designers collaborated on a limited edition leather bag for PUMA.

Betsey Johnson

Betsey Johnson (born August 10, 1942 in Wethersfield, Connecticut) is a fashion designer best known for her feminine and whimsical designs. She also is known for doing a cartwheel at the end of her fashion shows. She took many dance classes as a child and adolescent which inspired her love of costumes. After high school, Johnson studied at the Pratt Institute and then later graduated from Syracuse University where she was a member of the Alpha Xi Delta sorority.

In 1967 she married Velvet Underground's John Cale. They divorced later in the year. She had a daughter, Lulu, in 1975 who now works with her. She is a survivor of breast cancer and is a breast cancer awareness advocate. She has also had numerous facial plastic surgeries.

She resides in New York but once a week each month she spends time in her house in Mexico, which she has dubbed "Villa Betsey". Betsey also converted an old, small hotel in Mexico into a house which she rents out to interested people; this is called "Betseyville", and can accommodate 8-10 people.

Marc Jacobs

Marc Jacobs (born April 9, 1963 in New York City) is an American fashion designer. He attended the High School of Art and Design and graduated in 1981. From there, Jacobs entered the Parsons School of Design in New York City. At Parsons, Jacobs won the Perry Ellis Gold Thimble Award in 1984, and in the same year was also awarded the Chester Weinberg Gold Thimble Award and the Design Student of the Year Award.

While still at Parsons, Jacobs designed and sold his first line of hand knit sweaters. His first collection that he designed was for Reuben Thomas, Inc. under the Sketchbook label. At this time in

1984, Jacobs formed his partnership with Robert Duffy, Jacobs Duffy Designs Inc., which continues to this day. In 1986, backed by Kashiyama USA, Inc., Jacobs designed his first collection bearing the Marc Jacobs label. In 1987, Jacobs received the distinct honor of being the youngest designer to be awarded the fashion industries highest tribute: The Council of Fashion Designers of America (CFDA) Perry Ellis Award for New Fashion Talent.

Marc Jacobs and Robert Duffy joined Perry Ellis in 1989. Robert as the President and Marc as the Vice-President of women's design to create the designer collection and in addition, he oversaw the design of the various women's licensees. In 1992, the Council of Fashion Designers of America, once again bestowed Jacobs with a great honor: The Women's Designer of the Year Award.

Following his studies at the Parsons School of Design, he became prominent on the fashion scene when he designed a "grunge" collection for Perry Ellis, leading to his immediate dismissal. Jacobs is currently the artistic director for Louis Vuitton, a position he assumed in 1997. At Vuitton Jacobs has spearheaded such notable collaborations as Stephen Sprouse's graffiti bags, Takashi Murakami's pastel-colored accessories, and the first ready-to-wear line marketed under the Louis Vuitton imprimateur (designed by Jacobs). His own clothing lines, Marc Jacobs and the less expensive diffusion line Marc By Marc Jacobs (which he created in 2000), are also extremely popular.

Jacobs has sometimes bucked prevailing fashion trends. In Spring 2004/2005, when designers were following the "safari theme", he made his collection completely lady-like and the catwalk which the models walked on had an archway of 450,000 roses. Jacobs' Fall 2005 collection received sharply mixed reviews. In 2006, he is set to bring out a watch collection this year under the brand of Marc Jacobs. These watches will feature classic and timeless aesthetics with a slightly vintage feel. His clothes are available in a few boutiques around the world including New York, Los Angeles, Boston, San Francisco, Tokyo, Hong Kong, and Taipei. In 2007, he was ranked as 8th on Out magazine list of "50 Most Powerful Gay Men and Women in America".

On March 12, 2007, Jacobs checked into rehab for treatment of drug and alcohol abuse.

Calvin Klein

Calvin Richard Klein (born November 19, 1942) is a well-known American fashion designer. In 1968, he launched the company that would later become Calvin Klein Inc.

In addition to clothing, Calvin Klein also gave his name to a range of perfumes, including CK One and CK Be (fragrances for both genders), now owned by Coty Inc. Swatch Group manufactures watches and jewelry under the Calvin Klein and Calvin Klein Jeans brands.

Derek Lam

Derek Lam is a fashion designer from San Francisco, California. He is a graduate of the Parsons School of Design.

Lam started out as an assistant for Michael Kors in the 90s. In 2005, Lam won the CFDA Perry Ellis Swarovski Award for new designers and started his own line of clothes. In addition to clothes, Derek Lam also has a line of shoes and jewelry.

He is known for his pretty, girly fabrics backed by clean, crisp silhouettes. Signature pieces include raw silk sheath dresses with plunging necklines, wide-leg trousers in various wool's and dainty cashmere pea coats cinched with stiff silk belts.

He now works with Tod's to create ready-to-wear. Tod's is now also licenced out to produce his bags and shoes.

Beth Levine

Beth Levine (born Elizabeth Katz) (1911-2006) was an American fashion designer most known for her designs from the 1940s through the 1970s. Under the label of her husband Herbert Levine she was the best-known American women's shoe designer from the 1950s to the early 1970s, and is still referred to as "The first Lady of American Shoes Design").

She was born on December 31, 1911 in Patchogue, New York, the third of five children of Anna and Israel Katz, Lithuanian immigrants who operated a dairy farm. In the 1930s, she moved to Manhattan and found work as a shoe model, then worked her way up from a stylist to head designer for I. Miller. She served as a Red Cross volunteer during World War II.

She met Herbert Levine when she applied for a job designing shoes for another shoe manufacturer in 1944 and married him three months later. He was head of the firm, and this gave her designs the chance to come to center stage. They founded a new company under the name Herbert Levine in 1948. Beth Levine described their vision for the company by saying, "We wanted to create a shoemaking niche. We were making very pretty shoes that nobody needed, but everybody wanted".

Although the company was named after publicity-savvy former-journalist Herbert, Beth Levine's name was still featured as the primary shoe designer for their products. She was given the Coty Award in 1967 for design innovation.

The Levines' greatest influence is considered to be the re-introduction of boots to women's fashion in the 1960s and the popularization of the shoe style known as mules. When Nancy Sinatra wore Levine boots in publicity shots for the 1960s hit song These Boots Are Made for Walkin' demand for fashion boots leaped so much that Saks Fifth Avenue opened a special section its shoe department called Beth's Bootery.

Beth had recognized how much women admired the delicacy and femininity of high fashion shoes when she modeled them on her tiny (size 4B, European size 35) foot. She set out to create designs that would make women with average shoe sizes look more delicate and feminine in their shoes, and in the process changed the silhouettes of American fashion. She experimented with cutting away more and more of the leather to expose more and more of the foot, in the process creating shoes that were regarded as both sexier and more elegant than her predecessors.

In addition to three First Ladies, Jackie Kennedy, Lady Bird Johnson and Pat Nixon, the clientele also included movies stars such as Bette Davis and musicians like Barbara Streisand. Beth Levine worked to ensure that the wives of former presidential rivals John F. Kennedy and Richard Nixon never ran into each other at her studio, and once frantically had to rearrange their fitting schedules when she discovered their visits would overlap.

Innovations

Fashion innovations introduced by the Levines include:

- Boots as Haute Couture. Once highly stylish, boots lost favor in fashion after World War I as skirts became shorter and new manufacturing styles allowed shoes in a variety of styles to be made less expensively. In the mid-1960s the Levines added fashion boots to their line, starting a trend which remains current four decades later. Nancy Sinatra wore Levine boots for publicity shots and on stage during her period of fame for the song These Boots Are Made for Walkin'. Shirley Maclaine used them for dance numbers in Sweet Charity, and Raquel Welch wore them in her television variety specials.
- Spring-o-Lator mules, where an elastic strip allowed the wearer to keep the shoes securely on while wearing stockings despite the lacl of any straps at the side or back of the shoes. Through much of the 1950s and 1960s a wide range of shoe designers used Beth Levine's Spring-o-Lators in their shoe lines. Television characters such as Della Street (portrayed by Barbara Hale) in the popular Perry Mason series often made Spring-o-Lators part of their trademark wardrobe.
- Stocking boots (panty hose with heels attached, as well as boots made from materials like vinyl and acrylic.
- Clear plastic shoes, a style that inspired later designers including Charles Jourdan.

Although the company closed in 1975, many Beth Levine designs remain on display in museums in Europe and North America.

Beth Levine died of lung cancer on September 20, 2006, aged 91.

Mainbocher

Mainbocher (1891-1976) (born Main Rousseau Bocher) was an American couturier who operated fashion houses in Paris and later New York from the 1930s through the 1960s. He is best known for designing Wallis Simpson's wedding dress and trousseau for her 1937 marriage to the former Edward VIII (the Duke of Windsor) which was photographed by Cecil Beaton

Mainbocher's wedding dress worn by the Duchess of Windsor on the wedding day.

Mainbocher was a native of Chicago, where he studied art at the University of Chicago and the Chicago Academy of Fine Arts. He served in the Army in the first World War and stayed on in Paris after the war, working as a fashion illustrator for Harpers Bazaar and later as a fashion editor for French Vogue.

In 1929, he established his own fashion house, designing expensive, elegant haute couture dresses and gowns for an exclusive clientele, and charging them for the privilege of viewing his collections. He designed much of the Duchess of Windsor's wardrobe, naming a color, Wallis blue, for her, and created the first strapless evening gown.

In 1939, he relocated his business to New York on 57th Street next to Tiffany's, and continued to design for generations of discerning women of means like Gloria Vanderbilt through the 1960s.

After he achieved fame for dressing some of the world's most famous women, Mainbocher was commissioned to design the costumes for Ethel Merman in the 1950 Broadway musical Call Me Madam. Merman recounts in her memoirs that she took her mother to her first fitting for her costumes. Mainbocher would not permit Merman's mother in the fitting area saying he did not allow outside persons in the areas where he created. When Merman inquired why he would not allow her mother when he allowed another old woman in the room, Mainbocher replied, "But that is my mother."

Recently, Mainbocher and twenty-three other American fashion designers were honored with bronze plaques on New York City's "Fashion Walk of Fame" in the legendary garment district.

Norman Norell

Norman Norell (born Norman David Levinson April 20, 1900 in Noblesville, Indiana - died in New York, October 25, 1972) was an American fashion designer, known for his elegant suits and tailored silhouettes.

The son of a haberdasher, from early childhood Norell had an ambition to become an artist. After spending a short period at military school during World War I, he studied fashion design at the Pratt Institute.

In 1922, he joined the New York studio of Paramount Pictures where he designed clothes for Gloria Swanson and other stars of silent movies. He then worked as a costume designer on Broadway, making the costumes for the Ziegfeld Follies and the Cotton Club, as well as for the Brooks Costume Company and for wholesale dress manufacturer Charles Armour. In 1928, he was hired by Hattie Carnegie and remained with her until 1941.

In 1943 Norell won a Coty Fashion Award and began teaching at the Parsons School of Design, where he was previously a student. Shortly afterwards Anthony Traina invited him to form the fashion company Traina-Norrell, with Traina looking after the business side and Norell the fashion side. By 1944, Norell had launched chemise dresses, evening dresses, fur coats, sequined evening sheaths, fur slacks and empire-line dresses.

Today, he is considered by many in the world of fashion to be one of the foremost fashion designers in US history, on a par with the legendary French couturiers.

Patrick Porter

Patrick Porter (November 18th 1977 -) is an american singer/ songwriter, novelist, poet, and painter. Born in Murfreesboro, Tennessee and raised in the isolated mountain town of Bailey, Colorado, Porter began playing music at a young age, often acting as a sit-in drummer for his father's biker bar band. As a teenager Porter began to write his own songs, recording and distributing hundreds of homemade cassettes of wildly varying disposition and sound quality. As a result of these demos, Porter was signed to Camera Obscura Records, an Australian indie label who released his first full-length CDs: the shadowy, lo-fi Reverb Saved My Life and Reconsidered, a disc recorded with the shoegazer group Phineas Gage.

After moving to New York in 2003, Porter recorded a handful of discs known as the "New York Trilogy": Lisha Kill, Maybe Waltz and Skylan Mo. In 2006 he signed with Greyday Records, an indie label in Portland Oregon, who released the Die Wandaland LP, in September 2006.

Porter is also a poet and novelist of note. His first book of poetry, The Intrusive Ache of Morning, was published in 2001 by Chicago's

Press of the Third Mind. His second, Nervous Halo, was published a year later on the late Paul Dilsaver's Arts and Academic Press. He has also written two novels, Kristallnacht and Apocalypse Later.

Porter began painting in the summer of 2006 while living in New York City, selling watercolor/crayon paintings in Union Square Park to make extra money. By the end of the year he was painting full-time and continues to work consistently both through galleries and private commissions.

Zac Posen

Zac Posen (born 1980) is a contemporary fashion designer. Posen grew up in New York City, attending Saint Ann's School. He went to design school at Central Saint Martins in London, where he began to conceive his distinctive aesthetic. At 16, he interned at the Metropolitan Museum's Costume Institute, under the tutelage of Richard Martin, followed by an internship with Nicole Miller and a position at Tocca. In 2001, he was one of the new names at the Gen Art Fresh Faces in Fashion show.

In the early 2000s, Posen had success with designs worn by prominent young actresses including Natalie Portman, Liv Tyler, Gwyneth Paltrow, and Claire Danes. In 2004, Posen was awarded the CFDA Swarovski-Perry Ellis Award for Ready-to-Wear after his first major ıunway show. Posen is as much an entrepreneur as a design success; by 2005 many major stores were carrying his collections. In 2006 renowned fashion historian Didier Ludot granted him the honor of showing his work in his Palais Royal stores during Paris Fashion Week.

Posen's garments frequently appear in magazines such as Vogue and Elle.

At the 2006 Academy Awards, Best Actress nominee Felicity Huffman wore a Zac Posen gown to the ceremony. At the 2007 Academy Awards, Gwyneth Paltrow and Portia de Rossi wore Zac Posen gowns to the ceremony. Posen lives in Greenwich Village with his boyfriend, Brian Callahan.[1]

Collette Dinnigan

Collette Dinnigan (born 1965 in South Africa[1]) is an Australian fashion designer. Born in South Africa, Dinnigan was raised in New

Zealand and later moved to Australia. She has had an "on-again, off-again" relationship with Richard Wilkins, with whom she had a child Estella in 2004. While fashion designing is a big part in her life, now Estella is an even bigger part. Collette designs for all ages, infants to bridal wear.

She is related to the famous Irish gaelic footballer Rory Dinnigan who was recently involved in a medical controversary where he was found to be using prostetic arms to aid his performance. He currently plays for the Dublin Dragoons and is said to be in contact with Collette on a semi-regular basis.

Collette's bridal wear is the most famous, which has featured in Vogue Magazine. Her evening wear is also quite popular in Australia. Collette Dinnigan graduated from the Wellington Polytechnic College in New Zealand where she majored fashion design, then migrated to Australia in 1985 to work with the Australian Broadcasting Commission's (ABC) fashion studios in the Costume Department in Sydney. She was noted for her attention to detail and the historical flavour she bought to costume design and fabrication.

Her friends influenced her in her decision to become a fashion designer. When she was in an accident and was confined to her bed, she had made lingerie for her friends. They were so well received she decided to head down a career of fashion design. She had studied the makings of a historical dress while working for the ABC, and this influenced her work greatly. She also takes inspiration from items associated with luxury, such as musk, espresso and moonstones.

In 1990, she established the label Palladium, then launched the self-named Collette Dinnigan label. Her label drew inspiration from classical vintage styles; which spoke of luxury and were distinctly feminine. Her style can vary, but her trademark is her tulle, chiffon and lace dresses, inspired by the art deco period. Her products are usually very feminine, delicate and finely tailored.

Collette Dinnigan describes her label's style as being romantic bohemian and timelessly elegant, based on the reworking of historical fabrics. Her products are designed to be suggestive of the body, rather than revealing; thus achieving the sense of confidence, sensuality and individuality.

During the early 1990, Dinnigan's label went international; being sold across Australasia, and in America and Asia. In 1995, Collette

Dinnigan targeted European markets, starting with the fashion epicentre: Paris. She was the first Australian-based designer to present a ready-to-wear range on the catwalks of Paris. In 1996, she was elected as Australian 'Designer of the Year'; in 1997 she won the Louis Vuitton Business Award. By 1998, she had also won the 'Award for Excellence Award' by Fashion Group International and was given a place in the Business-woman's Hall of Fame. She held the position of Chairperson of The New South Wales Small Business Development Corporation from 1998 to 2000. For three consecutive years, the Collette Dinnigan label was recognised as one of Australia's 50 Most Beautiful Exports. She has gone on to win innumerable award for her creativity, originality and distinctive style and designs.

In today's world, at 42 years of age, Collette is highly successful, with her products sold in around 80 boutiques across the globe as well as in retail giants such as Myer and David Jones and remains the only designer invited by Chambre Syndicale du prêt-a-porter des couturiers et des createurs de mode to mount a ready-to-wear parade on Parisian catwalks. Her label has been recognised by the Powerhouse Museum as being most symbolic of Australian design. At present, she has opened a store in London, in a bid to reach the UK market.

Alannah Hill

Alannah Hill is an extremely successful fashion designer who focuses on creating whimsical clothing. She has become known for her feminine, flirty and magical style. Her clothing is sold around the world, with many boutiques in Australia.

Alannah Hill was born in Tasmania, but at the age of 17, relocated to Melbourne to further her career in hairdressing. After this career was not all as she expected, Alannah started working at a small store in Chapel St. From there, she started designing her own fashion label into what she has now.

Alannah Hill has a son, Edward, who is about 4 years old. Alannah Hills' style can be summed up by her intensely whimsical website designed by Melbourne based design and creative agency Lemonade

Alex Perry

Alex Perry is an Australian fashion designer who has been nicknamed as 'Australia's Most Glamorous Designer'.

After graduating from East Sydney Fashion Design Studio in 1984, Alex worked as a model agent representing some of Australia's most beautiful women for some of the world's most elite agencies. In 1992 Alex opened his first atelier creating expensive gowns, jewelled corsets and sexy sheaths. Vogue Australia photographed these gowns that were to become the Alex Perry trademark signature in his first editorial shoot.

Perry relocated his salon in 1994 to Double Bay, Sydney where he built up his impressive clientele to include high profile celebrities, social identities and personalities. Elle Macpherson, Linda Evangelista and Claudia Schiffer lead the long list of 'Perry Girls' who had donned the designer's magnificent ball gowns and sensational red carpet eveningwear. Most recently international Perry Girls Jennifer Lopez and Nelly Furtado both chose to perform on stage and walked the red carpet in Alex Perry gowns.

Alex Perry was a designer at the inaugural Mercedes Australian Fashion Week held in May 1995, and is the only designer to show each year since. Over the past eleven years the Alex Perry fashion shows evolved into what has been described as "the most glamorous show of the week". Perry's runway shows have featured supermodels such as Linda Evangelista, Megan Gale, Kate Fisher, Alyssa Sutherland, Nicole Trunfio and Lily Cole.

After being established as Australia's premier Couturier, Alex Perry launched his first "ready to wear" collection in 1998. The Alex Perry experience is now accessible to a wider audience and currently available nationally at David Jones Department Store, capital city stores. The collection of special occasion pieces has been designed with dinner, cocktails, the races and red carpet moments in mind. Familiar Alex Perry Couture signatures of boned corsetry, hand ruching and sexy, feminine silhouettes are all-important elements of the ready-to-wear collection.

Alex Perry ready-to-wear is also available at selected boutiques internationally including United States, United Arab Emirates, Saudi Arabia, Indonesia and Hong Kong. In May 2002, Alex Perry launched his Sydney salon at The Strand. Alex Perry's debut accessories collection was launched in 2006 and is available at the Strand Arcade store. The collection features glamorous stilettos, jewelled clutch handbags and bijoux earrings for evening and bridal.

Alex is currently represented by Chic Media and was seen on: Network 7 "50 Years of Television - Red Carpet reportage", Network 7 co-host "Melbourne Cup Fashions on the Field", commentary of Prince Charles & Camilla's Royal Wedding, co-host for Network 9 "Australian Fashion Awards", co-host of Network 7's "Ultimate Make Over". Alex is also the only judge to appear in all 3 seasons of Foxtel's highest rating Australian show "Australia's Next Top Model".

Dirk Bikkembergs

Dirk Bikkembergs (born January 2, 1959) is a Belgian fashion designer. Dirk Bikkembergs was born in Cologne, Germany, where his Flemish father was stationed at the time. After his high school career, Dirk Bikkembergs was interested to attend law school because he found "lawyers so chic" but eventually decided to start studying at the Royal Academy of Fine Arts in Belgium. In 1982 Bikkembergs graduated, together with other Belgian designers Ann Demeulemeester, Dries van Noten, Dirk van Saene, Walter van Beirendonck and Martin Margiela. Together they came to be known as the "Antwerp Six" by the fashion world.

In 1985, after winning the Canette d'Or award for Best Young Designer in Fashion, Dirk Bikkembergs was given the opportunity to create his own men's shoes collection. His first line featured perforated soles and highly original laces, creating an uproar at the time. Dirk also got himself noticed at the British Design Show in 1986.

In 1989 Dirk Bikkembergs went to Paris and launched his first menswear collection, followed by the women's collection in 1993.

The influence of Dirk Bikkembergs' origins is palpable in his designs. Many of his clothes betray a preference for military aesthetics. He loves robust materials and simple shapes. Other characteristics of his collections are the austere lines, the abundant use of leather and many virile details such as belts. Dirk's first women's collections were (apart from size) identical to his menswear lines.

To say Dirk Bikkembergs likes movement is an understatement. The tall designer divides his time between Belgium, France, Italy, Germany, London and New York and is rarely seen in any one place for more than a week. He describes himself as a workaholic and once said in an interview with ID magazine: "I am married to fashion and will remain faithful."

Dirk Bikkembergs has become particularly popular with young people since 2000 after he launched his fashion line 'Bikkembergs Sport', including the t-shirts with the famous footballer. This so-called 'sport-couture' has given Bikkembergs the opportunity to design the clothing for the Inter Milan football club. He is currently the owner of Eccellenza football club S.S.D. F.C. Bikkembergs Fossombrone from Fossombrone, a small town in the province of Pesaro e Urbino.

He was the first fashion designer who received permission to hold a fashion show in the famous FC Barcelona football stadium Nou Camp.

Raf Simons

Raf Simons (1968-) is a Belgian fashion designer. He studied industrial design, but after a few years of self-study, he became a menswear designer in 1995. Initially, he worked with Walter Van Beirendonck in Paris, where he was exposed to the work of Martin Margiela and Jean-Paul Gaultier.

His collections (menswear only) are strongly influenced by youth culture albeit in an indirect way. He often combines strongly cut classic menswear with baggy streetwear-influenced items. Simons' style has been described as highly influential. He is being cited as one of the most important innovators in contemporary menswear by the international press. He presents his collections twice a year, usually in Paris, but works and lives in Antwerp, Belgium. In his early years, his runway shows were unconventional: models running down a street or walking in a parking lot, on a bridge, around a photography studio. His Raf Simons collection is sold at Barneys in New York.

Jil Sander In summer 2005 he was appointed as creative director for the Jil Sander label, owned by the Prada Group.

Critical Review of Raf's Work at Jil Sander

New York Times Fashion Writer Cathy Horyn respects Raf's work at Jil Sander. As she wrote about his Fall 2007 collection, "On Tuesday a little-known Belgian designer named Raf Simons had the full attention of the fashion world. Mr. Simons's collection for Jil Sander, his third since becoming creative director 18 months ago, was perfect. It will make everything else, I bet, seem a little contrived, a little clunky, a little silly."

She also considers him in the ranks of older, established designers. As she wrote: "There are plenty of designers who have shown that you don't need the crutch of a club or a book to design original clothes, among them Mr. Alaïa, Karl Lagerfeld and Raf Simons."

Dressing Alpha Career Women

Style.com's Sarah Mower wrote about his Fall 2007 collection that he is one of the only designers whose clothes are appropriate for the high-powered career woman: "Jil Sander may be the last designer resource for alpha-female corporate dressing left unbowed in the twenty-first century it's certainly the only one that dares to air a full range of navy pantsuits on a runway. That unflinching Belgian pragmatism regarding the need for upper-echelon career clothes has, after three seasons, become Raf Simons' brand-stabilizing trademark, alongside the stamp of calm conceptualism he's bringing to the house." As she wrote about his Spring 2007 collection, "Simons took on challenges that other designers have been frantically avoiding: working on a pantsuit, coming up with strategies to modernize a dress, making clothes that just might apply to the life of a high-achieving woman."

In W's March 2007 issue, Ellen Degeneres admitted to wearing Raf's clothes. "I usually wear Jil Sander, or I wear Marc Jacobs, or I wear Viktor & Rolf.... I love Raf Simons, but I didn't know he was even doing the [Jil Sander] collection."

In New York, Raf's Jil Sander collection is sold at the Jil Sander Store, Bergdorf Goodman, Barney's, Jeffrey, and Linda Dresner. From his Spring 2007, there is a waitlist at Bergdorf's for the Jil Sander sequin skirts and dresses. For Spring 2007 accessories, Barneys and the Jil Sander store sell the collection's bags and shoes, whereas other stores only sell shoes. His first collection for the label, Fall 2006, sold well: the only pieces of Jil Sander that made it to the Barney's Warehouse Sale were the "sharkskin" blazers and a few pairs of pants. The coats, shirts, sweaters, and dressers had sold in the store.

Bridge Collection

He also announced the creation of a second own menswear line, "Raf by Raf Simons", to be launched in 2006.

Walter Van Beirendonck

Walter Van Beirendonck (Brecht, 4 February 1957) is a Flemish fashion designer. He graduated in 1980 from the Royal Arts Academy in Antwerp. Together with Dirk Van Saene, Dries van Noten, Ann Demeulemeester, Marina Yee (graduated in 1981) and Dirk Bikkembergs (graduated in 1982) he became known as the Antwerp Six.

Since 1983, he issues his own collections. They're inspired by the visual arts and literature, but also by nature and ethnic influences. His unusual color combinations and a strong graphic influence are characteristic for his collections. In 1997, he designed the costumes for the U2 "Popmart Tour". In 1999, he was awarded the honorary title of "Cultural Ambassador of Flanders". In 2001, he was the curator for the exhibition Mode 2001 Landed-Geland in Antwerp.

Martin Margiela

Martin Margiela (born April 9, 1957 in Leuven, Belgium) is a Belgian fashion designer. He studied at Antwerp's Royal Academy of Fine Arts, graduated 1980 and worked as a freelance designer for five years after graduation. Between 1985 and 1987 he worked for Jean Paul Gaultier, before showing his first collection under his own label in 1988.

Margiela has a store in the West Village in New York City and also sells at Barneys. In his store, salespeople wear white lab coats.

Nicolas Ghesquiere, the designer of Balenciaga, has said on several occasions that he is a fan of Margiela and often wears Margiela's clothes.

D-squared and Margiela use the same Japanese distributor and thus their sample sales are held together in New York City.

Christopher Bailey (Fashion Designer)

Christopher Bailey is Design Director of the largest British luxury goods brand, Burberry. Born in 1971, Bailey graduated from the BA Fashion Design course at The University of Westminster in 1990, before going on to attend London's Royal College of Art, graduating with a Masters in Fashion in 1994. Moving to New York, he worked for Donna Karan before becoming Senior Designer for Gucci womenswear in 1996.

Christopher Bailey was awarded British Fashion Designer of the Year in 2005. Since his arrival at the label, Burberry has earned a record $167 million in profits.

Burberry

Burberry is a British luxury fashion house, manufacturing clothing and other apparel. Its distinctive check pattern has become one of its most widely copied trademarks. The company has branded stores and franchises around the world, and also sells through concessions in third party stores. It also runs a catalogue business and has a fragrance line. Both HM Queen Elizabeth and HRH The Prince of Wales have granted the company Royal Warrants. Today, Burberry's trademark products are its fashionable handbags and exclusive fragrances. The current Design Director is Christopher Bailey. The First Store to open in Austin, Texas, opened July 13, 2007 at 10:00 am at the Domain

Jane Norman

Jane Norman is an English clothing company, selling clothing aimed at women. In early 2006, Jane Norman reported a 45% rise in profits over 2006, and released plans to open 100 more stores around the country, having already almost doubled their number from the year before, to 116. The company was founded by Norman Freed, who then sold it on to Graphite Capital in 2003 for £70m. On July 30, 2005, the company was purchased by Baugur for £117.4m.

Andrew Groves

Andrew Groves (born February 27, 1968) is an English fashion designer based in London who was notorious during the 1990's for his runway collections at London Fashion Week. His first on schedule show was called "Ourselves Alone", translated Gaelic "Sinn Féin" and Groves sent out his models in a mixture of grey suits, white shirts, orange sashes and charred green taffeta. He mixed the colours of unionism and republicanism. One model poured lighter fluid over her clothes and appeared to set herself on fire. Outside the show were 30 foot burning crucifixes.

His next show Cocaine Nights featured a dress made of razor blades modelled by a model walking on a catwalk of sugarlike cocaine. This was seen as an act of direct provocation at the time since President Bill Clinton had recently deplored the fashion industry's glamourisation of drugs. As well as designing runway collections Groves also designed costumes for Robbie Williams and The Spice girls.

Paul Smith (Fashion Designer)

Sir Paul Smith, RDI, (born in Beeston, Nottingham on July 5, 1946) is an English fashion designer, whose business and reputation is founded upon his menswear. Smith only took up fashion design after having been injured in a cycling accident. He set up his first shop in Nottingham in 1970. He gradually expanded his retail business, being the first fashion brand to open on Floral Street in London's Covent Garden in 1979, where his shop offered an eclectic combination of clothes and 'finds' for men which reflected his own magpie personality. The initial international growth of his business came in Japan, where his British designs have been particularly popular, while he expanded into three adjacent stores on Floral Street. A converted town-house in Notting Hill opened in 1998 now operates as his flagship store, but the company's operational heart remains in Floral Street.

The success of his business has been put down to his understanding of his dual roles of both designer and retailer; the success of his designs is attributed to his combination of the classic and the quirky, which he has described as "Savile Row meets Mr Bean", and which allow men to purchase relatively traditional (and hence commercially popular) designs but which offer a 'twist' of individuality.

Today there are 12 different collections; Paul Smith, Paul Smith Women, PS by Paul Smith, Paul Smith Jeans, Paul Smith London, R.Newbold (Japan only), Paul Smith Accessories, Paul Smith Shoes, Paul Smith Fragrance, Paul Smith Watches, Paul Smith Pens and Paul Smith furniture and 'things'. Designed in Nottingham and London, the Paul Smith collections are primarily produced in England and Italy while the fabrics used are mainly of Italian, French and British origin. The company today boasts annual revenue in excess of £300 million as of 2006.

Smith was knighted by Queen Elizabeth II in 2001, after nearly three decades as a menswear icon. His collections of clothing and accessories for both men and women are usually identified by the presence of Smith's signature multi-coloured pinstripe motif somewhere on each item. Paul Smith is credited with introducing a number of trends within the realms of fashion and 'lifestyle' including the revival of boxer shorts and of the Filofax in the early 1980s.

Paul Smith's collections are wholesaled to thirty five countries and has fourteen shops in England. Paul Smith shops are found in London, Nottingham, Paris, Milan, Moscow, New York, Los Angeles, Hong Kong, Singapore, Taiwan, Thailand, the Philippines, Korea, Kuwait, UAE - and over two hundred throughout Japan. Paul remains fully involved in the Japanese business; designing the clothes, choosing the fabrics, approving the shop locations and overseeing every development within the company. Paul Smith also has impressive and diverse showrooms in London, Paris, Milan, New York and Tokyo.

Smith's menswear collections cater largely to men of tall, slim builds - a niche market that very few high street designers have targeted. Apart from his multi-coloured stripes, Paul Smith has created waves in the fashion world with his "naked lady" designs - pictures of a naked lady "hidden" inside cuffs or wallets, for example.

Likewise the Paul Smith sock collections, which contain some designs that use his signature stripes, are particularly sought after.

Matthew Williamson

Matthew Williamson is an openly gay fashion designer based in the United Kingdom.[1] His collections are shown twice a year during New York Fashion Week, and they often have an Indian influence, perhaps related to the time Williamson spent working in India for the clothing store Monsoon.

He counts celebrities such as Cat Deeley, Sienna Miller, Kelis, Jade Jagger and Plum Sykes amongst his friends, but has often been criticised by others in the fashion industry for using them to promote his designs.

French Connection (clothing)

French Connection is a company founded in the United Kingdom in 1969 which sells clothing and accessories in many parts of the world.

"FCUK"

In April 1997, French Connection began branding their clothes "fcuk" (usually written in lowercase). Large stores are in Leeds and London. Though they insisted it was an acronym for French Connection United Kingdom, its similarity to the word "fuck" caused controversy. French Connection fully exploited this and produced an extremely popular range of t-shirts with messages such as "fcuk this", "hot as fcuk", "mile high fcuk", etc. There were also a number of regionally specific messages, such as "fcuk in hull" (bearing similarity to "fucking hell") and "no fcukin worries" (in Australia). The company recently announced that the "fcuk" label is to be phased out. Apparently they first discovered the acronym when a fax was sent from their Hong Kong store FCHK to FCUK.

In 2001, during the introduction of French Connection in San Francisco, big banners hung on the front of the newly opened store saying "San Francisco's first fcuk."

Mulberry

Mulberry (Morus) is a genus of 10-16 species of deciduous trees native to warm temperate and subtropical regions of Asia, Africa and North America, with the majority of the species native to Asia.

The closely related genus Broussonetia is also commonly known as mulberry, notably the Paper Mulberry Broussonetia papyrifera. Mulberries are fast-growing when young, but soon become slow-growing and rarely exceed 10-15 m tall. The leaves are alternately arranged, simple, often lobed, more often lobed on juvenile shoots than on mature trees, and serrated on the margin. The fruit is a multiple fruit, 2-3 cm long. Mulberries begin as white to pale yellow with pink edges. They are red when ripening. A fully ripened mulberry is dark purple to black, edible, and sweet with a good flavor in several species.

Azzedine Alaia

Azzedine Alaia (Arabic:?? ????? ????? , original - Alaïa, pronunciation - Aliya) is a Tunisian-born fashion designer, most successful in the 1980s. Azzedine Alaia was born in Tunis, Tunisia in 1940. He studied sculpture at the Ecole des Beaux-Arts, Tunis. After his graduation, Alaia began working as a dressmaker's assistant. Alaia soon began dressing private clients, and in 1957 Alaia moved to Paris to work in fashion design. In Paris he worked for Guy Laroche for two seasons and for Thierry Mugler until the late 1970s. In 1980 he produced his first ready-to-wear line and was voted Best Designer of the Year by the French Ministry of Culture. By 1988 he had opened boutiques in Beverly Hills, New York, and Paris. His seductive, clinging clothes were a massive success, and he was named by the media 'The King of Cling'. Stars such as Tina Turner, Raquel Welch, Madonna, Brigitte Nielsen, Naomi Campbell, and Stephanie Seymour were all regular customers of Alaia's.

Alaia was referenced in the mid-90's teen hit Clueless starring Alicia Silverstone. When mugged at gunpoint, Silverstone's charecter protests to kneeling in a parking lot because she is wearing one of the famous clingy dresses designed by the "totally important designer."

In the mid-1990s, Alaia virtually vanished from the fashion scene. His clothes are available in Barneys New York alongside

Proenza Schouler, Balenciaga, and Dolce & Gabbana. His shoes are sold at Bergdorf Goodman. Carine Roitfeld was photographed during February 2007 fashion week in one of his coats, wwith the New York Times declaring that she was the only woman at any of the fall 2007 shows that "looked like the future." Victoria Beckham stated that Alaia is her favourite designer and wore the designer's work, a gift from husband David Beckham, to two Academy Award parties in February 2007.

Coco Chanel

Gabrielle Bonheur "Coco" Chanel (August 19, 1883 - January 10, 1971) was a pioneering French fashion designer whose modernist philosophy, menswear-inspired fashions, and pursuit of expensive simplicity made her arguably the most important figure in the history of 20th-century fashion. Her influence on haute couture was such that she was the only person in the field to be named on TIME Magazine's 100 most influential people of the 20th century

Jacques Doucet (fashion designer)

Jacques Doucet (1853 - 1929) was a French fashion designer, known for his elegant dresses, made with flimy translucent materials in superimposing pastel colors.

He was born in Paris in 1853 to a prosperous family whose lingerie and fine linens business, Doucet Lingerie, had flourushed in the Rue de la Paix since 1816. In 1871, Doucet opened a salon selling ladies apparel. An enthusiastic collector of eighteenth-century furniture, objets d'art, paintings and sculptures, many of his gowns were strongly influenced by this opulent era. A designer of taste and discrimination, Doucet valued dignity and luxury above novelty and practicality and therefore gradually went out of popularity during the 1920s. By far his most original designs were those he created for actresses of the time. Cecile Sorel, Rejane and Sarah Bernhardt (for whom he designed her famous white costume in L'Aiglon) all often wore his outfits, both on and off the stage. For the aforementioned actresses he reserved a particular style, one which consisted of frills, sinuous curving lines and lace ruffles the colors of faded flowers.

A passionate collector of art and literature throughout his life, by the time of his death he had a magnificent collection of Post-Impressionist and Cubist paintings (including "Les Demoiselles d'Avignon", which he bought direct from Picasso's studio), as well as two libraries of manuscripts by contemporary writers, both of which he left to the French nation.

While little-remembered today, in his time he was equalled to the likes of Charles Worth and Jeanne Paquin and even now is remembered by fashion historians as one of the great old masters of fashion design.

Charles Jourdan

Charles Jourdan (1883-1976) was a French fashion designer born in the same year as Coco Chanel, and known best for his designs of women's shoes starting in 1919. His name reached its greatest notoriety in the years since his death under the leadership of his sons, first with an emphasis on the use of innovative materials and later for more conservative designs. After 2000 the company went into decline and was sold to investment bankers.

Originally trained as a shoemaker, after World War I Jourdan opened a shoe shop in Romans in the Drome region of France, the center of France's shoe industry. His lines of women's shoes prospered, and this became the focus of his career. After only two years Jourdan moved his shoe company into a factory on Boulevard Voltaire in 1921 and employed over 30 people in Romans.

In the 1930s, Jourdan was the first shoe designer to place advertisements in the high-end fashion magazines, which helped to identify his name as a haute couture house. In 1947 his three sons Rene, Charles and Roland joined the company, and in 1950 they expanded beyond France and began selling designer shoes in the United Kingdom.

Jourdan and his sons opened his first boutique in Paris in 1957, although the company headquarters remained in Romans. They were granted a license to design and manufacture shoes under the Christian Dior brand in 1959 and in more recent years have also created designs under the Pierre Cardin label.

The company has for many years focused on being viewed as setting trends and innovating in fashion design, and it can be debated whether Herbert Levine and Beth Levine inspired this innovation or learned from it; both may be true. Jourdan and the Levines are arguably the most innovative designers to use new materials in women's shoes in the period since World War II. In the 1960s and early 1970s Jourdan used its magazine advertising campaigns to advance its avant-garde image by using imagery from the surrealist photographer Guy Bourdin. In 1975 ready-to-wear clothing and handbags were added to the Jourdan line, although the company has remained best-known for its shoes.

Charles Jourdan died in 1976, but the company continued under the leadership of his sons. During this decade Roland Jourdan began to lead the company's designs, taking the basic pump, lengthening the toe and adding simple buckles to increase both its delicacy and its tailored image. By this time Jourdan boutiques were open in major cities across Europe and in North America. Roland Jourdan retired in 1981, and the company subsequently was known for more conservative designs.

Jourdan gained unintended publicity from the exposure of Imelda Marcos' excesses in shoe fashion in 1986, among them many Jourdan stilettos. The company has also created a limited number of perfumes, including a scent called Stiletto (after the stiletto heel) in 1996 to recognize the 75th anniversary of the firm. To honor Paris the bottle was shaped like the Eiffel Tower.

The flagship store for the Romans-based manufacturer was moved to the Champs-Elysees in Paris in 1999, but it remained open for less than two years due to financial troubles caused by a switch in emphasis from design to retailing. In mid 2002 the company filed for bankruptcy with over $9 million in debt and was reorganized as the Jourdan family sold its stake to a Luxembourg investment fund, Lux Diversity. Sales had fallen to only 65,000 pairs per year.

Patrick Cox, a Canadian who had launched his own shoe label, was named head designer of Charles Jourdan in 2003. In 2005 he left the firm and was replaced by Josephus Thimister.

Christian Louboutin

Christian Louboutin (born 1963) is a well known French shoe designer.

Biography

Christian Louboutin was interested in women's fashion since he was a small child. In 1979, as he was walking alongside the streets of Paris, he noticed a billboard that instructed women tourists not to scratch the wooden floor in front of the Museum of Oceanic Art.

Louboutin felt personally bothered by this sign and, as a consequence, he would draw shoes with compressed buckles and with soles. He admits to having spent a lot of time as a Teenager drawing these types of shoes in his school notebooks. These shoes would become the base of Louboutin's sales as a designer.

Later on, Louboutin began attending parties and dance halls in Paris, offering his shoes to women at these events and venues. Most of the ladies rejected his shoes, claiming to have no money. Louboutin then decided to attend various designing schools, such as Chanel's and Saint Laurent's.

Louboutin later opened a boutique shop in Paris; his store became distinguished not only because of his clientele, but also because he offered free coffee to shoppers. Such other sellers as American company Neiman Marcus began to sell Louboutin's designs. Louboutin shoes also have a trademark red leather sole, making them instantly recognizable.

Louboutin, who has been interviewed by fashion reporters such as Jacques Brunel, has seen his celebrity status expand to such places like Monte Carlo, Singapore and the United States, among others. He includes Princess Caroline of Monaco and Catherine Deneuve among his friends.

Christian Louboutin currently has 3 boutiques in the United States. Two can be found in New York. One location is Downtown on Horatio Street and the other is on Madison Avenue. The third location is in Beverly Hills, California.

Paul Poiret

Paul Poiret (20 April 1879, Paris, France - 30 April 1944, Paris) was a fashion designer based in Paris before the First World War, during the Belle Epoque. He was taken on by the fashion designer

Jacques Doucet as a draftsman. When he completed his apprenticeship with the House of Worth in 1904 he opened up his own fashion house, and by 1905-07 had produced a revolutionary style.

He was famous for designing luxurious oriental and Art Deco gowns. He also launched the suspender belt, flesh-colored stockings, culottes, and the modern brassiere. About his creation of the hobble skirt, he said, "It was in the name of Liberty that I proclaimed the fall of the corset and the adoption of the brassiere which, since then, has won the day. Yes, I freed the bust, but I shackled the legs." He also presented the first sheath and sack dresses. Moreover, Poiret was noted his use of vibrant primary colors, breaking from the soft colors common during the late Edwardian period. "He was the first couturier to launch his own perfume[,] named Rosine, after his oldest daughter."

Poiret's signature was the rose, which was a decorative motif on his label and appeared periodically on his creations (lapels and elsewhere). His rose most often designated a piece of which he was particularly proud. Paul Iribe, a graphic artist and jewelery designer was hired to design Poiret's label, which was a simple rose drawing accompanied by the text, "Paul Poiret a Paris."

Poiret was notorious for throwing lavish parties and plays featuring his designs. For one of his famous parties, the June 24, 1911, "The Thousand and Second Night" (based on The Arabian Nights), he required his over 300 guests to dress in Oriental costuming. Improperly dressed guests were requested to either outfit themselves in some of Poiret's 'Persian' outfits or to leave.

In 1909, Raoul Dufy was commissioned by Poiret to design stationery for the house, and also designed textile patterns used in Poiret's garments.

Pauline Trigere

Pauline Trigere (1909-2002) was a French-born fashion designer, known for her crisp, tailored cuts and innovative ideas.

The daughter of a tailor, Trigère was able to operate a sewing machine by age 10 and often assisted her dressmaker mother. Shortly after leaving school, Pauline was employed as a trainee cutter at

Martial et Armand in the Place Vendôme, Paris. While there, she met American buyer Adele Simpson, who told her about the wonders of the New York fashion world. In 1937, aged 25, she moved to New York where she first found work at Ben Gerschel and later became assistant designer at Hattie Carnegie.

In 1942, Trigère decided to open her own fashion house, which was managed by her brother Robert. Her first small collection of 12 custom-made dresses was bought by a group of US department store executives and by 1945, Trigère was a respected New York label. She began producing ready-to-wear lines during the late 1940s. In the 1950s she started to produce costume jewelry to accompany her outfits, like many other fashion houses at the time. Her clientele included many famous women such as the Duchess of Windsor, actress Claudette Colbert and singer Lena Horne. Trigère is also known for designing Patricia Neal's sophisticated wardrobe in Breakfast at Tiffany's. Today, Trigere's vintage dresses and jewelry are greatly sought-after and have been worn recently by the likes of Winona Ryder.

Max Mara

Max Mara, or The House of Max Mara, is an upscale, luxury Italian women's fashion house most famous today for its high-fashion ready-to-wear clothing.

History

Achille Maramotti was born on January 7, 1927 in Reggio Emilia in Italy. At 20, Maramotti began designing couture clothing and officially established the Max Mara House in 1951. Originally the fashion house specialized in men's formal wear, however has since become a women's fashion house.

Today, Max Mara is one of the largest and most popular Italian fashion houses. Max Mara has spawned nearly 20 labels under its name, however, Max Mara's luxury women wear remains the most profitable while its trendy, youth Max&Co. division is also gaining international popularity. In 2005, the Max Mara Fashion Group generated over $1 billion in revenues.

According to Forbes Rich List of 2005, Maramotti was one of the world's richest men with a fortune of $2.1 billion. Maramotti passed away at 78 on January 12 of 2005. Max Mara remains as one of the most influential brands in fashion today and Maramotti's two sons are now the chief executives, managers, and artistic directors.

The company currently operates 25 boutiques in the United States in Arizona, California, Florida, Georgia, Hawaii, Illinois, Maryland, Massachusetts, Michigan, Nevada, New Jersey, New York, Texas, Virginia, and Washington. The fashion house's major competitors include Dior, Prada, and Gucci.

Franco Moschino

Francisco Moschino (born February 27, 1950 - September 18, 1994) was an Italian fashion designer remembered for his unusual designs.

He was born in Abbiategrasso, Lombardy, Italy, located 14 miles from Milan. Before becoming a fashion designer, he attended Accademia delle Belle Arti in Milan to study fine arts in 1967 hoping to become a painter. To finance his studies, he worked as a freelance fashion illustrator. Eventually, his interest shifted from paints and canvases to fabric and tailoring. His fashion career began in 1971 when he became an illustrator for Gianni Versace, and continued to work for him for another six years. In 1977 he became a designer for Cadette.

He found his own company Moonshadow in 1983, and launched Moschino Couture in the same year. At first, he designed casualwear and jeans, but his line eventually expanded to lingerie, eveningwear, shoes, menswear and perfumes. In 1988, he launched a less expensive Cheap and Chic line. His designs were very innovative and unusual such as quilted black denim miniskirt with plastic fried eggs decorating the hemline, quilted jacket decorated with bottle tops, plug-socket drop earrings, and bodices made out of safety pins. Because of this, he dubbed as Jean-Paul Gaultier of Italian fashion for his highly innovative designs but their styles are different; while Gaultier experiments with different fabrics and shapes, Moschino used basic forms and traditional methods. He also spoofed high fashion lines through his clothes. For example, "Expensive jacket" was embroidered in gold across the back of a cashmere jacket, and "Bull chic" on a matador-styled outfit. He also mocked the fashion classics such as the Chanel jacket with garish trimmings and details. Ironically, people rushed to wear his clothes, thus becoming successful and famous in the industry he satirized. Since his early death in 1994, Rosella Jardini has directed Moschino which continues to be popular to this date. His clothes are worn by celebrities such as Gwyneth Paltrow, Alicia Silverstone, and Anna Friel.

Emilio Pucci

Emilio Pucci, Marchese di Barsento (November 20, 1914 - 1992) was an Italian fashion designer.

Fashion Career

Born in Florence, Italy, the son of an Italian marchese, Pucci studied in both Italy and the USA, eventually gaining a doctorate in political science in 1941. Pucci was a member of the Italian olympic ski team of 1934, and in 1935 won a skiing scholarship to Reed College in Oregon. He first ventured into clothing design at Reed by creating the ski team's uniforms. He graduated from Reed with the class of 1937.

In 1947 he was photographed by Toni Frissell, a photographer working for Harper's Bazaar, wearing skiwear Pucci had designed himself. Upon learning this, Frissell's editor asked Pucci to design skiwear for a story on European Winter Fashion, which ran in the winter 1948 issue of the Bazaar

The exposure encouraged him to create and sell clothes for women, and he opened a couture house in 1950 on the Isle of Capri and also expanded with a couture location in Rome. Pucci became well known for his signature use of bright colours, bold patterns, and striking designs. Popular early creations were a line of wrinkle-free printed silk dresses and the still popular Capri pants.

From 1954 to 1968 he designed flight attendant uniforms for Braniff Airlines. These avant-garde creations were designed as individual components to be added or removed as weather dictated.

The uniforms included turtlenecks, t-shirts, crop jackets and culottes. Among the more unusual innovations was a "bubble helmet" a clear plastic hood worn by flight attendants between terminal building and aircraft to protect their hairdos from rain and the blast of jet engines.

Political Career

In addition to his life of fashion, Pucci was elected to the Italian Parliament. While a Member of Parliament, Pucci was hired by New York ad agency Jack Tinker and Associates to re-design the hostess wardrobes for Braniff International Airways. Pucci would end up designing seven complete outfits for Braniff hostesses, pilots and ground crew between 1965 and 1977. Pucci incorporated Alexander Girard's "BI" logo into some of his prints.

Elsa Schiaparelli

Elsa Schiaparelli (September 10, 1890 - November 13, 1973) was a Parisian fashion designer of the 1920s and 1930s. She was born in Rome, Italy, of Italian and Egyptian heritage. She was a great-niece of Giovanni Schiaparelli, who discovered the canals of Mars.

Career

Elsa Schiaparelli was one of the most influential clothing designers of the 20th Century. Schiaparelli opened her first salon, "pour le Sport," in 1927, and as the name indicates specialized in sportswear. In 1931, her design of a divided tennis skirt for star player Lili de Alvarez shocked the staid tennis world when Alvarez wore what was the forerunner of shorts at the Wimbledon Championships. Schiaparelli became famous for her black knit sweaters with a white bowtie pattern sewn into the sweater. She had a flair for the unusual and even hired Salvador Dalí to design fabric, producing a white dress with a lobster print. Schiaparelli was the first to use shoulder pads, animal print fabrics (in 1947), and zippers dyed the same colors as the fabrics. She is also well known for her surrealist designs of the 1930s, especially her hats, including the Dalí design resembling a giant shoe and one a giant lamb chop, both which were famously worn by the Franco-American Singer sewing machine heiress Daisy Fellowes, who was one of Schiaparelli's best clients and who owned a pink gemstone that inspired the color shocking pink. She collaborated with many surrealist artists, Salvador Dalí, Jean Cocteau, and Alberto Giacometti, between 1936 and 1939.

She designed a number of perfumes in addition to clothing; the first and most famous of which, named Shocking, was created in 1936. Shocking is famous less for the fragrance itself than for its packaging: besides a box colored a shocking pink, the bottle itself was in the shape of a woman's torso, based on the curvaceous body of one of Schiaparelli's clients, film star Mae West. For West, she designed costumes for the film Every Day's a Holiday (1938). She also designed Zsa Zsa Gabor's costumes for the film Moulin Rouge (1952). In 1935 Schiaparelli moved to a salon overlooking the Place Vendome in Paris. Her output slowed by World War II and with title of trendsetter going to younger designers such as Christian Dior. In 1954, her couture house declared bankruptcy and she moved to the United States.

Schiap, as she was known to her friends, also designed costume jewelry. She was known for her vivid use of color and juxtaposition of shapes and textures. Schiap collectors seek Schiaparelli clothing, including lambs wool or fur coats, scarves, hats, shoes, perfume bottles, advertisements by Vertes and more.

She was briefly married to Count William de Wendt de Kerlor (1883-), a Franco-Swiss psychic medium once described as "a persuasive but inconstant Theosophist", and moved with him to Greenwich Village in New York City, where she sold clothing designed by the French couturier Paul Poiret. They had one child, Maria Luisa Yvonne Radha, known as Gogo, who was born in New York City in 1919.

Nicola Trussardi

Nicola Trussardi (June 17, 1942 - April 15, 1999) was an Italian fashion designer and entrepreneur.

Career. Trussardi was born in Bergamo, Lombardy. A graduate in economics at the Catholic University of Milan, in 1970 he took over his family's glove-making business founded in 1910 by his grandfather Dante Trussardi, and turned it into a major company that helped contribute to the popularity of the made-in-Italy label throughout the world. He expanded Trussardi's product line beyond gloves to include luxury accessories, and in 1973 he created Trussardi's spiky greyhound logo. A few years later, Trussardi launched a line of leather jackets, the first step toward a ready-to-wear line which, by the 1980s, encompassed womenswear, menswear, sportswear and children's wear.

Trussardi's Fashion House has a remarkably wide range of design activities: it has designed interiors for the airline company Alitalia, cars for Alfa Romeo, telephones, and even helicopters. In 1988, it outfitted the Italian athletes competing in the 1988 Olympic Games in Seoul, Korea. Trussardi was killed when he lost control of his Ferrari and hit a lamp post; he died instantly in Milan.

Initiatives

Trussardi has undertaken many other initiatives, including the creation of the Palatrussardi in Milan, which has hosted a number of pop and rock concerts, including that of Frank Sinatra, Liza Minnelli, and Sammy Davis, Jr. Other projects included a specially fitted-out Mini, produced by Innocenti.

The Nicola Trussardi Foundation is a no profit institution for the promotion of contemporary art and culture. Under the direction of president Beatrice Trussardi. Since 2003 the Foundation has decided to concentrate its resources on the realization of contemporary art events in the public spaces of the city of Milano.

Donatella Versace

Donatella Versace (born May 2, 1955) is an affluent Italian fashion designer, like her famous brother, Gianni Versace, the founder of the Versace clothing empire. Her current title is Vice-President of the Versace Group and Chief Designer of the fashion line. She holds a great amount of Versace stock, totalling 20% of the entire stock market assets of Versace. Her brother, Santo Versace, owns 30%. Donatella's daughter Allegra Versace got 50% of the company stocks after Gianni Versace died, the two were very close and he testamented his half to Allegra.

Biography

Early life and fashion debut

Donatella Versace was born in the Italian city of Reggio di Calabria, the youngest of three children in her family, her father being a personal financier to the Italian aristocracy. In the mid 1970s, Donatella followed her 25-year older brother, Giovanni ("Gianni"), to pursue knitwear design in Florence, Italy. Donatella had planned to work for her brother as Public Relations, but she was more valuable to Gianni as a "muse and critic", according to Donatella during an interview with Vogue. Through her closeness to her brother's enterprises, Donatella plunged into the fashion world. A decade later, during the 1980s, Gianni launched a perfume dedicated to her, Blonde, and gave her her own diffusion label, Versus, which remains a well-known Versace inner line.

The growth of Donatella and Versace

Donatella is accredited as the first designer to use notable celebrities to broadcast her clothing into the world on the catwalk and other public mediums such as advertisements, instead of using unknown models. Another member of the growing Versace success was Santo Versace S.p.A., Donatella's brother, who is also a fashion designer and the owner of Finanziaria Versace, an established Versace branch. Donatella soon proved to be the public relations giant within the Versace label and spread its name throughout Europe and most of the United States. Donatella chose to place some of her good friends, Madonna, Christina Aguilera and Demi Moore, in high esteem in the Versace advertising sector, making them and other A-List celebrities the persona and image of Versace.

Tragedy in Miami

On July 15, 1997, outside the re-constructed Versace Mansion, also known as Casa Casuarina, in Miami, Florida, Gianni Versace was shot dead by Andrew Cunanan, a suspected serial-killer who committed suicide before apprehension was possible. Her brother's murder was not only a blow to the South Beach, Miami community but also to the fashion industry. Donatella and other family patriarchs temporarily moved the family to a secluded, private resort in the Caribbean. Consequently, the Spring-Summer 1998 Collection was cancelled as were the indirect operations of the company. The Official Funeral of Gianni Versace was held at the Roman Catholic Milan Cathedral in Milan, Italy, where over 2,000 mourners attended a traditional service, which was originally highly controversial. Notable guests in attendance were Diana Princess of Wales, Sir Elton John, Naomi Campbell, Giorgio Armani, Carolyn Bessette-Kennedy, Sting, Luciano Pavarotti, Carla Fendi, Karl Lagerfeld and many other famous fashion designers. Elton John and Sting sang a setting of Psalm 23, "The Lord is My Shepherd", broadcast to millions of viewers worldwide.

Promotion and success

A year and three days after Gianni's death in July 1998, Donatella Versace mounted her first couture show for the Versace Atelier at the Hotel Ritz Paris. She built her runway over the hotel's swimming pool, as her brother had done every season, though this time using sheer glass. She now oversees the production of a dozen collections each year, though these days, Donatella is just as famous for her celebrity entourage and glittering parties. Regular guests include Sir Elton John, Liz Hurley, Catherine Zeta-Jones and Kate Moss. Even Prince Charles attends Donatella's parties for the famous and elite throughout Europe.

Branching into other fields, the company has created the grand, luxurious Palazzo Versace resort on the Gold Coast of Australia. Another growing symbol of the Versace style, the world's tallest hotel, the Burj al-Arab in Dubai, United Arab Emirates (UAE), boasts a broad collection of Versace furniture and beddings in its expensive and lavish rooms.

Plans for the Palazzo Versace Dubai were announced in May of 2005. Gianni Versace SpA, Sunland Group Ltd. and Emirates International Holdings have announced the Palazzo Versace resort to be constructed in the Arabian Bays on the Dubai Creek in Dubai, United Arab Emirates. The second Palazzo Versace will boast a number of suites and luxury villas, including an exclusive spa. Official plans are to begin construction in 2006 and have the hotel completed sometime in the year 2008. The interior of the hotel will be furnished with various Versace collections. As Creative Director, Donatella will carry out final plans and design strategies for the hotel and resort compound. This will be the second Pallazo Versace hotel ever to be built, and the second hotel in Dubai to boast a wide range of Versace collections.

In October of 2002, Gianni and Donatella's most famously designed Versace clothing were displayed in a special exhibit of the historical Victoria and Albert Museum of London to be honored for extraordinary fashion success and symbolism worldwide.

Gianni Versace

Gianni Versace (December 2, 1946 - July 15, 1997) was an accomplished Italian designer of both clothing and theater costumes. He was influenced by Andy Warhol, Ancient Roman and Greek art as well as modern abstract art; he is considered one of the most colorful and talented designers of the late 20th century.

Gianni was the founder of famous fashion tag Versace. The first boutique was opened in Milan's Via della Spiga in 1978, and its popularity was immediate. Today, Versace is one of the world's leading international fashion houses.

Versace designs, markets and distributes luxury clothing, accessories, fragrances, makeup and home furnishings under the various brands of the Versace Group.

Biography

Early life

Gianni Versace was born in Reggio di Calabria, Italy, where he grew up with his older siblings Santo and Donatella, along with their father and dressmaker mother, Francesca.

Gianni began his apprenticeship at a young age, helping his mother find precious stones and gold braid with which to embroider dresses. He studied architecture before moving to Milan at the age of 25 to work in fashion design.

In the mid-Seventies, his knits drew the attention of head-hunters at Genny and Callaghan. Complice hired him to design their leather and suede collections, and a few years later, encouraged by his success, Versace presented his first signature collection for women at the Palazzo della Permanente Art Museum of Milan. His first menswear collection followed in September of the same year. After presenting his menswear collection he joined Jorge Saud, who would become later, also partner with Giorgio Armani.

Personal Life

Gianni Versace met a model Antonio D'Amico (born 1959 in southern Italy, raised in Milan) in 1982. The couple embarked on a long-term relationship that lasted 11 years, until Versace's untimely death. During that time Antonio worked as designer for the Versace sports line.

Versace's will left his male partner D'Amico with a pension of 50 million lire (about $33,000) a month (for life), and the right to live in any of Versace's homes in Italy and the United States. D'Amico now runs his own fashion design company.

Death

One July morning in the summer of 1997, returning from his customary walk on Ocean Drive, he was gunned down outside his ocean-front mansion in Miami Beach, Florida. He was murdered by spree killer Andrew Cunanan, who committed suicide shortly after the murder. Police reported that Andrew Cunanan had committed suicide using the same handgun that had been used to murder Gianni Versace. Versace was buried in Lake Como, Italy.

In September 1997, Versace's brother Santo Versace, together with Jorge Saud were announced as the new CEOs of the Versace holding. Gianni's sister, Donatella Versace, is the new head of design. Elton John dedicated his 1997 album The Big Picture to Versace.

Hussein Chalayan

Hussein Chalayan MBE (or, in keeping with the original spelling of his name, Hüseyin Ça?layan) (born 1970) is a British/ Turkish Cypriot fashion designer.

He was born in Nicosia (Lefko?a in Turkish) in 1970. He graduated from the Turkish Maarif College of his hometown, and his family having moved to England in 1982, obtained British citizenship and later studied design in London. While finishing his studies at the Central St. Martin's School of Art in 1993, his senior year collection, "The Tangent Flows", was displayed in Browns Windows.

In 1995, Chalayan beat 100 competitors to clinch a top London fashion design award. In the contest, organised by the company "Absolut", Chalayan, aged 25, won financial backing to the tune of £28,000 (GBP) to develop creations for the British capital's Fashion Week in October 1995.

Along with his own line, he also recently designed for TSE knitwear. His personality is calmer than his fellow British designers, yet his shows can be thought provoking and intense. His designs, which can be based on experiments and even abstractions of existing items such as meteorological charts, are often minimal and elegant.

Twice named 'British Designer of the Year', Chalayan also won much praise from trade publications around the world. He remains highly innovative and active, busy and present in various centers of the fashion business, especially in London and ?stanbul, the last being the hometown of yet another famous name in the business, R?fat Ozbek.

Chalayan was created a Member of the Order of the British Empire (MBE) on 17 June 2006. His father, Ata, runs the Park House Guest House in Warwick.

Alexander McQueen

Alexander McQueen CBE (born Lee Alexander McQueen, 17 March 1969) is an English fashion designer.

Biography

Born in the East End of London, the son of a taxi driver, McQueen started making dresses for his three sisters at a young age and announced his intention of becoming a fashion designer.

Career

McQueen left school at 16, landing himself an apprenticeship with Savile Row tailors Anderson & Sheppard, then working for Gieves & Hawkes and the famous theatrical costumiers Angels and Bermans. Whilst on Savile Row, McQueen's clients included Mikhail Gorbachev and Charles, Prince of Wales. At the age of 20, he spent a period of time working for Koji Tatsuno before traveling to Milan, Italy and working for Romeo Gigli.

McQueen returned to London in 1994 and applied to London's most prestigious fashion school, Central Saint Martins College of Art and Design to work as a pattern cutter tutor. Due to the strength of his portfolio he was persuaded by the Head of the Masters course to enroll on the course as a student. He received his Masters degree in Fashion design and famously, his graduation collection was bought in its entirety by influential fashion stylist Isabella Blow, who was said to have persuaded McQueen to change his name from Lee to Alexander (his middle name) when he subsequently launched his fashion career.

Design history

McQueen's early runway collections developed his reputation for controversy and shock tactics (earning the title "enfant terrible" and "the hooligan of English fashion"), with trousers aptly named "bumsters", and a collection entitled "Highland Rape". It has also been claimed that he was on income support and that he needed to change his name for his first show so that he could continue to receive benefits.

Givenchy appointment

The president of LVMH, Bernard Arnault caused a stir when he instated McQueen as head designer at Givenchy in 1996, succeeding John Galliano. Upon arrival at Givenchy, McQueen had the nerve to insult the founder by calling him 'irrelevant'. Thus, his first couture collection with Givenchy was unsatisfactory, with even McQueen telling Vogue in October 1997 that the collection was "crap". McQueen toned down his act at Givenchy, but continued to indulge his rebellious streak, causing controversy in Autumn 1998 with a show which included car-robots spraying paint over white cotton dresses, and double amputee model Aimee Mullins striding down the catwalk on intricately carved wooden legs. McQueen stayed with Givenchy until March 2001, when the contract he said was "constraining his creativity" was ended.

Accomplishments

Some of Alexander McQueen's accomplishments include being one of the youngest designers to achieve the title "British Designer of the Year", which he won three times between 1996 and 2003. He has also been awarded the CBE, as well as being named International Designer of the Year at the Council of Fashion Designer Awards. December 2000 saw a new partnership for McQueen with Gucci Group acquiring 51% of the company, and McQueen serving as Creative Director. Plans for expansion have included the opening of stores in London, Milan, and New York, and the launch of his perfumes Kingdom, and more recently My Queen. In 2005, McQueen collaborated with Puma to create a special line of sneakers for the shoe brand.

Personal life

In the summer of 2000, McQueen married his twenty-four-year-old lover George Forsyth, a documentary filmmaker. The ceremony, which took place in Ibiza on a yacht owned by a friend of supermodel Kate Moss (who was also bridesmaid), was covered by the press in much the same way as any other celebrity wedding.

Luella Bartley

Luella Bartley is a London-based designer who launched an upscale women's clothing line in 1999. Her collections, shown in New York since 2001, often feature a fusion of street style and preppy sophistication.

In January 2006, Bartley became the first designer to create an affordable collection of women's apparel and accessories for Target Corporation's GO International line, focusing on oversized sunglasses and kitschy prints. Bartley's designs were regularly featured in defunct teen fashion magazine ELLEgirl.

Current Life As of 2007

Luella Bartley was born in 1974 in the English town of Stratford-upon-Avon, the birthplace of Shakespeare. The graduate of Central

Saint Martins short-lived British Vogue editor still lives in London today. She resides in the company of her fashion-photographer boyfriend, David Sims, and their two children, Kip and Stevie. She has also been showing in New York since 2001. Bartley's early and first few shows featured friends like Sadie Frost walked the catwalk while model pal, Kate Moss, watched and supported from the front row. Her interests include surfing and horseback riding.

Career

Luella attended Central Saint Martins for a short time, which led her to the fashion journalism course at the college. Luella got her start in the fashion industry with a steady job in the fashion department at The Evening Standard(an English newspaper). While there, she made her way up through the ranks, and after four years, she got a job at British Vogue where she worked for a yeah and a half. Luella's first collection (for S/S 2000), named 'Daddy I Want a Pony', was informal and held at her friend's flat. Indeed, it was hard to distinguish between the guests and the models. Luella eventually made her London Fashion Week debut in February 2000. Her line picked up momentum with licensing deals with Italian maufacturers tat allowed her to expand her brand's presence to the point where models like Gisele Bundchen were opening the AW'02 show at NY Fashion Week. Her profile was further enhanced by her partnership with British leathergoods company Mulberry, for whom she designed a line of bags. Following the success of the collaboration, Bartley signed a deal with majority Mulberry shareholder Club 21 to produce a small line of accessories that eventually grew to include clothing and a complete accessory collection. Luella has also collaborated with Vans, Churches, Sony and M.A.C. In 2006 she won the Designer of the year from both Elle and Glamour Magazine, and acheived a nomination for Designer of The Year at the British Fashion Awards.

The Label

Since the launch of her line in 1999, Bartley's London-based design has consistently delivered. She is best known for her fluent street-chic aesthetic, to the "squaky-clean badasses and pretty punks." Serving as her internal muse, is the compliant Brit "It" girl who just loves to be adorned in nothing less than a classic pink button-down shirt-usually tucked into skintight jeans or-another favorite, under one of Bartley's signature striped sweaters. Bartley is known for her eclectic theme combinations of "punk motorcycle jackets with gingham skirts; little black dresses with pearls for polka dots; preppy navy, red, and white."

Collections

'Dial F for Fluoro', a show which helped launched 2001's trend for graffiti chic. This collection completely commenced brand awareness to an international level. At this point, Bartley hailed as London's hot, young, and fresh designer. Bartley decided to take a risk and began, what is now called 'The Luella Roadshow.' She bascially takes her team and shows at venues in Milan and New York. The titles, as Luella later explained, of her shows are a hangover from her earlier days in journalism. Bartley was also asked, by Bottega Veneta to present her collection 'Looking Hard in the Yard' in Milan for the autumn/ winter2000 season.

John Galliano

John Galliano, CBE, RDI, (born November 28, 1960) is a British-Gibraltarian fashion designer.

Early life and career

Born Juan Carlos Antonio Galliano in Gibraltar to a Gibraltarian father and a Spanish mother, he moved to London as a child and attended Wilson's School in Wallington. In 1984, he graduated in fashion design from St. Martin's School of Arts, with a collection inspired by the French Revolution called Les Incroyables, that received positive reviews and was bought in its entirety and sold in the London fashion boutique Browns. Following that, he started his own label under his name and began his career as a fashion designer. He was awarded British Designer of the Year in 1987, 1994 and 1995. In 1997, he shared the award with Alexander McQueen, his successor at Givenchy. Fashion guru Susannah Constantine has worked for Galliano in the past.

Career

In the 1990s, Galliano relocated to Paris in search of financial backing and a strong client base. In 1995, he was appointed as the designer of Givenchy by Bernard Arnault owner of luxury goods congolmerate LVMH, thus becoming the first British designer to head a French haute couture house. Less than two years later, on October 14, 1996, LVMH moved Galliano to Christian Dior. His first couture show for Dior coincided with the label's 50th anniversary, on January 20, 1997.

He has been quoted as identifying his love of theatre and femininity as central to his creations "my role is to seduce" he has said. Galliano has reputedly cited Charlize Theron as a muse and has been creating couture dresses for her to wear to red carpet events such as the 2006 Academy Awards and the 2005 Golden Globes. She is also part of the ad campaign for Dior's "J'Adore" perfume, while Riley Keough, granddaughter of Elvis Presley, fronts his "Miss Dior Cherie" perfume, and Kate Moss, in photographs by Nick Knight, his ready-to-wear campaigns. Cate Blanchett and Nicole Kidman have also worn dresses created by him to the Academy Awards in the past. Currently, between his own label and Dior, Galliano produces six couture and ready-to-wear collections a year and a new mid-season range under his own name "G Galliano".

Personal life

Galliano says he follows a rigorous exercise regime which sees him rise at 6am each morning to complete a gruelling, 40-minute aerobic session with his personal trainer, before embarking on a 10-minute stretch, doing 150 push-ups and a six-mile jog along the banks of the Seine River. "Working flat out, it was a necessary step to take," he once said. "It helps to concentrate the mind and I find that I have so much more energy and focus." In 2000, he said that he also had found his inspiration for the couture collection of boho-meets-hobo chic he unveiled that January during his jogging sessions, when running past the homeless people lining the river. He added that he hoped to expose the pure decadence of couture by "turning it inside out". Similarities between Galliano and the fictional amoral fashion designer Mugatu, with his "Derelicte" homeless fashion show, from the movie Zoolander have been pointed out by some comentators.

Vivienne Westwood

Dame Vivienne Westwood, DBE, RDI, (born Vivienne Isabel Swire in the village of Tintwistle in Glossop, Derbyshire, on 8 April

1941) is an English fashion designer largely responsible for modern punk and new wave fashions[1].

She is linked with the Sex Pistols via Malcolm McLaren and their SEX/Seditionaries boutique on King's Road, in London during the 1970s.

Biography

Westwood was seventeen when her parents bought a post office in the North of England. She studied at the Harrow School of Art (later to become the University of Westminster) for one term. Vivienne went on to attend Trent Park College and later taught at a primary school in North London. She loved teaching.

Vivienne's first husband was Derek Westwood, with whom she had one child named Ben. Their marriage lasted three years before she met Malcolm McLaren, later known for being the manager for punk band The Sex Pistols. The two had a son named Joseph, and Westwood continued to teach until 1971, when Malcolm decided to open a shop, Let It Rock (also known as Sex, Too Fast To Live Too Young To Die, Seditionaries) where Westwood began to sell her outrageous designs. During this period, Westwood, McLaren, and artist Jamie Reid were influenced by the Situationists. She still owns the shop, which is at 430 King's Road, and sells her Anglomania label from there. The shop is now known as World's End.

The punk style began to gain notoriety when the Sex Pistols wore clothes from Westwood and McLaren's shop at their first gig. The "punk style" included BDSM fashion, bondage gear, safety pins (taking inspiration from Richard Hell, a personality in the early New York punk rock scene), razor blades, bicycle or lavatory chains on clothing and spiked dog collars that were used as jewellery, as well as outrageous make-up and hair.

The inclusion of more traditional elements of British design, such as tartan fabric, amongst the more unusual elements of her style only served to make the overall effect of her designs more shocking.

Together, Westwood and McLaren revolutionised fashion, and the impact is still felt today. She has only a few exclusive shops including one in Leeds. Westwood worked historical factors into her collection by using historical 17th-18th century original cutting principles and modernising them. This collection was about 'gold and treasure, adventure and exploration'. Other influences in Westwood's work have included ethnic Peruvian influence, feminine figure, velvet and knitwear. A historical influence has always shown in her work.

In December 2003, she and the Wedgwood pottery company launched a series of tea sets featuring her designs. Her first major retrospective of her work was shown in 2004-2005 at the Victoria and Albert Museum, London, and the National Gallery of Australia. The exhibition is made up of around 145 complete outfits, grouped into the themes which have dominated her work from the early 1970s to the present day and were drawn from her own personal archive and the V&A's extensive collection. They range from early Punk garments to glamorous 'historical' evening gowns. The retrospective is touring the world and is set to continue until 2008.

In September 2005, Westwood joined forces with the British civil rights group Liberty and launched exclusive limited design T-shirts and baby wear bearing the slogan I AM NOT A TERRORIST, please don't arrest me. Westwood said she was supporting the campaign and defending habeas corpus. "When I was a schoolgirl my history teacher, Mr. Scott, began to take classes in civic affairs. The first thing he explained to us was the fundamental rule of law embodied in habeas corpus. He spoke with pride of civilisation and democracy. The hatred of arbitrary arrest by the lettres de cachet of the French monarchy caused the storming of the Bastille. We can only take democracy for granted if we insist on our liberty", she said. The sale of the £50 T-shirts raised funds for the organisation.

Her Autumn/Winter 2005/06 Propaganda Collection drew inspiration from her archive, reinterpreting designs using Wolford's exclusive knitting technology, who she has worked in close collaboration with since 2003. Westwood accepted a DBE in the 2006 New Year's Honours List "for services to fashion", and has thrice earned the award for British Designer of the Year.

In May 2006, Westwood wrote a poem and provided personal photographs eulogising Swallows Wood, a Nature Reserve near

Tintwistle where she was born and grew up. The Reserve is threatened with destruction by the construction of the Longdendale Bypass.

Vivienne Westwood for Nine West

For Fall 2006, Nine West presented a series of special designs from three designers which were held for one month only each. September 2006 saw Vivienne Westwood for Nine West. The collection featuring, a ballet flat in two colors, two open toe shoes, shoetie, boot, two belts, two bags, and a skirt were featured in ninewest.com, select Nine West stores, and select Macy's. On September 12, 2006 Vivienne Westwood made an appearance in Macy's Herald Square to present her collection.

Julien MacDonald

Julien MacDonald (born March 19, 1972) is a Welsh fashion designer.

Biography

Born in Merthyr Tydfil, MacDonald was taught knitting by his mother, and soon became interested in design. He was also interested in a career as a dancer, but instead studied textiles at Brighton and went on to the Royal College of Art where he gained a Masters. Soon after he graduated, Karl Lagerfeld recruited him to work for Chanel. He also worked freelance creating knitwear for Alexander McQueen and Owen Gaster.

In 2000, he was appointed as successor to Alexander McQueen as chief designer at the Paris Haute Couture house of Givenchy, and in 2001 he was named British Fashion Designer of the Year. His creations have been worn by stars such as Joely Richardson, Kylie Minogue, Geri Halliwell,Dame Shirley Bassey, Carmen Electra and Naomi Campbell. He was also selected by British Airways to redesign their flight attendants' uniforms. He also acts as a judge on the British version of Project Runway, known as Project Catwalk, which is broadcast on Sky One. In June 2006 he was awarded an OBE in the Queen's Birthday Honours for services to fashion.

Controversy

MacDonald has attracted much criticism for his extensive use of fur, including one incident in which he and Paris Hilton were flour-bombed. He has stated that fur provides the majority of his revenue and that his label would collapse were he not to use it. In February 2007, Macdonald was again criticised for the prominent use of fur in his autumn collection, causing further outrage when he claimed that "People who don't like fur can p*ss off. I love fur. It's a beautiful natural product from animals."

Zandra Rhodes

Zandra Lindsey Rhodes, CBE, RDI, (born 19 September 1940 in Chatham, Kent) is an English fashion designer, most prominent in the 1970s, known for her unusual clothes in loud colours.

Zandra Rhodes was introduced to the world of fashion by her mother, who was a fitter in a Paris fashion house and a teacher at Medway College of Art. Zandra studied first at Medway and then at the Royal College of Art in London. Her major area of study was textile design. Her early textile fashion designs were considered too silly by the traditional British manufacturers, so in 1969, she established her own retail outlet in the fashionable Fulham Road in West London. Zandra's own lifestyle has proved to be as dramatic, glamorous and extroverted as her designs. With her bright green hair (later changed to a pink and sometimes a red), theatrical makeup and art jewelry, she has stamped her identity on the international world of fashion.

She was one of the new wave of British designers who put London at the forefront of the international fashion scene in the 1970s. Her designs have always been clear, creative statements, dramatic but graceful, bold but feminine. Zandra's inspiration has always been from organic material and nature. Her innovative approach to the construction of garments can be seen in her use of reversed exposed seams and in her use of jeweled safety pins and tears during the punk era.

Zandra designed for the late Diana, Princess of Wales, and continues to design for royalty and celebrities. She has a loyal, if small, following in the USA. Over the years, she has had many academic and professional honours bestowed upon her and was made a Commander of the British Empire by the Queen in 1997.

She has made San Diego her other home and it was the San Diego Opera that commissioned her to design the costumes for her first opera, The Magic Flute in 2001. Zandra is the founder of the Fashion and Textile Museum in London which opened in May 2003. On 22 September 2006, she appeared as herself on the long-running BBC Radio 4 soap opera The Archers.

Mary Quant

Mary Quant OBE FCSD (born February 11, 1934 in Kent, England) is an English fashion designer, one of the many designers who took credit for inventing the miniskirt and hot pants. Born to Welsh parents, Quant studied illustration at Goldsmiths College before taking a job with a couture milliner. She is also famed for her work on pop art in fashion.

Early Career

In October 1955, she teamed up with her husband, Alexander Plunkett-Greene, and an accountant, Archie McNair, to open a clothes shop on the Kings Road in London called Bazaar.

Following the positive reaction to a pair of "mad house pyjamas" designed for the opening, and dissatisfied with the variety of clothes available to her, Quant decided to make her own range of clothing. Initially working solo, she was soon employing a handful of machinists, and by 1966 she was working with 18 different manufacturers concurrently.

The Miniskirt

Skirts had been getting shorter since about 1958 - a development Quant considered to be practical and liberating, allowing women the ability to run for a bus. The miniskirt, for which she is arguably most famous, became one of the defining fashions of the 1960s. The miniskirt was developed separately by Andre Courrèges, and there is disagreement as to who came up with the idea first. Mary Quant named the miniskirt after her favourite make of car, the Mini. In addition to the miniskirt, Mary Quant is often credited with inventing the colored and patterned tights that tended to accompany the garment, although these are also attributed to Cristobal Balenciaga.

The Swinging Sixties

Regardless of whether she invented these items, Quant was one of their major popularisers, largely thanks to the fact that Bazaar was a popular haunt for the fashionable "Chelsea Set" of "Swinging London". By 1961, Quant had opened a second Bazaar in Knightsbridge and by 1965 she was exporting to the USA. To keep up with demand, Quant went into mass-production, setting up the Ginger Group.

Quant's popularity was at its peak in the mid 1960s, during which time she produced the dangerously short micro-mini skirt, "paint box" make-up, and plastic raincoats. She was described as being the leading fashion force outside Paris. In 1970 Bernard Levin called her the "High Priestess of Sixties fashion". At the height of her fame in the 60s, she anticipated that pubic hair would be a "fashion emphasis" in the coming decade, a suggestion that was scorned by many, though, as Levin observed, "none was so sure of the basis of his ridicule as to deny the possibility". In 1966, Quant was appointed an OBE for services to the fashion industry.

Later Career

In the late 1960s, Quant launched hot pants, which was her last big fashion development. Through the 1970s and 1980s she concentrated on household goods and make-up.

In 1988, Quant designed the interior of the Mini (1000) Designer (Originally dubbed the Mini Quant, this name was switched when popularity charts were set against having Quant's name on the car). It featured black and white striped seats with red trimming. The seatbelts were red, and the driving and passenger seats had Quant's signature on the upper left quadrant. The steering wheel had Quant's signature daisy and the bonnet badge had "Mary Quant" written over the signature name. The headlight housings, wheel arches, door handles and bumpers were all nimbus grey, rather than the more common chrome or black finishes. 2000 were released in the UK on 15 June 1988, a number were also released onto foreign markets, however the numbers for these are hard to come by. The special edition mini came in two body colours, jet black and diamond white. She is also a Fellow of the Chartered Society of Designers, and winner of the Minerva Medal, the Society's highest award. In 2000, she resigned as director of Mary Quant Ltd., her cosmetics company, after a Japanese buy-out. There are over 200 Mary Quant Colour shops in Japan, where Quant fashions continue to enjoy more popularity.

Valentino

The Paris years

Garavani became interested in fashion while in middle school in his native Voghera, Lombardy Italy, when he apprenticed under his uncle Rosa and a local designer Ernestina Salvadeo, an aunt of noted artist Aldo Giorgini).

At 17 Valentino moved to Paris to pursue this interest with the help of by his mother Teresa de Biaggi and his father Mauro Garavani. There he studied at the Ecole des Beaux Arts and at the Chambre Syndicale de la Couture Parisienne.

His first Paris choice was Jacques Fath, then Balenciaga. He then found apprentice jobs with Jean Desses where he used to help style icon countess Jacqueline de Ribes sketch her dress ideas. He then joined Guy Laroche for 2 years. At Desses, Valentino sketched furiously, between helping with window dressing and greeting clients for the daily 2:30 p.m. private showings. Most of his early sketches were lost. At a Rome exhibition in 1991 a smattering went on display and current clients at that time such as Marie Hélène de Rothschild and Elizabeth Taylor marveled that the DNA of Valentino's style was already apparent in the layers of white pleats and animal prints.

After five years, Valentino left Jean Desses under a cloud over an incident about prolonging a vacation in St. Tropez that still makes him wriggle uncomfortably today. Rescued by his friend Guy Laroche, he joined his "tiny, tiny" fashion house. Anyway just when he had been offered the French equivalent of a green card and after discussions with his parents, he decided to return to Italy and set up in Rome in 1959.

In 1959 Valentino thus moved back to Italy with his lover, french socialite Gerald Nanty and opened a fashion house in Rome on the posh Via Condotti with the backing of his father and an associate of his. More than an atelier, the premises resembled a real "maison de couture", being it very much on the line of what Valentino had seen in Paris: everything was very grand and models flew in from Paris for his first show.

On 31 July 1960 Valentino met at the Café de Paris on the Via Veneto in Rome Giancarlo Giammetti. One of three children, Giammetti was in his second year of architecture school, living at home with his parents in the haut bourgeois Parioli section of Northern Rome. His father owned an electronics store near the Via Veneto. That day Giammetti gave Valentino a lift home in his little Fiat and a friendship as well as a long-lasting partnership started. The day after Giammetti was to leave for Capri for vacation and by coincidence Valentino was also going to there so they met again in the island 10 days later. Giammetti would shortly after abandon the University for good to become Valentino's business partner.

Giammetti's entrepreneurial genius will prove fundamental to the worldwide expansion and success of the House. Thanks to Giammetti Valentino was able to focus on the creative aspect of design leaving all business intricacies to Giammeti. When Giammetti arrived, the business situation of Valentino's atelier was not brilliant: in one year he had spent so much money that his father's associate pulled out of the business so that Valentino had to fight against bankruptcy. Valentino already had a passion for luxury and would thus spend too much money on expensive fabrics never thinking about the financial aspects of his fashion business.

Valentino and Giametti were told to start a new company and so they did. Under Giammetti's wing Valentino business got under control and things were ready for international success.

Breakthrough in Florence

Valentino's international debut took place in 1962 in Florence, the Italian fashion capital of the time. His first show at the Pitti Palace was welcomed as a true revelation and the young couturier was submerged by orders from foreign buyers and enthusiastic comments on the press.

After the breakthrough show in Florence, Valentino started to dress the ladies of the international best-dressed crowd such as his acquaintance from the Paris years Countess Jacqueline de Ribes and New York socialites Babe Paley and Jayne Wrightsman.

In 1966, confident of his client base, he moved his shows from Florence to Rome and there, two years later, he had one of his greatest triumphs, an all-white collection, which became famous for the "V" logo he designed.

In 1964 Jacqueline Kennedy bought six of his couture dresses, all in black and white, to wear during her year of mourning after J.F.K.'s death. Jackie had seen countess Gloria Schiff, twin sister of the Rome-based fashion editor of American Vogue and Valentino's friend Consuelo Crespi, wearing an ensemble in two pieces in black organza at a party. Jackie called Gloria Schiff to know the name of the designer and found out it was some Valentino. In September 1964, Valentino had a show at the Waldorf-Astoria for a benefit. Since Jackie wanted to see the clothes he sent his saleslady, along with a model, to Jackie's apartment on Fifth Avenue. Mrs. Kennedy ordered six outfits and from then on she became a devout client and a friend. Valentino later on would also design the white dress that Jackie wore to her wedding with Greek tycoon Aristotle Onassis.

Throughout the 1970s Valentino spent considerable time in New York City where his presence was embraced by social personalities such as Vogue's editor-in-chief Diana Vreeland and art identities such as Andy Warhol. Valentino and Giammetti were together for 12 years. Neither ever discussed their relationship with anyone outside their closest circle of friends-not even with their mothers. Valentino's mother, Teresa, moved from Voghera to Rome to help with the business. Eventually both his parents moved to Rome and lived with Valentino. Teresa Garavani and Lina Giammetti lived with their sons until the women died, Teresa in 1977 and Lina in 1996.

The Accademia Valentino

1989 marked the opening of the Accademia Valentino, designed by Architect Tommaso Ziffer, a cultural space located near his atelier in Rome, for the presentation of art exhbitions. The next year, encouraged by their friend Elizabeth Taylor, Valentino Garavani and Giancarlo Giammetti created L.I.F.E., an association for the support of AIDS-related patients, which benefits from the activities of the Accademia Valentino.

From HDP group to Marzotto group

In 1998 Valentino and his partner Giancarlo Giammetti sold the company for approximately $300 million to HdP, an Italian conglomerate controlled, in part, by the late Gianni Agnelli, the head of Fiat. In 2002, Valentino S.p.A., with revenues of more than $180 million, was sold by HdP to Marzotto Apparel, a Milan-based textile giant, for $210 million. It was rumored that HDP was displeased with Valentino's and Giammetti's personal expenses, a claim Giammetti has bristled at: businessmen have a perspective of fashion which is completely old-fashioned, they believe fashion is a little show with models-beautiful girls they would like to know-who walk on the runway. They don't know how much work is behind it, and how important the image of the founder and the designer is for the company. You cannot talk about the dresses of Valentino without thinking about him, and when you think about him, you think about the glamorous life he leads, and all that adds to the product.

Glamour for Glamour

It is difficult to deny that Valentino in his long career has created some of the most sophisticated dresses to be seen and worn, particularly for the evening, the time of the day in which his flamboyant and opulent style has expressed itself at the best, however, when it comes to considering the general output of his work, and its relevance in the history of fashion, things change. Compared to the influence and innovations of such great masters as Christian Dior, Coco Chanel, Elsa Schiaparelli and ultimately Yves Saint Laurent, Valentino's style can be seen as much more conservative and fixed. His concept of elegance and beauty is basically an exercise in glamour for the sake of glamour itself. Inventive as it may be it lacks the modernity, the conceptual depth and the daring spirit that has marked the work of the above mentioned designers, particulary that of the most influential of his contemporaries (and in general the most influential post war designer), Saint Laurent. When one looks retrospectively to his collections,(and the recent celebration in Rome is an occasion to do this) it is possible to see clearly that he has always designed thinking only and exclusively for women of the so called jet set, the vacuous and glittering world of the great socialites, towards which he always had a particular craving. The Italian designer has never translated the Zeitgeist into his fashion, remaining constantly hooked to the more abstract imperative of a glamourized concept of femminility. In this sense, there are no sociological traces to be found in his creations, as there are in the collections of the four French masters or, more recently, in those of Jean Paul Gaultier and Gianni Versace, two of the most acute interpreters of fashion as a mirror reflecting social and cultural changes. All of Valentino's talent has been put at the service of a romanticised notion of what the upper crust of society is, and consequently, of how a women belonging to it must dress and behave. This woman is more the fabrication of Hollywood in the 30ies-40ies (and all of his work, this is it's main limit, is foundamentally tied to the period of the mythical stars such as Greta Garbo, Gloria Swanson, Merle Oberon and Joan Crawford), than anything else. At 75 years of age, Valentino cannot but go on doing what he has already done, even if most of his creations (but this issue concerns haute couture as a whole) seems anachronistic and too elaborate for today standards of life, even for the very rich for whom they are produced.

Legion d'Honneur

On Thursday, 6 July 2006 President Chirac of France awarded Valentino with final jewel in the crown of his achievements: Chevalier de la Legion d'Honneur from the country where he arrived as a 17-year-old Italian boy - and fell in love with haute couture. "I am very honored," said Valentino, who has gleaned awards from across the world from his native Italy to America. "French people are charming, adorable but not extremely generous with foreigners, but they believe in what they do. I feel proud in exchange because what I did in restoration is something I did for La France." (Herald Tribune) Valentino was referring to restoring Wideville, his Louis XIII chateau outside Paris.

Patrons of the art

Both Valentino and Giancarlo Giammetti are renowned for their extensive collection of art spread among their homes around the world including Picasso, Cy Twombly, Balthus, Damien Hirst.

High Living

Valentino and Giametti's lifestyle has always been flamboyant to the extreme. John Fairchild, editor-at-large at Women's Wear Daily and W, told Vanity Fair: Valentino and Giancarlo are the kings of high living. Every other designer looks and says, 'How do they live the way they do?' I don't think they made the money that Valentino and Giancarlo did, because Giancarlo knows how to make money. If they did, they didn't spend the money like Valentino. No other designer ever did. When the terrorism first started in Rome - the period when the Red Brigades were kidnapping people - Valentino was riding around in a bulletproof Mercedes. And do you know what color the Mercedes was? Red. My God, I thought, you must want to get blown up.

Valentino's Big Family

An enlarged family: Giancarlo, Carlos, Charlene, Anthony and Sean

Observers have often noticed how Valentino always seems to move surrounded by a court of friends which has become a real family for him. This court always comprises his business associate and ex boyfriend Giancarlo Giammetti, his current boyfriend American bag and jewel designer Bruce Hoeksema, Brazilian brothers Sean and Anthony de Souza, the sons of his PR Carlos de Souza and socialite Charlene Shorto de Ganay, Souza's ex-wife, who is also Valentino's Paris-based pr woman. Souza met Valentino and Giammetti in 1973. Valentino and Giammetti are also the godfathers of Anthony and Sean. Giammetti confided to Vanity Fair that "this family has stayed together because of me, because when Valentino gets mad he cuts - that is that. I remember when Carlos left and moved to Brazil and married Charlene. Valentino refused to speak to him, but I always talked to Carlos. Then one day Carlos called and said he had a baby boy, Sean. I handed the phone to Valentino, and he started to cry and cry".

Bruce Hoeksema

As affirmed in an interview with American Vanity Fair he has a love relationship since 1982 with American jewel and bag designer Bruce Hoeksema, a former model and vice president of the house of Valentino until 1998.

Daniela, Naty, Georgina & Rosario

Valentino's "family" often includes other close friends like Valentino's PR Daniela Giardina, Spanish socialites like Nati Abascal, a former model, and Rosario Nadal y Fuster-Puigdorfila, wife of prince Kyryl Saxe Coburgh Gotha of Bulgaria, who met Valentino in her native Mallorca via Carlos de Souza at a club. Another close friend is his former PR countess Georgina Faucigny-Lucinge Brandolini d'Adda of the Agnelli family, who worked for Valentino for 18 years before leaving for Balmain.

The Valentino entourage often travels together everywhere around the world for vacation, moving from one or the other Valentino and Giammetti's various homes around the world and in summer time to the yacht, where Giammetti, for a period in the 90s, made everyone except Valentino do needlepoint. Architect Tommaso Ziffer, a close friend of Giancarlo Giammetti, and actress Gwyneth Paltrow are also part of the group. Since Marzotto group's acquisition of Valentino from HDP group, Matteo Marzotto and her socialite mother countess Marta Marzotto often join the party.

Maude, Margot, Monty, Molly, Milton and Maggie

Valentino adores dogs to the point that he once named a second line of clothing after his late pug Oliver. Today Valentino owns six pugs: the mother, Molly; her sons, Milton and Monty; and her daughters, Margot, Maude and Maggie. When traveling on his 14-seat Challenger jet, three cars are needed to move Valentino and his entourage to the airport: one to move Valentino and Giammetti, another for the luggage and the staff and a third to transport five of six Valentino's pugs as one of them, Maude, always travels with Valentino.

Giammetti told Vanity Fair: Valentino is embarrassed to be seen traveling with so many dogs. People look at him enough as it is. He often asks his valets to bring the pugs out of the car after he has boarded the plane, sometimes in two shifts so that there seem to be fewer animals. After take-off Maude is released by a butler. She runs forward and jumps up on Valentino's lap, but before she can settle in, another staff member appears with a light-blue linen cloth, which he unfurls and placed under the dog to minimize the effects of shedding. At lunchtime Maude is returned to her fellow pugs.

Movie:The Devil Wears Prada

In 2006 Valentino did a cameo role as himself in the hit movie The Devil Wears Prada. One of the DVD's featurettes is called "Getting Valentino" and shows an interview of the designer and Valentino backstage with the movie's actresses, Meryl Streep and Anne Hathaway , and his associate Giancarlo Giammetti and his PR Carlos de Souza and Charlene Shorto de Ganay.

Valentino Museum

During the festivities for the 45th year of Valentino's career the Mayor of Rome Walter Veltroni accounced that the site of the Valentino museum will a building in via San Teodoro in Rome between the Palatine hill and the Bocca della Verità (mouth of truth).

45 years of Valentino: 6 - 8 July 2007, Rome

In order to celebrate the 45th anniversary of Valentino's career a fashion extravaganza took place in Rome between 6th and 8th July 2007. Festivities started on Thursday 5th July with a dinner for Valentino's assistants and employees at Ristorante Gusto and ended on Sunday 8th July with the launch of a perfume and a brunch at the French Academy of Villa Medici.

The main five exclusive golden invitation cards have been sent from the Valentino headquarters for the main weekend's events:

- 6 july 2007 at 7:30 pm: inauguration of the exhibit "Valentino in Rome, 45 years of style" designed by Patrick Kinmonth and Antonio Monfreda at the ancient sacrificial altar Ara Pacis showcasing Valentino's most important creations from the past 45 years. Valentino has gone through his archives and his clients' closets to narrow down his choices to about 300.
- 6 july 2007 post-exhibit gala dinner at the Temple of Venus in the Imperial Forum. Dating back to 135 A.C. and dedicated to

Emperor Hadrian the forum had never been opened to any event. Oscar-winning designer Dante Ferretti (The Aviator, Gangs of New York, The Age of Innocence) Dante Ferretti re-created the monument's long-lost columns in fiber glass, a special procedure called anastilosys, and choreographed a spectacular performance by high-wire ballerinas (costumed in exaggerated versions of the designer's ball gowns or signature lipstick-red evening dresses), who moved with poetic grace to Maria Callas's haunting arias, with the Coliseum, bathed in red and mauve light, as a breathtaking backdrop. The plexigas structure remained for the summer for tourists to enjoy. Culture Minister Francesco Rutelli also revealed that Valentino contributed to the restoration of the Temple with a donation of 200,000 euros.

- 7th july at 5.00 pm: fashion show for 1000 people. For the first time after 16 years Valentino's Haute Couture fashion show will not take place in Paris during the HC fashion week but in Rome. Socialite and longtime Valentino fan Marina Palma took over the fashionable Bolognese restaurant for a tribute lunch before the international guest list set off for the designer's bravura couture runway show. The fashion setting was two halls called Sala Incisa and Sala Baglivi of the restructured 16th century Santo Spirito in Saxia complex, next to Castel Sant'Angelo and the Vatican. Valentino showed about 61 couture dresses, a record number considering a HC show never shows more than 40 gowns. The collection referenced many of the leitmotifs revealed in the retrospective at Ara Pacis and was a tour de force of the flawless and unmatchable techniques that Valentino's brilliant workrooms. The music segued from Mahler's Fifth to Maria Callas's hauntingly beautiful rendition of Puccini's 'O Mio Babbino Caro' as Valentino took his bow. An impressive roster of fellow designers who had gathered to pay homage-Karl Lagerfeld, Giorgio Armani, Donatella Versace, Tom Ford, Diane von Furstenberg, Carolina Herrera, Zac Posen, Manolo Blahnik, and Philip Treacy among them led the standing ovation, which drew tears from the habitually unflappable designer, who embraced Giancarlo Giammetti on the runway.'It was the most fantastic collection,' said Princess Firyal of Jordan backstage. 'I'm about to cry, too.

- the post-show gala dinner and ball took place in the Parco dei Daini at the Villa Borghese. There Dante Ferretti had created a spectacular Brighton Pavilion-inspired tent, with palm-tree columns and red, black, and mirrored walls, in the gardens. Guests included Princess Caroline of Monaco, Anna Wintour,Farah Diba, Karl Lagerfeld, Uma Thurman, Princesses Marie-Chantal of the Hellenes and Rosario of Bulgaria, as well as Mayor Walter Veltroni. Other movie stars flocked too: Eva Mendes in a black version of the designer's iconic 1965 red crepe sheath (the original was encased in a giant red Perspex box at the entrance to his retrospective), Sarah Jessica Parker in black draperies, Sienna Miller, in a ostrich-feather crinoline gown, Jennifer Hudson in a gown with a train. Socialites included Daphne Guinness in a black-and-white lace flamenco dress with silver platforms and ostrich-feather eyelashes and Lita Livanos, Sheetal Mafatlal, and Rena Sindi, Nada Kirdar, Lynn Wyatt (in the red taffeta ruffles of a dress Valentino made for her 25 years ago that she found in her attic), Allison Sarofim in a coral-beaded 1960s Valentino.Singer Annie Lennox held a surprise concert.
- Sunday, July 8: Valentino launched the house's latest perfume, Rock 'n Rose Couture and a giant book.

In addition to the celebration in Rome, a tribute book written by Vanity Fair writer Matt Tyrnauer will be published in July by Taschen.

Valentino movie at Sundance Movie Festival

Tyrnauer is also set to release a documentary about Valentino, three years in the making, at Sundance movie festival.

Timeline

- 1959 Having completed his fashion studies and an apprenticeship with Jean Desses and Guy Laroche, Valentino starts up his first studio in Rome
- 1960 Begins his collaboration with Giancarlo Giammetti, who manages the commercial development of the House of Valentino

- 1962 His first collection at the international fashion Gotha in the Palazzo Pitti, Florence, is a triumphant success
- 1965 Valentino is recognized as the top name in Italian Haute Couture
- 1967 He is awarded the Neiman Marcus Prize in Dallas (the equivalent of an Oscar in the world of Fashion)
- 1968 Valentino's reputation is secured with the enormous success of his "Collezione Bianca", the first clothes and accessories to have the magic "V" label Designs the wedding dress worn by Jacqueline Kennedy for her marriage to Aristotle Onassis.
- 1969 Begins his Boutique line of clothes and opens the first Valentino shop in Milan
- 1970 Launch of his first Ready-to-Wear collections Opening of Valentino boutiques in Rome and New York
- 1971 Opening of the first menswear shop in Via Condotti
- 1975 First fashion show of his Ready-to-Wear collection in Paris
- 1976 Opens a boutique in Tokyo
- 1978 Launch of the Valentino perfume at a gala evening in Paris, at the Theater des Champs Elysees
- 1982 Publication of the book "Valentino", edited by Franco Maria Ricci 20 September, Valentino presents his Autumn/ Winter collection at the Metropolitan Museum in New York
- 1984 Valentino celebrates his twenty-fifth year in the business and receives an official award from the Minister for Industry
- 1985 He is awarded the Grand'Ufficiale dell'Ordine al Merito by the President of Italy
- 1986 Receives the highest decoration possible in Italy, the Cavaliere di Gran Croce, from the President
- 1989 First show of the Haute Couture collection in Paris
- 1990 In February, Valentino and Giancarlo Giammetti found L.I.F.E (initials in Italian for "Fighting, Informing, Building, Teaching"), an association working for the fight against Aids. The Accademia Valentino is also officially opened to the public with an exhibition of painters of the Roman School Exhibition of "The Art of Cartier" at the Accademia Valentino

Publication of the book "Valentino: Trent'Anni de Magia", by Leonardo arte.

- 1991 To celebrate his 30th year in the fashion business, an exhibition entitled "Valentino: Thirty Years of Magic" is organized in Valentino's honour by the Mayor of Rome at the Capitole Museum, while the Accademia Valentino presents a retrospective of his designs. Creation of the perfume Vendetta for men and women.
- 1992 Exhibition at the Accademia Valentino entitled: "La seduzione da Boucher a Warhol" The "Valentino: Thirty Years of Magic"' exhibition is invited to go to New York to coincide with the fifth centenary celebrations of the discovery of America. Valentino is invited by the Chinese government to stage a show in Beijing* 1994 In January, Valentino presents his first ever costume designs at the Eisenhower Theatre in the John Fitzgerald Kennedy Center, Washington, for an opera entitled "The Dream of Valentino", based on the life of the movie star Rudolf Valentino
- 1995 Valentino's return to Italy is celebrated on 14 January in Florence with a fashion show at the Stazione Leopolda, over thirty years his first show at the Palazzo Pitti. The Mayor of Florence awards him the "Premio speciale dell'arte nella moda"
- 1996 Valentino is named Cavaliere del Lavoro
- 2004 launch of V perfume which will be followed by V for men
- 2006 Opens a boutique on Newbury Street in Boston
- 2006 President Chirac awards Valentino of the Legion d'Honneur
- 2007 Opens a boutique in Bangkok

Fendi

Fendi is an Italian fashion designer brand founded in 1918. Fendi boutiques can be found all over the world- including stores in Dar Es Salaam, Ulanbataar, Baku, Harlem, N'Djamena, and Lesotho.Today, Fendi is owned by LVMH Moët Hennessy Louis Vuitton S.A. group, with creative director Darius at its helm. Fendi's trademark is sofas and women's clothing.

History

Fendi began in 1918 when Adele Casagrande opened a leather and fur shop in Via del Plebiscito in central Rome. When Adele married Edoardo Fendi in 1925, they made a decision to change the name to Fendi. The business prospered, and a new shop was opened in Via Piave in 1932. By 1946 Paola, 15, the eldest of the couple's five daughters, went to work for the firm, followed by her sisters Carla, Anna, Franca, and Alda.

In 1965 a marriage between the Fendis and German designer Karl Lagerfeld was sealed, and it proved to be fortuitous for both. Lagerfeld immediately created the inverted FF logo that joined the growing list of international status symbols, and then set about, aided and abetted by the sisters, to revolutionize the treatment of fur and other clothing.

What had once been a precious but stiff and heavy garment was transformed into a light, soft, easy-to-wear and above all flattering outfit. The team went on to invent new ways of working with fur, tanning, dying, and treating, taking previously unused skins and turned them into fashionable garments. By 1966 Fendi had presented its first couture fur collection, designed by Lagerfeld. It was an immediate success with foreign buyers. Marvin Traub, president of Bloomingdale's, discovered Fendi's leather goods and introduced them to the United States. Other outlets soon followed, and today Fendi is largely represented through high-end department stores.

In 1969 Fendi presented its first ready-to-wear fur collection at Palazzo Pitti in Florence, bringing continuously evolving techniques and imaginative designs to lower-priced furs without sacrificing quality. When the sisters could not find the fabric clothes they wanted to show under the furs their ready-to-wear line was born, again to great success.

The company's accessories are now found on the arm of many stars and signature bags such as the Spy, buckled B-bag, and embellished bucket bag are often in high demand sometimes creating long waiting lists.

BIBLIOGRAPHY

BOLEN, J. S. (1984). *Goddesses in every woman. A new psychology of women.* New York: Harper & Row. Italian translation, *Le dee dentro la donna. Una nuova psicologia femminile.* Rome: Astrolabio, 1991.

BRADFORD DE LONG, J. AND EICHENGREEN, B. *(May* 1992), *The* Marshall Plan: *History's Most Successful Structural Adjustment Plan,* Discussion Paper Series No 634, Centre For Economic Policy Research.

BREWARD, C. (1995), *The Culture of Fashion,* Manchester, Manchester University Press.

BROOKS, R. A. (2002). *Flesh and machines: How robots will change us.* New York: Pantheon.

CALEFATO, P. (1996). *Mass moda* [Mass fashion]. Genoa: Costa & Nolan.

DREY, M. (1997). *Escape velocity: Cyberculture at the end of the century.* New York: Grove.

DUGGAN, C. andWAGSTAFF, C. (eds) (1995), *Italy in the Cold War: Politics, Culture and Society 1948–58,* Oxford, Berg.

DULLES, A. (1993), *The Marshall Plan,* Oxford, Berg.

ECO, U. (1973), 'Social Life as Sign System' in Robey, D. (ed.), *Structuralism, an Introduction,* Oxford, Oxford University.

EICHER, J.B. and EREKOSIMA, T.V. (1993), 'Taste and 19th Century Patterns of Textile Use Among the Kalabari of Nigeria', paper presented at a conference on 'Cloth, The World Economy and the Artisan: Textile Manufacturing and Marketing in South Asia and Africa, 1780–1950', Dartmouth College, Hanover, New Hampshire.

EICHER,J.B. and EREKOSIMA, T.V. (1996), 'Indian Textiles in Kalabari Funerals', *Asian Art and Culture*. Washington, DC: Smithsonian Institution Press; 68–79.

ELLWOOD, D. (1985), *Italy 1943–1945*, Leicester, Leicester University Press.

ELLWOOD, D. (1992), *Rebuilding Western Europe: America and Postwar Reconstruction*, London, Longman.

ELLWOOD, D. and KROES, R. (eds) (1994), *Hollywood in Europe: Experiences of a Cultural Hegemony*, Amsterdam, VU University Press.

EVANS, W.C. and THORNTON, M. (1989), *Women and Fashion: a new look*, London, Quartet Books.

FINKELSTEIN, J. (1991), *The Fashioned Self*, Cambridge, Polity.

FLUGEL, J.C. (1950), *The Psychology of Clothes*, London, Hogarth.

FORTUNATI, L. (1995). *The arcane of reproduction*. New York: Autonomedia.

FORTUNATI, L. (1999). Abbigliamento tecnologico [Technological clothes]. In *Enciclopedia "L'Universo del Corpo"* ["The universe of the body encyclopedia"] (Vol. 2, 11–12). Rome: Istituto dell'Enciclopedia Italiana.

FORTUNATI, L.(1998). *Revêtirdeste chnologies* [Wearing technologies]. *Réseaux, 90*, July–August, 85–91.

GARBER, M. (1992), *Vested Interests: Cross-Dressing and Cultural Anxiety*, London, Penguin Books.

HEIDEGGER, M. (1971),'The Origin of the Work of Art' in *Poetry, Language, Thought*, trans. Hofstadter, A., New York, Harper Row.

LAVER, J. (1966), *Dress* 2nd ed., London, John Murray.

LEE-LEVIN, P. (1965), *The Wheels of Fashion*, New York, Doubleday.

LEVITT, S. (1986), *Victorians Unbuttoned*, London, Allen and Unwin.

LIAUT, J.-N. (1996), *Cover Girls and Supermodels: 1945–1965*, trans. Robin Buss, London: Marion Boyars.

MAEDER, E. (1988), *Hollywood and History,* London, Thames and Hudson.

MAIER, C. (ed.) (1978), *The Origins of the Cold War and Contemporary Europe,* New York, New Viewpoints.

MCCARDELL, C. (1956), *What Shall I Wear? The What, Where, When and How Much of Fashion,* New York.

MCROBBIE, A. (1991), *Feminism and Youth Culture: From 'Jackie' to 'Just Seventeen'*, Boston: Unwin Hyman.

MEISEL, S. (April 2000), 'The Moving Image', *Vogue*: 98.

MILWARD, A. (1984), *The Reconstruction of Western Europe 1945–51,* London, Methuen.

NELLI, H. (1983), *From Unrrigrants to Ethnics: the Italian-Americans,* Oxford, Oxford University Press.

NYSTROM, P. (1928), *The Economics of Fashion,* New York, Ronald Press.

SMART MARTIN, A. (1993), 'Makers, Buyers and Users – Consumerism as a Material Culture Framework', *Winterthur Portfolio,* Vol. 28, 2–4, Sunmer-Autumn.

SPARKE, P. (1982), *Ettore Sottsass Jnr.,* London, Design Council.

SPARKE, P. (1988), *Italian Design 1870 to the Present,* London, Thames and Hudson.

SPIGEL, L. (1989), 'The Domestic Economy of Television Viewing in Postwar America', *Critical Studies in Mass Communication,* 6: 17–55.

STEELE, V. (1988), *Paris Fashion: a Cultural History,* New York, Oxford University Press.

STEELE, V. (1991), *Women of Fashion: Twentieth Century Designers,* New York, Thompson, P. (1988), *The Voice of the Past: Oral History,* Oxford, Oxford University Press (first published 1978).

TCMLINSON, A. (ed.) (1990), *Consumption, Identity and Style: Marketing, Meanings and the Packaging of Pleasure,* London, Routledge.

WILSON, E. (1985), *Adorned in Dreams: Fashion and Modernity,* Berkeley: University of California Press.

WILSON, E. (1985), *Adorned in Dreams: Fashion and Modernity*, London, Virago.

WILSON, E. and Taylor, L. (1989), *Through the looking Glass: a History of Dress from 1860 to the Present*, London, EEC.

WOOLF, S.J. (ed.) (1972), *The Rebirth of Italy 1943–50*, London, Longman.

YOHANNAN, K. (1998), *Claire McCardell: Redefining Modernism*, New York, Harry N. Abrams.

ZAMAGNI, V. (1993), *The Economic History of Italy 1860–1990*, Oxford, Clarendon.

INDEX

F

G

H

I

J

K

L

R

S

T

U

V

W